Just-in-Time: Making It Happen

Just-in-Time: Making It Happen

Unleashing the Power of Continuous Improvement

William A. Sandras Jr.

FOREWORD BY WALTER E. GODDARD

John Wiley & Sons, Inc.
New York · Chichester · Brisbane · Toronto · Singapore

ISBN 0–471–13266–7

Printed in the United States of America

10 9 8 7 6

Contents

Acknowledgments

The implementation of JIT/TQC is a team effort. The content of this book is in large part a result of knowledge gained through teamwork during my career. Over the years I have learned much from many managers, peers, and employees at Hewlett-Packard, Oliver Wight, and at client companies.

I especially want to mention Terry Johnson, formerly with Hewlett-Packard and now with Oliver Wight's TeamJIT, and his team of employees who not only successfully implemented many of my ideas, but who contributed to my learning with many ideas of their own. Joe Conrad, Max Davis, and Jerry Harmon, former Hewlett-Packard managers of mine encouraged and facilitated our pioneering JIT/TQC efforts in repetitive, job shop, new, and mature factory environments.

I also owe a debt of gratitude to a number of people at client companies, many of whom I consider personal friends. They are at Tellabs, Hallmark, McDonnell Douglas, Beckman Instruments, NCR, GE, Harris, Tektronix, Michelin, Formica, and at several startup companies destined to be famous. They helped prove the general applicability of the implementation process explained in this book, and have provided very informative stories and examples.

A number of these same colleagues, plus others, helped to review this book for content, accuracy, omissions, and clarity. In addition to their official titles, they were the true champions and coordinators of the JIT/TQC efforts for their company and division. They include:

Grace Pastiak
Manager of Manufacturing Operations
Tellabs, Inc.

George Killianey
Director of Material Services
Beckman Instruments, Inc.

John Saathoff
Corporate Director, Materials Management
Harris Corp.

James C. Sanders
Manager of Manufacturing Engineering
Hallmark Cards

Carl Okeson
Corporate Manager of Inventory & Technical Planning
NCR

John Lee
JIT Coordinator
McDonnell Douglas
(now retired, but he achieved a personal objective of leading a successful implementation of JIT/TQC before leaving.)

Robert Hall
Professor of Operations Management
Indiana University

Reviewers from the Oliver Wight Companies include:
Walt Goddard, President of Oliver Wight Education Associates
Roger Brooks, Executive Vice President of Oliver Wight Education Associates
Darryl Landvater, President of Oliver Wight Video Productions
Tom Wallace
James Correll
Norris Edson
Bill Belt
Bruce Harvey, previously with Hewlett-Packard
Bill Boyst, previously with Northern Telecom
Pete Landry, previously with Xerox
Cecil Bradshaw, previously with Steelcase.

In addition, I appreciate the contribution of Walt Goddard for writing the foreword to this book.

I also want to thank my publisher, Dana Scannell, General Manager of Oliver Wight Limited Publications for the support and priority he has given this effort. Thanks also to Ron Schultz, a writer, who took my thoughts and, by painstakingly working back and forth with me over many months, organized and made readable sense and continuity out of them. Rachel Snyder should also be recognized for her work as production coordinator, and Larada Johnson for her help with the figures.

And finally, I want to thank my wife, Konnie, for her logistical and emotional support throughout the countless hours this project required.

Foreword

Walter E. Goddard
President, Oliver Wight Education Associates

THE CONTINUOUS CHANGE MACHINE

"To see the way a machine works, you can take the covers off and look inside. But to understand what goes on, you need to get to know the principles that govern its actions." This insight comes from David Macaulay, author of the book, *The Way Things Work*.

Bill Sandras, in this book, takes the covers off the Continuous Change Machine known as Just-in-Time/Total Quality Control (JIT/TQC). Bill describes how JIT/TQC works, the principles that hold it together, the motor that propels it, and what you, the operator, must do to drive it. A distinguishing contribution is Bill's methodology, "one less at a time." It's a controlled process, a constant series of small steps, each evaluated before the next one takes place, which creates a safe, economical, and rapid way to drive continuous improvements into your company. With this approach, the concepts of Just-in-Time/Total Quality Control are combined with a practical, proven process which converts the philosophy into progress.

What's the potential for your company? A quick way to assess this is to analyze your inventories. All inventories can be divided into two categories. At any point in time, either value is being added or it is not. Inventory that is moving from one place to another and inventory that is simply sitting, waiting for something to happen, is not gaining any value. Whereas, inventory that is being worked on is in a value-added state. For years, I've surveyed executives attending my Top Management classes, asking them to estimate the size of their sitting inventory. They typically feel that 70–90 percent of their total inventory investment is sitting.

The sitting inventory is a gold mine of opportunities. Mining it yields the following: More responsive deliveries for customers, faster throughput in the factory, quicker feedback on problems, accelerated introduction of new products, improved ability to respond to changes, less space, and simpler planning. Added together, the results mean greatly reduced costs, better customer service, and higher quality. The sitting inventory is waiting for you. Applying the proven approaches described in this book will enable you to remove it.

It's not just material, however, that sits. It's also customer orders in order entry, engineering changes and blueprints in engineering, requisitions and purchase orders in purchasing, invoices and receivables in accounting, new programs and changes to existing ones in data processing, new tooling and tooling requiring repair in maintenance, orders to be picked in stockrooms and finished goods, memos to be typed in the secretarial pool, and all of the things accumulating in your "in basket." The principles and techniques of JIT/TQC can be applied to reduce wasteful activities in these and all other facets of your business.

JIT/TQC also strives to speed up the moving inventory in addition to reducing the sitting inventory. Transferring inventory from one location to another adds cost but does not add any value to a product. All economical changes which shrink the distance that things move and/or increase the speed, be they transportation or manufacturing operations, produce significant improvements.

Many practitioners and many companies have contributed to the JIT/TQC body of knowledge that exists today. Bill describes Henry Ford's efforts at the River Rouge plant as being an excellent example of high-velocity manufacturing. Toyota Motor Car Company also deserves special recognition for its pioneering efforts. For many years people have analyzed how Toyota is using JIT/TQC. A prominent ingredient is the "pull technique" called Kanban. It is important to understand how this technique works (see chapter 3) but it is also important to recognize that it is not a stand-alone operating system. Two other elements must be in place for it to generate improvements.

First, management must understand and accept the principle that producing inventory prematurely is undesirable. In fact, it may be better to have an idle operator and an idle machine than to produce material ahead of time. Certainly this is also wasteful, therefore undesirable as well, but it may be less wasteful than premature inventory. To many executives, this is radical thinking. Generation after generation of operating the company in a traditional manner has conditioned us to the opposite—let's keep the operators busy and machines humming.

Implementing JIT/TQC does not mean operators will be idle. Before wasting any resources, all other alternatives should be exhausted. Help out in another area, perform maintenance, do housekeeping, practice setups, work on problem-solving, etc., are all excellent choices. Idle operators are not good but producing inventory that is not needed until later may be worse. Executives must embrace this principle to utilize the Kanban technique properly.

The second element is to reduce the levels of inventory authorized by Kanbans. Bill was the first person I heard who said, "Kanbans are bad; the objective is to get rid of them." If a company simply maintains them, they are not getting better. "One less at a time" is the way to do it.

As productive as JIT/TQC is, however, it needs a partner since it lacks planning capability. The generally accepted approach for planning resources is Manufacturing Resource Planning, MRP II. All manufacturing companies need a wide variety of resources. They include material, labor, equipment, tooling, space, money, and specifications. Missing only one hurts. It hurts productivity, it hurts deliveries, it can hurt quality, and it generates costly corrective actions. To have each resource available, economically, when needed, requires an effective planning system. Planning matched sets of resources is MRP II's forté. It's a process linking long-term aggregate plans to short-term detailed actions to insure that all activities and resources required to accomplish the company's objectives are properly coordinated.

Welding the strengths of JIT/TQC's abilities to continuously improve the process with MRP II's capabilities of planning resources becomes a powerful force for improving performance. "Matched sets of resources, flowing faster"—that's the best few words that I can put together to describe what happens when the two are used properly.

Does it sound too good to be true? Sound like one more promise that will turn out to be a mirage? All hype and no substance? What you need to do is evaluate what other companies have already demonstrated—it's not an untested theory. Bill cut his teeth on MRP II and JIT/TQC while working for Hewlett-Packard, another leading-edge company. Subsequently, he has helped a long list of other companies, ranging from commercial to defense, small to big, repetitive to job shop, make-to-stock to make-to-order, metal-bending to chemical, and from assembly to process. This book is laced with their names, their experiences, and their results.

To successfully operate the Continuous Change Machine, the four main controls are:

- It is started by a vision—a leader who can visualize what's achievable when everyone in his company works as a team to eliminate all aspects of waste.
- Its fuel is understanding—knowing how the process works.
- It moves when you have an action plan—a step-by-step roadmap showing where to begin, what to do, and where to go.
- It accelerates when you apply resources and dedication—the expenditures are small in comparison to the benefits, yet, changing your company requires commitment, education, and support.

As the Continuous Change Machine helps your company become increasingly more competitive, it also produces an invaluable by-product—the pride that comes with doing your job better.

For detailed instructions, read on.

Preface

Moving from traditional manufacturing approaches to JIT/TQC is much like progressing from walking to learning to ride a bicycle. You can read about the history of two-wheeled vehicles and watch others race on television, but to really appreciate the power of the process, you need to do it yourself. Making the transition is a little difficult and emotional first, but it is not really dangerous. Unfortunately, you cannot "sort of try out JIT/TQC" any more than you can "sort of ride" a bicycle. Both require a commitment.

You do not have to compete in the Tour de France the first time you attempt to ride a bicycle. You can select a controlled environment for learning and practicing. But, a full commitment is still required to obtain the necessary balance and realize the velocity improvements that are possible by riding a bicycle. Likewise, you do not have to immediately convert your entire facility to JIT/TQC, but to realize its full potential, you must make a full commitment to follow the process in the controlled environment of a well designed pilot. To achieve a breakthrough in performance there is no half step between walking and riding, just as there is no half step between traditional and JIT/TQC processes.

Much has been written about the philosophy of JIT/TQC, but little has been written regarding the process, and even less about how to implement the process. This book is written to help you bridge the gap from philosophy to practice. It is not a theoretical book. It is based on extensive experience—broad experience leading significant changes during more than twenty years of work in manufacturing companies. These changes have included moving from manual to computerized information processing, and designing, implementing, and then using Manufacturing Resource Planning systems. The last ten years have been dominated with JIT/TQC activities. Five of them were spent gaining hands-on JIT/TQC experience as a manager in manufacturing, design, marketing, materials, and information systems, with close ties to finance and personnel. Those five years were spent learning, implementing, interfacing, and using JIT/TQC in three new and mature factories, encompassing repetitive and job shop operations. The most recent years have been as a consultant, working at all levels with all areas in a wide variety of client companies, helping them unleash the power of continuous improvement.

In this book you will see that the underlying purpose of JIT/TQC is to continuously improve your ability to economically respond to change. You will see the philosophy explained in the context of accelerating velocities through a manufacturing pipeline. But, the most significant contribution of this book lies in the explanation of the "one less at a time" process that makes the philosophy practical. Neither JIT nor TQC are just philosophies. The real power of both lies in implementing their processes.

This book is written to help you transform the philosophy into practice. It thoroughly describes a proven implementation process that has repeatedly improved quality, throughput time, and other important measures tenfold. This magnitude of improvement has been for well-run companies; less disciplined companies have even more to gain. The changes do not require technical breakthroughs, capital outlays, or much out-of-pocket expense. But they do require a change in thinking. I don't promise the changes to be easy—competing is not easy either—but I do offer a breakthrough implementation process that is fast and economical and that will consistently produce results while unleashing the power of continuous improvement in your operation.

This book attempts to strike a rational balance. JIT and TQC are not the only things a company must do to compete, but it now appears unlikely that a company will remain competitive for long without the improvements JIT and TQC make possible. You will see how JIT/TQC provide a fertile environment for practical automation and a logical stepping-stone to cost-effective computer-integrated manufacturing. And you will see how it is to be used in conjunction with powerful planning tools such as Manufacturing Resource Planning.

It is important to realize that JIT/TQC will affect manufacturing no more than it does any other functional area. The constraints to higher velocities lie throughout every area and level in the company. Every person should become aware of the forthcoming changes and their associated responsibilities. Every member of the implementation team should thoroughly read this book to help guide them during the implementation of the JIT/TQC process, and to help them understand how to resolve some of the more difficult constraints to higher velocities, to help them avoid the most serious obstacles to unleashing the power of continuous improvement, and to steer them away from the most tempting pitfalls.

Others not on the team, or not immediately affected by the initial changes may choose to read only selected portions. If you choose not to read the entire book at first, at least read chapters 1–3 to understand the philosophy, process, changes, results, and responsibilities you can expect. Then read the chapters with subjects appropriate to your responsibilities. Finally, read chapters 12–14 on performance measures, the vision, and taking the next step.

All good ideas ultimately degenerate into hard work. This book is for those of you who want results. It is a how-to book. It will show you how to unleash the power of continuous improvement in your people through the use of JIT and TQC. I wish you much success and excitement and enjoyment in your JIT/TQC journey!

William A. Sandras
Productivity Centers International
4490 Monitor Rock Lane
Colorado Springs, CO 80904
Telephone: (719) 685-5405
FAX: (719) 685-5406

Just-in-Time:
Making
It Happen

Chapter One

Introducing High Velocity Performance

Accept change or remain behind in a state of shock.
—**Alvin Toffler**

The morning sun is rising behind a cowboy sitting on his horse, overlooking a dry riverbed. Years of experience show in the weathered lines of his face. Other riders, their horses pawing the ground aimlessly, are still wiping the sleep from their eyes. Suddenly, the first cowboy raises his hat above his head, lets out a sharp yip-yell, and charges down the embankment on his horse. Quickly the others follow. The thunder of pounding hooves and the shouts of cowboys fill the air. Dust is everywhere.

The message in this scene is simple. In business you either make dust—or you eat it!

This book is for those of you who are ready to make dust. Alvin Toffler wrote, "Accept change or remain behind in a state of shock— misunderstanding the new equipment, the new ways and the new ideas." Let me add, however, that merely acknowledging the need to change is not enough. To survive, our companies must successfully implement those changes that will continuously improve our competitive position.

Faced with the relentless onslaught of global competition, manufacturing must decide not *whether* it should change but *how*. Maintaining the status quo is a fatal option. As one factory manager explained to his employees, "We can either hide in the corner or rise to the competitive challenge." The painful fact is, there is no more business as usual. The choice in manufacturing has narrowed to whether *you control* how your business changes or you let the *competition control* the changes for you. Enter Just-in-Time and Total Quality Control (JIT/TQC).

Of course, JIT/TQC is not all your company will need to compete, but it is now clear that you will not remain competitive for long without its breakthrough capabilities. Leading competitors throughout the world have adopted a continuous-improvement philosophy. Even more important, they have converted that philosophy into action by aggressively implementing processes that make that philosophy practical and self-sustaining. These processes have allowed them to utilize every worker's potential to eliminate waste. The results have been breakthrough achievements in quality, delivery responsiveness, and cost.

This book will help you understand the *philosophy* of Just-in-Time and Total Quality Control (JIT/TQC). Its main focus, however, will be to help you *implement* these *processes*. This *is* a how-to book. It is a book for those who are willing to work to compete, not those looking for a panacea. It is a book for those who want to change aggressively, continuously, safely, and with a purposeful direction. It is for those who want to make dust, not eat it!

The process of change is not simple. In many ways, significant change is akin to trauma. In daily life, when we are confronted by a traumatic situation, our first reaction is often shock. Then we deny it could ever happen to us. Slowly, though, reality begins to set in and we realize that to cope we have to change our behavior. It is the same in adjusting to JIT/TQC.

In 1980, we came face-to-face with just such a dilemma at Hewlett-Packard in Vancouver, Washington, and we were driven to make a virtual about-face.

We had just gone through the process of consolidating all our personal-computer printer manufacturing, and we were busily turning out high-quality products. Not too long after our consolidated operations began, an ad appeared from a company called Epson. The ad stated simply that Epson was selling a new printer. It gave the retail price. There should be nothing too surprising about hearing from a new competitor. What did surprise us was that Epson's retail price was unbelievably close to our factory cost.

How could they do it? It was impossible. Shock! Denial! The printer must be a piece of junk. It was, of course, anything but junk.

Epson continued to sell that printer at what was basically our cost. We had watched other manufacturers' markets being eroded by other foreign competitors, and we worried that the same might happen to us. We finally had to accept that something was fundamentally different. Reality sets in. We had to learn this new ball game. Our task, then, was to close the education gap on those new processes that seemed so impractical, yet which produced these unbelievable results. We had to change our behavior.

We had heard rumors about new Japanese processes, but what little information we were able to scrape together back then just didn't seem practical. We had heard that inventory is wasteful, movement is wasteful, and inspection is wasteful. We had heard about processes serving immediate needs, with lot sizes of one, zero defects, and negligible setups. It was a nice philosophy and theory, but none of these ideas made much practical sense. We started attributing these things to Japanese culture and to their lower labor rates. Excuses!

Epson probably has no idea how much it had to do with Hewlett-Packard/Vancouver's involvement with JIT/TQC. But if HP/Vancouver hadn't learned about the philosophy of Just-in-Time and Total Quality Control and then successfully implemented the process, the Vancouver division might never have survived the intensely competitive personal-computer printer market, much less emerged as the successful global competitor that it is today.

This story was told at a JIT/TQC seminar conducted for Beckman Instruments. Beckman builds a variety of complex medical-laboratory diagnostic and bio-analyzing systems. When the story was finished, a woman from Beckman's marketing department stood up and told the audience that she had just returned from a trade show, where she had encountered the same phenomenon. A foreign competitor had built a machine that was functionally equivalent to Beckman's, and it was retailing for close to Beckman's cost. The threat is never more real until it hits close to home.

Many readers may be aware of a similar global encroachment story that threatened Xerox. Another happened at Tellabs, a Lisle, Illinois-based manufacturer of high-speed telecommunications products. When the divestiture of AT&T hit the telecommunications industry in 1983, the marketplace was prepared for a new era of giant profits. Tellabs had just posted one of its biggest years. "The perception was," says Tellabs' president Mike Birck, "that all of a sudden there would be an enormous marketplace that would just suck manufacturers in and create wealth beyond all measure. We certainly know now that that didn't happen."

What Birck, and the telecommunications industry in general, had not counted on was the incredible influx of global competition. Tellabs was suddenly faced with not just 15 or 20 national competitors, but close to 100 international rivals. Price became the competitive factor. Within a few years, though, the competitive battleground also included quality and delivery responsiveness.

Tellabs knew something had to be done to ensure its survival. Bold steps needed to be taken. The company sent its vice president of manufacturing to hear Hewlett-Packard's president, John Young, speak and was initiated into the world of JIT/TQC. It too had experienced first hand the volatile, highspeed changes that international competition can bring to the marketplace. Tellabs was determined to survive and thrive.

That company decision opened the door to doing business in a fashion no one had ever thought possible. It was a real breakthrough and the results were dramatic. In Tellabs' JIT/TQC pilot project, work-in-process (WIP) inventory was reduced by 80 percent. Lot sizes shrank from batches of 100 to 300 down to 40, a 60 to 75 percent drop. Throughput time went from twenty days to an amazing two days, a 90 percent reduction. Assembly-space requirements for the pilot products fell from 7,500 square feet to three manufacturing cells of 500 square feet each, an 80 percent reduction. As plant manager Bob Pastiak put it, "Everything happened at once. We got increased volume, better productivity, and better quality." Improvements are still continuing at Tellabs.

Global competition factors are not the only pressures that can inspire a company to adopt JIT/TQC. As mentioned earlier, Beckman Instruments had a run-in with foreign competition, but initially the company turned to JIT/TQC because the United States government was rapidly reshaping the way in which medical lab testing was to be reimbursed.

Beckman's customers in the 1970s were primarily hospital and research-lab technologists. The company was driven by technology. "We sold to those people interested in having the latest technology," said Dennis McDonald, manager of strategic projects for Beckman's Brea, California, operations.

During this period, doctors performing blood tests on their patients would normally order all the tests possible on a blood sample. The procedure was very expensive, however, and the government finally decided enough was enough and put a lid on the kind of testing these providers—Beckman's customers—could do. The government reimbursed only those tests that were targeted as clinically significant to a specific problem.

"All of a sudden, our total market changed," McDonald recalled. "Our customers were now the hospital administrators, and their intent was to get the most for their money. It became a price market not a technology market."

Up to that point, Beckman had experienced a fairly dynamic growth. Rather suddenly, everything came to a dead halt. "We had to completely redefine our business," McDonald said. "It was very painful. We had to start thinking about how we were going to face a whole new era as we approached the 1990s. We had to start managing our business better. We had to put together our strategies to deal with this evolution. That's when we started to look more closely at JIT/TQC."

HIGH VELOCITY MANUFACTURING

An excellent way to understand the capabilities of JIT/TQC is to picture a pipeline running through the factory. At one end, we pay our suppliers for material entering the pipeline. At the other end, our customers pay us for the products we ship. Our goal is to reduce the time between payment on one end and receipt on the other. Therefore, we need to move material through the pipeline more quickly. A fat pipeline will allow us to make shipment, but only sluggishly. With a narrower pipeline we can make the same rate of shipments if we accelerate the velocity of flow through the pipeline. A faster throughput time will also allow us to be more responsive to changes in the marketplace.

The Ford Motor Company River Rouge factory provides an excellent example of high velocity through a manufacturing pipeline (see figure 1.1). In 1926, this plant was able to go from raw ore to an engine to a car to cash in forty-one hours! Years later, Taiichi Ohno, at Toyota in Japan, built on Ford's philosophy and processes and developed the Toyota Production System. Today's version of the Ford and Toyota systems is called Just-in-Time/Total Quality Control.

We must realize, however, that in reducing the diameter of the pipeline and increasing velocities, we invariably uncover constraints. To further reduce the diameter of the pipeline without eliminating each

Figure 1.1
High Velocity Manufacturing

Mon.	7 PM	Boat Docks Loaded With Iron Ore Conversion Begins
Tue.	10:55 AM	Ore Conversion Complete Foundry Processes Continue
	12:55 PM	Cast Into Cylinder Blocks Cooling And Cleaning Begins
	5:05 PM	First Machining Operation Begins 58 Operations In 55 Min.
	6:00 PM	Block Enters Assembly
	7:45 PM	Motor Assembly Complete Shipped To Car Assembly Factory
Wed.	8:00 AM	Motor Enters Car Assembly Line
	Noon	Dealer Takes Delivery Of Car Payment Received

ORE TO PAYMENT IN 41 HRS. (INCL. 12 SHIPPING)!

- SOURCE: TARGET, FORD

constraint we encounter will slow the rate of flow and jeopardize shipments. We must, therefore, employ methods to determine the location and cause of these constraints. Once we successfully eliminate a constraint, we can then safely progress on our journey toward higher velocities. That is, of course, until we run into the next constraint, which, in turn, must also be eliminated.

It is true, however, that if we allow ourselves the luxury of a fat pipeline with low velocities, life is more comfortable. We are usually able to make shipments; constraints do not appear as often; and when they do, there is less turbulence. Ignorance of constraints may be blissful; unfortunately, it is not competitive.

In a competitive environment, the status quo is easy to maintain. It is also fatal. If the competition's processes are capable of achieving velocities ten times our own, enabling them to respond quickly and consistently with high quality while still delivering cost-effective shipments, we are indeed vulnerable. Traditional rates of improvement will only briefly prolong our inevitable decline. Competition may not be pleasant, but that is the way business works on this planet. The question is not whether we are able to make shipments with our traditional processes, but whether we will be able to obtain future orders to ship against.

THE PHILOSOPHY OF JUST-IN-TIME

JIT/TQC is designed to continuously improve our ability to economically respond to change. Constraints occur as our attempts to increase our velocity threatens to negatively affect quality, delivery, or cost. These constraints appear in the form of waste.

In a JIT/TQC environment, waste is defined as any activity that does not add value for the customer. It is the use of resources in excess of the theoretical minimum required (manpower, equipment, time, space, energy). Waste can be excess inventory, setup times, inspection, material movement, transactions, or rejects. Essentially, any resource that is not actively involved in a process that adds value is in a waste state.

Shigeo Shingo, one of the Japanese founding fathers of improved manufacturing methods, detailed what are now known as his Famous Seven Wastes. They are the following:

1. Waste of overproduction
2. Waste of waiting
3. Waste of transportation
4. Waste of stocks
5. Waste of motion
6. Waste of making defects
7. Waste of processing itself (when the product should not be made or the process should not be used).

Just-in-Time, however, is not just another project to eliminate waste. It is not just another scheme to motivate the work force or to reduce defects. It is not just another inventory-reduction project. It is not just another method to shrink throughput times, space, or setup times. It is not just a project for production or purchasing. It is not a project at all!

Just-in-Time is a process. It is not a list of things to do, but a process to help you prioritize what to do.

To repeat, the purpose of Just-in-Time is to improve a company's ability to economically respond to change. As the pipeline shrinks, Just-in-Time will highlight and prioritize those constraints that impede the flow and block the company's ability to quickly and economically respond to change. In addition, once each constraint is made visible, Just-in-Time forces action to eliminate it, thereby stimulating the use of Total Quality Control.

After following the JIT/TQC philosophy, process, and procedures outlined in this book, Beckman Instruments achieved a 92 percent reduction in throughput times for a complex medical diagnostic instrument they introduced. Manufacturing this piece of equipment involved optics, robotics, electronics, fluid handling and mechanical assemblies. The company then realized similar results in its sheet-metal area and is now applying JIT/TQC to the manufacture of reagents, chemical compounds that initiate blood testing reactions.

The Harris Company achieved an 86 percent reduction in lead times in an integrated-circuit assembly area, with similar results in a wafer-fab area. It also accomplished an 87 percent lead-time reduction in its manufacture of long-range radios. Hallmark Cards achieved an 85 percent reduction in its "Shoebox" greeting-card line and is poised for the same results in other areas. Tellabs obtained a 90 percent reduction in lead times. NCR and Hewlett-Packard have also achieved similar results at several factories throughout the world and in a variety of product lines. Tektronix is fast approaching the same numbers in the manufacture of single- and multilayered printed circuit boards, having already incrementally reduced lot sizes from a maximum of 270 to 50, with a goal of 10 or less.

The improvement in defects per million ranged from 40 percent at Beckman to 90 percent at Tellabs. Factory floor space reductions, not counting warehouse space that was saved, ranged from 45 percent at one NCR facility to 65 percent at Tellabs.

The increased velocity resulted in millions of dollars in inventory reductions for even the smallest companies and divisions mentioned.

These companies did not adopt JIT/TQC to achieve a 10 percent improvement: they sought a tenfold improvement.

The time from education of the implementation team to pilot turn-on ranged from 45 days at Beckman to 170 days at one NCR facility that converted a major circuit-board assembly area in one step. These results occurred within the first few months of a significant JIT/TQC pilot. Each pilot was designed to immediately address the most difficult challenges to a breakthrough. This will be discussed in detail in Chapter 4, when we examine the breakthrough pilot specifications.

Tellabs converted its entire factory over to JIT/TQC in ten months, and the whole $120 million company was using JIT/TQC within about eighteen months. Beckman had a significant pilot in eight divisions in eleven months. Harris, NCR, Hewlett-Packard, and Hallmark are also focusing on implementing JIT/TQC quickly and successfully throughout their entire companies. They each recognize the competitive advantage it can offer.

As time progresses, each company continues to improve and to obtain similar results in other areas. These results include accelerating velocities through the supplier and customer distribution pipeline and through the sales and order-entry process.

Can every company expect impressive results? The answer is yes. There is no evidence at this time to indicate that one industry will have better results than any other. Certainly, any given company within an industry has as much a chance as its competitor.

Companies that have received similar results, including those listed here, come from a wide variety of environments. Some have assembly operations, while others have chemical, biological, or printing processes. Some work with metal, electronics, wood, paper, plastics, and rubber. Some have health regulations or defense contracts. Some have high-volume/low-variety product lines, while others have low-volume/high-variety. Some are considered high technology and others low. Some are multinational. Some are small. Some are unionized and others are not. Some dominate their markets, others want to. As I was developing this list, none of the companies that immediately came to mind were from the Far East, although there are certainly many good examples there as well.

According to conservative estimates, well-run companies should expect the results shown in figure 1.2. More and more are achieving tenfold improvement, in throughput times, quality, and inventory turns.

As we indicated earlier, JIT/TQC is not the only thing your company needs to compete, but it now appears unlikely that you will remain competitive for long without it. It appears that the biggest obstacle to achieving breakthrough successes with JIT/TQC is mental, not physical.

Figure 1.2
JIT/TQC Typical Results

50-90% REDUCTION IN THROUGHPUT TIMES
50-90% REDUCTION IN WIP
60-80% REDUCTION IN SCRAP AND REWORK
50-90% REDUCTION IN SETUP TIMES
30-60% REDUCTION IN MFG. SPACE REQUIRED
10-1000X IMPROVEMENT IN QUALITY SPECIFICS

THREE TO SEVEN YEARS

5-10X IMPROVEMENT IN OVERALL QUALITY
4-10X IMPROVEMENT IN INVENTORY TURNS
IMPROVEMENT IN RETURN ON ASSETS

JUST-IN-TIME IS NOT THE SAME OLD WAY

With such dramatic results, it should be evident that Just-in-Time is a different way of operating a company. Waste is not defined in the same way. It is not exposed in the same way, and people are not motivated to change it in the same way. Just-in-Time is a breakthrough from the limits of the same old way.

Traditional Steps in Manufacturing (The Same Old Way)

- We process material.
- We inspect it.
- We move it.
- We put it into queues.
- We put it into stock.

Suppose, for example, we need one plastic handset case to assemble a telephone. It has been decided, however, that a minimum economic order for the case is 500. We use one case and put 499 into inventory. It was not in the plans, but suppose the 499 sit for six months. How much more valuable are those handset cases to the customer six months later? There is, of course, no added value. Had those handsets been left in inventory for a month, it would have been better than six months, but they are still no more valuable to the customer after a month than when they were first built. One day would be even better than a month. Unless we are making a product like wine or whiskey, letting something age in inventory adds no value. No rational customer will pay more for an old product. Sitting inventory is 100 percent wasteful.

If we put the 499 pieces into a queue in front of a machine, it is still 100 percent wasteful. All we've done is establish another inventory location. By waiting, no matter how patiently, we add zero value to the product. As an added insult, we also have consumed valuable floor space, increased material handling, and raised the risk of obsolescence.

If we move our handsets from one operation to another in a building a quarter of a mile away and then bring them back, is the stock more valuable? Have we added any value during that half-mile trip? No, only delays and dust. Movement, according to Just-in-Time, is 100 percent wasteful. One company calculated that the combined movements to make its product totaled 3.7 miles— and this firm had a seemingly well-organized flow!

What about inspection? We now have all these well-traveled parts before us. The reality is, however, that each part is either good or bad before we ever inspect or test it. Our examination might increase the chance of damage but no amount of inspection can make it better. Just-in-Time teaches that inspection is 100 percent wasteful. One company's process involved one worker followed by three inspectors: one production inspector to catch defects before the quality-control inspector, who was then followed by a government inspector!

Finally, all that is left are the process steps. Those processes that cause scrap and rework are also wasteful. Only those that produce good products—that add value—are not wasteful. They are the only ones that add value for the customer. But we also create waste when we use good processes to make good products prematurely.

To some, this may sound like an incredibly impractical approach to manufacturing. Inventory may be wasteful, they argue, but it is absolutely necessary given the real-world conditions. Inspection wasteful?

What about customer expectations or legal requirements? If material handling is 100 percent wasteful, how do we move parts from one operation to the next? Magic? There is little wonder that people go into the trauma stages of shock and denial when they first hear about JIT/TQC. It's true that we can't manufacture products without inventory. What JIT/TQC eliminates, however, is that dominant portion of the inventory that is not in a value-added state—inventories that are sitting and moving about, striving to eliminate them if possible. It also attacks inventories in the process of being transformed in terms of improving cost and quality. JIT/TQC attacks the reasons for wasteful inventory[1]. JIT/TQC seeks to minimize all waste, not just the waste of inventory. Therefore, it also addresses the causes of the need to inspect, move, or engage in any other nonvalue-added activity.

Because of lot sizes and transportation, even if we do something to reduce inventories, aren't they still necessary to ensure shipments when we have fluctuating demands and variable processes? Certainly! There is no conflict between inventory being necessary and at the same time wasteful.

Just-in-Time does not require that we justify why things are necessary under today's conditions. It assumes we have good reasons for our past decisions. There is no need to feel guilty about having made them. However, we should feel guilty for trying to maintain the status quo in the future.

The question posed by Just-in-Time is, how can the processes be changed to eliminate the need for the non-value-added activity or inventory?

If we don't change anything, of course, inventory remains necessary. If we don't change the level of quality, inspection remains necessary. If we don't change the process flow, then product movement is also necessary. If nothing changes, the waste remains, and the competitive bells toll louder. There are plenty of excuses for maintaining the status quo.

---

[1] Throughout the book, the word "inventory" is generally used to denote materials, but readers, particularly those in nonmanufacturing areas, should be aware that inventories can exist in all processes. The engineering-change process typically has an inventory queue of changes waiting to be processed. Queues of customer inquiries, service calls, and insurance claims can also be considered inventory from a JIT/TQC perspective. The same applies to a backlog of requests in the information systems department or the maintenance department. The continuous improvement philosophy and, as we will soon see, the JIT/TQC process apply in all areas, not just production.

Unfortunately, there can be no more status quo. As Oliver Wight said, "In business there is no par, only competition."

PHILOSOPHY WITHOUT PROCESS

On one level, Just-in-Time is very easy to implement. Suppose our management gives us the objective to do Just-in-Time. Returning to our earlier example, if inventory is wasteful, we won't make 500 telephone handsets, we'll make just one. Management is pleased with our progress toward Just-in-Time. Of course, our product cost skyrockets when we can't amortize the long setup over a batch of units, but at least we have taken one step toward Just-in-Time. Next, if inspection is wasteful, we can easily eliminate it. Adequately performing inspection is difficult; stopping it is easy. Management is now ecstatic with our progress. Unfortunately, product quality, from the perspective of our customers, will probably plummet, but at least there will be no more inspection. And we've taken two steps toward Just-in-Time.

Next, we make one handset, we don't inspect it, and we send it to the customer on time! Management is preparing to reward us. Unfortunately, that handset ends up being dead on arrival, which is hardly a satisfactory delivery performance, and our costs are rising. Things are worse than ever. Just-in-Time seems to be driving operations in the opposite direction from what we desire. Is Just-in-Time *the* answer? No.

Just-in-Time is *not* the answer. Neither is Total Quality Control (TQC), Manufacturing Resource Planning (MRP II), Total Productive Maintenance (TPM), Computer Aided Design (CAD), Computer Aided Manufacturing (CAM), Computer Integrated Manufacturing (CIM), Design for Manufacturability (DFM), or robotics. No panacea exists. The answer for manufacturing lies in our ability to continuously and economically

- increase the quality and reliability of our products, processes, and services
- improve our delivery dependability and responsiveness
- lower our costs for value delivered.

The JIT/TQC philosophy is to eliminate waste, but if we blindly follow the philosophy without understanding the process, we will make cost, delivery, and quality worse, not better.

JIT/TQC is not the only answer. It is, however, a simple and extremely powerful tool designed to expose, prioritize, and force elimination of constraints to our ability to quickly and economically respond to change. The direction is to maximize the value-added activities and eliminate the cost-only ones. In its purest form, that would mean lot sizes of one, no inspection, no movement, zero defects, and process variation.

Impossible to reach? Only to those who never try to take their understanding beyond the philosophy, or who never take the time to learn and practice the *process* that makes JIT/TQC practical. *Learning the JIT/TQC philosophy, without understanding the process is one of the biggest mistakes people make in implementing JIT/TQC.*

THE PROCESS OF JIT/TQC

The philosophy of JIT/TQC is to eliminate waste. The ultimate goal is zero waste. The unanswered question is, "how can we use JIT/TQC to help continuously improve quality, delivery and cost, when on the surface it will make all three worse?"

To meet the JIT/TQC goal of zero waste, we must learn how to economically manufacture "One Less at a Time." For example, imagine that in a segment of our manufacturing pipeline we have 1,000 telephones in process. What stops us from just as economically making high-quality shipments with a maximum of 999 in the pipeline? We can also imagine that we normally have thirty-five engineering changes in queue. What stops us from never letting that queue exceed 34?

To return to our previous setup example, let us say we have an economic process at a lot size of 500 handsets. Walking through the JIT/TQC process flow chart (see figure 1.3), we first ask, Is the order quantity greater than one? The answer is yes. The order quantity is 500. Next, following the chart, we ask, Is the process economical? Yes, over the years, we've determined that 500 makes good sense and is economical. Does the next block of the flow chart say, "Leave well enough alone"? No. This would be the approach of a status-quo mentality, which is fatal in a competitive environment. The JIT flow chart says, subtract one from the lot size. If the lot size is 500, we take one away and make it 499.

Now, we must again ask, Is the order quantity greater than one? Yes, it's 499. Is it economical? Yes. In fact we can't tell the difference. Even

Figure 1.3
Just-in-Time

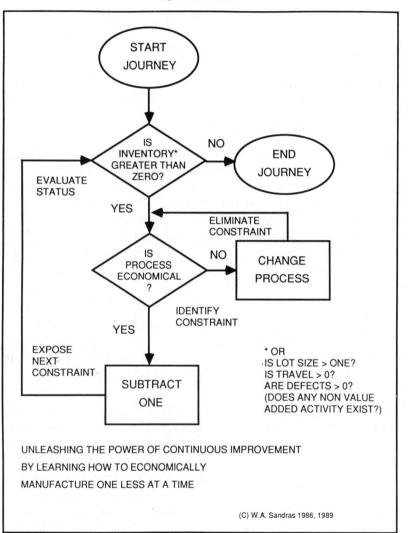

START
JOURNEY

IS INVENTORY* GREATER THAN ZERO?

NO

END
JOURNEY

EVALUATE
STATUS

YES

ELIMINATE
CONSTRAINT

IS PROCESS ECONOMICAL ?

NO

CHANGE
PROCESS

IDENTIFY
CONSTRAINT

YES

EXPOSE
NEXT
CONSTRAINT

SUBTRACT
ONE

* OR
·IS LOT SIZE > ONE?
IS TRAVEL > 0?
ARE DEFECTS > 0?
(DOES ANY NON VALUE
ADDED ACTIVITY EXIST?)

UNLEASHING THE POWER OF CONTINUOUS IMPROVEMENT
BY LEARNING HOW TO ECONOMICALLY
MANUFACTURE ONE LESS AT A TIME

(C) W.A. Sandras 1986, 1989

so, our velocity is $1/500$th higher. We can now economically respond to change slightly faster than before. We continue this process down to 350. Is the process economical? It's not grossly out of line, but it's becoming difficult to get the required work done, because we are spending so much time doing setups. We're starting to feel the constraint. The first rock has surfaced, so we turn to the "no" branch of the chart. Does it say, "Add inventory until the process goes back to where it is comfortable again"? No. It says, "Change the process." The constraint being felt is coming from setups. We're doing too many setups. They're starting to consume too much of the machine time. Now, we have to change the process. Just-in-Time is forcing us to see how we can have *more* setups in *less* time. As we continue through this flow chart we will expose layer after layer of constraints.

The first constraint to higher velocities exposed in this example is setup. We make a change and reduce our setup times. Is the process economical? Yes, we've made a substantial improvement and things are a lot better. Does that mean we've completed the job? No. It means we answer yes to the "economical" question and drop down again and take one more away.

We get down to 300 and hit another snag. Given the same level of output, we have 40 percent more activity in the stockroom, and we're driving costs up, not down. The answer is to change the material-handling processes. They have become a constraint, just as setups were earlier. Just-in-Time is driving us to store and control material at the point of use.

After solving that problem we get down to 250. Here, we find we have twice as many shop orders, purchase orders and related transactions. In essence, we have doubled our paperwork for the same amount of output. The paperwork process itself has become a constraint. Just-in-Time wants smaller lots and less paperwork. We've been taught since we were little children that you can't have your cake and eat it too. How can we do both? We can't unless we change the process. If we don't change the process, we'll have more paperwork, not less. This is precisely why the Just-in-Time process strives for the elimination of purchase orders and work orders as we know them today.

As we continue on through this process of "One Less at a Time," we accelerate the velocity of flow through the pipeline each step of the way. However, we also find constraints arising from transportation and distribution, preventive maintenance, the number of parts and suppliers, planning and forecast accuracy, and many other areas.

In the planning area, for instance, to manufacture products in a Just-in-Time environment, it is absolutely essential to be able plan what we want and when. Without an adequate planning system, our chances of running a successful Just-in-Time operation are nil. Though this will be discussed in greater detail in chapter 6, companies that don't have a Manufacturing Resource Planning system in place prior to using Just-in-Time frequently implement one later to improve their planning process. It has also been observed that companies that have a Manufacturing Resource Planning system already in place prior to Just-in-Time are often driven to use it better afterward.

It is important to realize that Just-in-Time is not a planning tool. But if planning is a constraint to higher velocities, Just-in-Time will prioritize its improvement as we go through the process of economically manufacturing "One Less at a Time."

Again, we must realize that just making shipments is no longer enough to survive. We have to make quality on-time shipments with continuously less waste if we're to stay in business. Therefore, Just-in-Time drives on-time shipments with "One Less" in the lot size, or in the pipeline. Each time we uncover a constraint and eliminate it, we achieve a new economic level of competitiveness. JIT/TQC is not an inventory reduction project, but the process of JIT/TQC does use step-by-step reductions in inventory to expose opportunities for improvement. Reducing the inventory in the pipeline not only saves money, it also lets us see the next opportunity. We can have our cake and eat it too.

As we narrow the pipeline, we must accelerate the velocity of the flow to continue to make shipments at our previous level. As we attempt to accelerate the velocity, we will invariably expose constraints that slow our progress. While these may feel like problems, we should view each constraint as an opportunity to become more competitive; then its elimination will constitute a noticeable step forward.

Once we become acquainted with the Just-in-Time process, we begin to perceive the many opportunities for improvement that we could not see before. These opportunities are shuffled together like a deck of cards. Each time we enter the "change process" block on the Just-in-Time flow chart see (figure 1.3) we are required to draw another card. Each card will define a prioritized constraint that needs to be eliminated

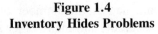

Figure 1.4
Inventory Hides Problems

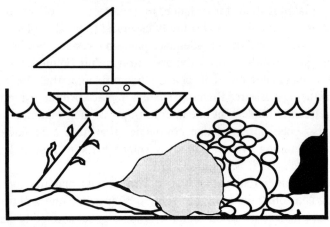

before we can continue our Just-in-Time journey, "One Less at a Time." We are expected to repeat our loops through the Just-in-Time process until there is no waste left. The process of improvement is continuous and relentless; it allows no place for complacency until we are perfect. It promotes the mentality and drives the action we need to function well in a competitive global environment.

The pipeline analogy of may seem oversimplified, but that is precisely how the JIT/TQC process works. A process does not need to be sophisticated to be effective! Chapters 3 and 4 will show how to convert that analogy into a simple visual control system.

Another way to represent the philosophy and process of JIT/TQC is through the use of an analogy depicting rocks in the water (see figure 1.4). As long as there is enough water to cover the rocks, you can sail along without any obstruction. The water represents inventory, while the rocks are problems, and smooth sailing means the company is easily making shipments. And you will make shipments, or your replacement will do it for you. Just making shipments, however, is not enough for survival. We must make them better in terms of quality, delivery, and cost in order to continue to compete.

Just-in-Time recognizes that extra inventory, in itself, is wasteful. Therefore, following the "One Less at a Time" process, it says, take a measure of water out, then take another measure out, then another. As the water level drops, a rock will eventually become exposed. Suddenly, the crew's energies are focused on the problem that lies ahead. The crew must change course to avoid the rocks until obstacles can be permanently removed, but they are now always aware of an obstacle in the path of a quicker route. Ignorance of a problem may be bliss, but awareness is more competitive.

Some might say that's a crazy way to try to make shipments. A clever sort might suggest using sonar or a diver to detect the problems. Then the problems could be fixed before the inventory was lowered. What's wrong with this approach? Nothing! That is what we should have been doing all along.

The only difficulty is, being human, we do only what is at the top of our priority lists. Inventory allows us to work on those problems we choose, while providing us the ability to alter the priority of others, often interorganizational ones. Still others go unnoticed altogether. If we send a diver down, the only person to see the problem is the diver. With Just-in-Time, the whole work group sees the problem. Suddenly, there is the added benefit of having a number of different minds coming up with possible ways to remove those rocks that have impeded our flow. With Just-in-Time we cannot distort the priority of the problems we are forced to address, choosing only those over which we seemingly have the most control. We must tackle each in the sequence presented. The fact that some are hard and some are easy makes no difference to JIT/TQC.

JIT/TQC is a people-intensive process. One of the greatest wastes I have encountered is the inefficient use of our people. We hire hands, but rarely use the heads that go with them. What JIT/TQC makes clear is that everyone in the company is a potential problem-solver. Not all problems require an engineering degree or management expertise. JIT/TQC uses the intelligence that is liberally and randomly distributed throughout the entire organization. Intelligence is not all concentrated at the top, or in engineering. When problems are highlighted, the object is to get everybody thinking about solutions. The more people are focused on a problem, the better the chance of making a breakthrough. The concept of the "thinking worker," which enlists the help of *everyone* who is involved in the process (including the thinking manager and professional), is essential to Just-in-Time and Total Quality Control. It will be reviewed in greater detail in chapter 10.

To reiterate, the Just-in-Time journey begins and advances as we learn how to economically make "One Less at Time." It does not begin with zero inventory, or zero inspection. Perfection is where you want to end up, not where you start, and you don't get there in one step. In fact, *JIT/TQC is a never-ending series of small, controlled steps, not one great leap forward.*

The process of "One Less at a Time" is as critical to Just-in-Time as the computer is to Manufacturing Resource Planning. We can do Manufacturing Resource Planning without a computer, but we can't do much. We can eliminate waste without the "One Less" process, but we are operating without JIT/TQC's built-in driver for continuous improvement. Good employees have always tried to improve, but performing JIT/TQC is not simply a matter of improving any way we choose. If that were the case we would have no need for a new term. The "One Less" process is the mechanism used by JIT/TQC to expose, prioritize, and force communications about constraints to our ability to more quickly and economically respond to change. *"One Less at a Time" is what makes JIT/TQC different* from the same old improvement methods of the past.

We know that numerous opportunities for improvement exist. Unfortunately, we can no longer recognize a large percentage of them, because they have become part of our everyday routine. Opportunities are spread throughout the entire company, but efforts to make progress are fragmented and too frequently limited to internal areas of responsibility. Many major opportunities go unaddressed, not only because they involve more than one organization, but because coordination of independent priorities is too difficult. We often learn to live with these problems instead of eliminating them.

The power of JIT/TQC lies in its ability to identify and prioritize constraints, and to force customer/supplier communications to eliminate them. Some of the constraints that often appear are shown in figure 1.5.

The arrows indicate the direction JIT/TQC dictates we take with each constraint to make it consistent with higher velocities and quality, delivery, and cost.

As will be demonstrated throughout this book, "One Less at a Time" is a constant, step-by-step methodology for making Just-in-Time work in *any* "production" environment. It is an effective process whether your product is electrical, mechanical, or chemical, or you are in an

Figure 1.5
"One Less at a Time" Drives . . .

↓ SETUP TIMES
↓ LOT SIZES
↓ MATERIAL HANDLING
↑ DELIVERY FREQUENCY
↓ MOVE DISTANCES
↓ TRANSPORTATION COSTS
↓ PAPER WORK
↑ QUALITY OF PRODUCT AND PROCESS
↑ PREVENTIVE MAINTENANCE
↑ PLANNING ACCURACY
↑ FORECAST ACCURACY
↑ SCHEDULE STABILITY
↑ FLEXIBILITY OF PROCESS & PERSONNEL
↓ NUMBER OF SUPPLIERS
↓ QUANTITY OF PART NUMBERS
↑ LINKS TO OTHER DEPARTMENTS
↑ LINKS TO SUPPLIERS
↑ LINKS TO CUSTOMERS

office environment processing claims, forms or orders. Just-in-Time and its "One Less" driver apply if your output is high-volume/low-mix, or low-volume/high-mix products. The Just-in-Time process doesn't care that we are going to make the same product or a different product every time. From a Just-in-Time perspective, what is important *is not that you repeat building the same product over and over, rather that you repeat your processes.* If you are populating fifty different circuit boards with components, from a process point of view, the fact that there are fifty different boards doesn't matter—you're still putting components on circuit boards. The same is true if you are printing fifty different forms or machining fifty different castings. The basic process steps repeat whether the same item is being replaced or a different item is the next to be completed.

It doesn't take a college degree to understand that if we can economically increase our velocities through our manufacturing facilities, we will become more responsive and therefore more competitive. This is especially true if we can extend that increased velocity from the final consumer down through our supplier's suppliers. Constraints, however, lie in all areas of the company, not just on the factory floor. The power of the JIT/TQC process lies in its simple ability to expose and prioritize constraints, to motivate the entire company population to eliminate them, and to provide visual feedback as progress is made. It is a powerful process, driving continuous improvement until all waste is eliminated. With Just-in-Time, there is no resting point or plateau between today and perfection. This is exactly the mentality and process required for a competitive environment.

THE PHILOSOPHY OF TOTAL QUALITY CONTROL

An essential partner in the Just-in-Time process is Total Quality Control.[2] Just-in-Time and Total Quality Control are two sides of the same coin. Whereas Just-in-Time exposes problems and forces us to do something about them, Total Quality Control is a tool used to understand those constraints for eventual elimination. It would be foolish to implement Just-in-Time without Total Quality Control. There is no reason to begin a process that exposes problems unless we have an effective procedure to make them go away. Total Quality Control is the process that we use to understand the cause of these constraints.

Armand V. Feigenbaum, president of General Systems Company, and author of the term "Total Quality Control," defines it as "an effective system for integrating the quality-development, quality-maintenance, and quality-improvement efforts of the various groups in an organization so as to enable production and service at the most economical levels which allow for full customer satisfaction."

"Quality" does not mean "best" in any absolute sense. It means "best" for certain customer conditions. Feigenbaum defines product quality as "the composite characteristics of engineering and manufac-

---

[2] People use a variety of names for Total Quality Control, just as they call Just-in-Time by different names. In this book, "Total Quality Control" encompasses the broadest philosophy down through the various processes to the narrowest technique.

turing that determine the degree to which the product will meet the expectations of the customer." Deming defined quality as "meeting or exceeding customer expectations." Juran described it as "fitness for use, and conformance to specifications." Crosby then refined that to a "conformance to requirements." There are new voices being heard too. In Japan, Taguchi describes quality as "the reduction of variability around target values," or, essentially, elimination of part variability.

It has been suggested that Total Quality Control can be used without Just-in-Time. That is technically correct. But in practice, most companies that try Total Quality Control without Just-in-Time achieve only limited success. When management is the sole driver for Total Quality Control, we sometimes see impressive results, but usually, we see only pockets of success. However, when driven by Just-in-Time and encouraged by management, Total Quality Control will more often permeate the entire organization. "When Just-in-Time and Total Quality Control are implemented together," says Roger Brooks, executive vice president of Oliver Wight Education Associates, "it far surpasses any superimposed, independent quality-improvement program."

Necessity is the mother of invention and the reality is, *Just-in-Time sets up the need to practice Total Quality Control.* The sum of the power of both of these processes is greater than their individual parts. They reinforce each other. Like Just-in-Time, Total Quality Control incorporates a philosophy aimed at continuous process improvements resulting in increased customer satisfaction.

A customer can be defined as either another company, another division or department within the same company, or the following operation. A supplier would similarly be defined as another company, another division or department within the same company, or the preceding operation.

The word "Total" applies to all levels, all employees, all functions, all processes, all output, all input, all suppliers and all customers.

"Quality" denotes the study of the characteristics of our products and processes. "Control" is the ability to make them behave as we intend. The better we understand our products and processes, the better chance we have of making them behave in a predictable manner.

It would be a mistake to limit our application of Total Quality Control simply to the production floor. It affects and improves all areas of the company, including customers and suppliers. In one case, a well-known

Just-in-Time facility was having trouble with inventory-record accuracy in the stockroom. Some of the material was in the warehouse and some was on the production floor. The company had not broken its older work-order system of issuing material into and out of the stockroom. A constraint arose as material began to move faster and in smaller lot sizes, causing an increase in the number of transactions and hence in the chances for error.

During the investigation of this problem, quality control charts were posted throughout production. But no data had been gathered on their inventory-record accuracy problem. They had done a good job of Total Quality Control in the production area, but they had no data on problems in other functions. Total Quality Control was used strictly on the production floor, but it applies in all areas.

THE PROCESS OF TOTAL QUALITY CONTROL

The process of Total Quality Control helps us understand how to break up a problem into prioritized pieces. This problem-solving approach is accomplished by following the Plan, Do, Check, Action circle (PDCA, sometimes referred to as the Deming circle). (See figure 1.6.) Numerous variations on the basic PDCA circle are in existence today.

This process will be explained in greater detail in Chapter 11. But for now, the first step is to describe the problem. The next phase is to quantifiably understand the current situation. Once we understand what's causing the problem, then we can begin to develop countermeasures. We must then verify that our countermeasures are working as expected. Finally, we must standardize the approach to prevent the problem from occurring in other areas.

There is no secret to Total Quality Control or to Just-in-Time. The attitudes and techniques are the same in any language and for any company. Those companies that have successfully pursued JIT/TQC are now recording defects not in percentages but in parts per million and, in some cases, billion. They have integrated both the philosophy and the processes of JIT/TQC into their business, and in so doing they have realized a continuous advantage.

WHAT IS THE DOWNSIDE?

JIT/TQC is not expensive. It doesn't take a long time to implement. You don't have to buy special computer hardware or software. The

Figure 1.6
TQC Process

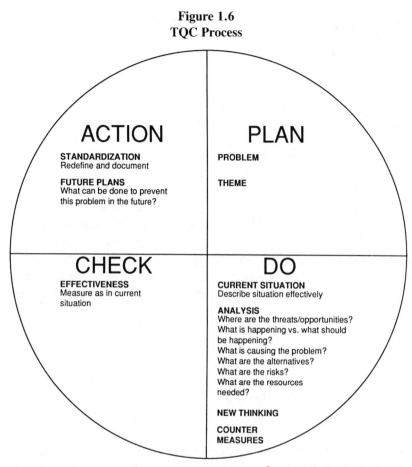

ACTION

STANDARDIZATION
Redefine and document

FUTURE PLANS
What can be done to prevent
this problem in the future?

PLAN

PROBLEM

THEME

CHECK

EFFECTIVENESS
Measure as in current
situation

DO

CURRENT SITUATION
Describe situation effectively

ANALYSIS
Where are the threats/opportunities?
What is happening vs. what should
be happening?
What is causing the problem?
What are the alternatives?
What are the risks?
What are the resources
needed?

NEW THINKING

**COUNTER
MEASURES**

Courtesy: Hewlett-Packard

downside of JIT/TQC, however, is that to seize its potential, you must tap every bit of leadership skill you possess in order to accomplish the attitude and process changes required. George Bernard Shaw once said, "Progress is impossible without change, and those who cannot change their minds cannot change anything."

It's one thing to maintain the status quo; it's another to lead yourself and others into a new environment. That's the hard part of JIT/TQC. There are a lot of administrators out there who haven't had to develop or use their leadership abilities. Leadership is not as critical in a status-quo environment. This is not to imply that in a JIT/TQC environment administrative skills are not important; Just-in-Time simply requires more. Extensive leadership throughout the organization will be needed to take a company into this new world.

Initially, JIT/TQC demands a certain amount of risk taking. However, the changes aren't as risky as one might imagine. In fact, it is difficult to think of any opportunity that will yield greater benefits, with such a small resource investment, in such a short period of time. The potential loss is minimal. The potential gain is enormous, especially if you implement JIT/TQC according to a proven process, such as the one described in this book. There is very little out-of-pocket expense. The only significant investment is time, and that is a priority decision each company must make.

Another element that relieves some of the sense of risk is that JIT/TQC is team dependent. At the heart of all successful breakthrough JIT/TQC implementations is a joining of company forces. Once the leadership drive to make these changes has been activated, then the environment to facilitate the changes in all functional areas must be established. There must be a willingness from all functional areas within a company to work together as a team. The motivation for these people to work together must come from the leader. This is the key to JIT/TQC: *one company* working together, not separate divisions battling for turf.

Manufacturing companies are often made up of a group of disparate islands. In one quadrant is manufacturing; in the others are engineering, finance, and marketing. Many times, these islands communicate not as parts of a whole, but as if they had totally separate agendas. As will be shown in chapter 2, the JIT/TQC implementation team helps breaks down those barriers. All functions need to be heard from and included, because everyone will be affected. Teamwork doesn't come easy, but the pilot approach helps to build the bonds necessary for people to work together.

There will be problems, but with JIT/TQC, the words *"problem" and "opportunity"* become synonymous. There is no better way to build a team than to ask a group of people to solve a common problem. I will discuss this in greater detail when I examine Total Quality Control in Chapter 11.

ESTABLISHING THE CORPORATE CULTURE

To establish the aggressive attitude necessary for seeking out constraints, a company culture conducive to change must be developed. For Beckman Instruments' first JIT/TQC discussions, George Killianey,

Beckman's JIT/TQC evangelist, arranged a meeting at a local hotel. The meeting was attended by the president of the company, the vice president of operations, middle managers, supervisors, and direct labor personnel from the proposed pilot area. It was a continuous chain from the top to the bottom. When Beckman's vice president of operations, Randy Davis, looked out at this audience to present a short introduction he was momentarily speechless. Beckman had never before gathered together a group composed of so many different elements of the company. They were indeed doing things differently.

Everyone attending that meeting could see that the president of the company felt JIT/TQC was important enough for him to dedicate his time to it, and the message traveled down. Beckman's president demonstrated his support and intent, and he has supported his company's JIT/TQC implementation from that first day on through its current phases. Employees need to see that level of commitment. They need to know that this is not just another fad, but something management has bought into with its time too.

Just-in-Time and Total Quality Control establish a consistent management operating philosophy. They both drive for continuous improvements, and both flourish with an emotional commitment from top management.

WHY CHANGE TO JIT/TQC?

There will always be those who believe that they will not be affected by change, that they will somehow escape paying the price of competition. That is the risky choice.

The president of Hewlett-Packard and Chairman of the President's Commission on Industrial Competitiveness, John Young said, "All of us face a new reality—*global competition.* It requires from us a new vision and a new resolve. If we can forge these, we can, and will, meet the challenge we face." As Walter Goddard, President of Oliver Wight Education Associates said, "In order to survive, we must break tradition."

Standards of performance that used to be acceptable are just not competitive today. An analogy can be made with the high jump. In 1948, using a scissors kick, John Winter of Australia set the men's Olympic high-jump record at six feet and six inches. Over the next twenty years, as jumpers used a process called the "roll," that record rose to just over seven feet. Then, in 1968, along came an American with a crazy approach called the "Fosbury flop." People said it was interesting but not practical. They were certain he wouldn't get very far with it. Besides it was dangerous, and was even against the rules. Today, jumpers routinely use the "flop," and the record is near eight feet. To the uninitiated, JIT/TQC, like the "flop," appears impractical. However, processes and policies need to change for a breakthrough to occur. There's nothing wrong with our old processes; it's just that some of them are no longer competitive.

Professors Steven C. Wheelwright and Robert H. Hayes, co-authors of *Restoring our Competitive Edge,* contend that manufacturing basically goes through four stages. In the first, the company is "internally neutral"; that is, it tries only to minimize the negative potential of manufacturing. During the second stage, when the company is "externally neutral," it seeks parity with its competitors. When manufacturing is achieving a credible level of support for the business, the company has entered the third stage and is "internally supportive." In the fourth and final stage the company becomes "externally supportive," maximizing manufacturing's competitive advantage.

JIT/TQC helps bring your company into this fourth stage, turning your manufacturing operations into a competitive weapon. Constraints to higher velocities, however, are not found only within manufacturing, but exist throughout the entire company. These too will require change. Essentially, you must seek to continuously improve your ability to economically respond to change. Everyone is involved.

It is important to realize that before the year 2000, the quest for continued improvement will be commonplace in manufacturing. We will also witness higher productivity from all assets, including labor. Transportation and distribution will take on added significance as waste is driven out of other portions of the system. We will see local manufacturing regaining a lost competitive advantage. The question you must ask yourself today is whether your company will be one of those to make it to the new millennium, or whether you will simply be the best scissor-kick high jumper in the world, locked into a way of doing things that is no longer competitive.

A PRESCRIPTION FOR LONGEVITY

What will follow is a prescription for longevity. It is a self-improvement program. It is a manufacturing diet. It is an opportunity to change a flabby, waste-filled operation into a toned and muscular manufacturing company. The only way to succeed is through hard work. But to paraphrase Dr. W. Edwards Deming, "Hard work is not enough. We must also know what to do." And even knowing what to do is not enough—we must also do it. This book will help you put the JIT/TQC philosophy into action. The reward is competitiveness. In the chapters to come, I will lay out a comprehensive, step-by-step approach for implementing JIT/TQC in your manufacturing company.

You are about to enter a new and different world of manufacturing, one that will affect all functional areas and transform the way you do business. It will vastly enhance your ability to see the opportunities for continuous improvement, and it will lead you to improved competitiveness. If you incorporate the ideas in this book, you will be asking yourself in a year's time the same thing those at Hewlett-Packard, Beckman Instruments, Hallmark Cards, Motorola, McDonnell Douglas, Harris, NCR, Tektronix, Tellabs and many other organizations are still asking themselves: How could we *ever* have operated differently?

Chapter 2

Organizing the Implementation Team

It is much easier to apologize than it is to get permission.
—Admiral Grace Hopper

BEGINNING THE PROCESS

Once a company decides to implement Just-in-Time/Total Quality Control, the next immediate step is *action:* act to form a team, act to educate the team, and act promptly to implement. When the management at Harris Company determined that JIT/TQC was the right answer for them, they took 110 days to implement the process into one of their semiconductor-assembly environments. As a rule of thumb, once the implementation team is educated, a company should initiate a pilot project within 120 days. Each company will, of course, have its own rate of change, but with JIT/TQC, the longer a company toys with implementation, the more difficult the transition becomes.

To make that transition and begin JIT/TQC, the essential first step is to form an *implementation team.* Such a team is usually built around a *champion.* Champions, according to authors Peters and Waterman, are "those individuals who believe so strongly in their ideas that they take it on themselves to damn the bureaucracy and maneuver their products through the systems and out to the customer." Admiral Grace Hopper made this same point in a story about how computers gradually were accepted into the military. She told about a Navy pilot who, on his own and with a private machine, had computerized the maintenance records of his plane. When someone asked if he was supposed to be doing that, he responded "I didn't ask." As Hopper's story made clear, "it is much

33

easier to apologize than it is to get permission. If you have walked all the way around a thing, and it is right, then go ahead and do it." She added, "Don't be afraid of sticking your neck out and taking a risk. A ship in port is safe, but that isn't what ships were built for. Be good ships, and sail out to sea and to new things. I know it works. It made me a rear admiral."

The champion is someone who is willing to step out and try something. This is a risk taker. What you're looking for when starting JIT/TQC, is a potential pilot area where there is a real leader, with good administrative skills. This person will make sure Just-in-Time is performed.

It is important to realize that a champion is not one to be appointed, he[1] emerges. He is often the one pushing for the change. Ideally, there are several champions spread from the upper management ranks down to the lower levels of the company. But when there is just one champion, that person should be prepared for it to get pretty lonely. The life span of a champion with no support is about six months. During that period, the champion will either acquire converts and obtain support to make something happen, be destroyed trying, or simply move on to a more fruitful environment.

As stated in chapter 1, JIT/TQC is not just a factory-floor process but a company-wide approach for eliminating waste and increasing velocity. Its implementation requires that *all* functional areas cooperate. This simultaneous involvement is vital. With JIT/TQC, you're trying to make a competitive *breakthrough* that, ultimately, will affect all areas and not be limited to production improvements.

The *implementation team* should consist of leaders who have a thorough knowledge of their respective areas, and they should have enough authority to make change happen. Members are usually middle managers and influential professionals, with some higher and lower levels

---

[1] People can be classified into two general categories: male and female. Any job category in this book—be it president, general manager, department head, professional, direct or indirect laborer (salaried or hourly employee)—can be very successfully performed by females, in this writer's opinion. In fact, a significant number of the most successful JIT/TQC implementations referred to in this book were led by women. The success of JIT/TQC does not depend on whether the leader is a male or female. However, for purposes of simplicity and ease of reading, "he," "him," and "his" will be used throughout the book to refer to any person, be it male or female. Therefore, if it pleases the reader, "he," can be read as "he or she."

Figure 2.1
Implementation Team

REQUIRED FOR PILOT:

COST ACCOUNTING
INFORMATION SYSTEMS
MANUFACTURING ENGINEERING
MATERIALS
(PLANNING, PURCHASING, SCHEDULING, STOCK)
PERSONNEL (HUMAN RESOURCES)
PRODUCTION
QUALITY

REQUIRED SOON (DESIRED FOR PILOT):

DESIGN ENGINEERING
FACILITIES
GENERAL ACCOUNTING
MARKETING
REGULATORY AGENCIES
UNION

REQUIRED SECOND PHASE:

CUSTOMERS (PERHAPS)
SUPPLIERS

USEFUL ALL PHASES:

CONSULTANT WITH JIT/TQC EXPERIENCE

included. Ideally all are strong leaders. The business areas that should be represented on the team are shown in figure 2.1.

Who should head up the implementation team? Often someone from manufacturing is in charge, but not always. In some instances, personnel, accounting, quality, materials, or systems have been instrumental in beginning JIT/TQC efforts. The key is to have a champion with the necessary leadership skills.

Ed McDevitt, vice president of manufacturing at Tellabs, thinks that the person they chose to head their implementation team was fundamental to the success of the project. They selected Grace Pastiak, a long-time employee with good corporate operational knowledge. She could cross corporate departmental boundaries easily and had the requisite organizational skills. Once she went to work, an implementation team was assembled, and within two months, the Tellabs pilot was on-line and breakthrough results were immediately achieved.

Whoever is in charge, however, it must be established from the outset that this is a team effort, built on the participation of all functional levels in the company. Though we will talk about the detailed pilot specifications in chapter 4, let us now examine why the involvement of these implementation members is so important.

Cost accounting's participation is necessary to help launch the changes that will be required in the way labor is collected, material is tracked and performance is measured. Information systems will have to help initiate the changes in planning, the shop floor control and other systems. A representative from manufacturing engineering is essential to implement modifications of existing processes and the factory floor layout. A person from materials will have to consider the impact of JIT/TQC on planning, scheduling, and purchasing. Personnel must be involved to discuss questions about labor grades, jobs, and compensation. Production's participation is required to address the changes in job responsibilities and layout and to explore ways for increasing velocities throughout the production process. Finally, a member from quality will have to evaluate the impact of JIT/TQC on that department's responsibilities as well as on inspection practices. That person will also be deeply involved in the Total Quality Control process.

If the pilot is centered around a new product, design engineering may have to be included on the implementation team from the beginning. If not, its active participation can begin after the first pilot is implemented. At this later time, however, what has been learned will have to be applied to existing and next generation product design.

If preventive maintenance presents a critical constraint and falls under the facilities organization, it too will need to be a part of the initial team. Otherwise, it should become actively involved once space is freed up in the factory.

General accounting typically enters the picture when it is time to link the JIT/TQC process into the supplier and customer network. At this time, accounts payable and perhaps accounts receivable become affected.

Marketing is normally included when the order-entry process needs to be accelerated and changed organizationally, or once opportunities surface to capitalize on the competitive marketing advantages JIT/TQC has provided.

If your company is unionized or must deal with governmental regulatory agencies, the relevant organizations should be informed of your plans not too long after starting. Some unionized companies actively involve the union in planning the first pilot, because it is during this stage that plans are developed to minimize labor grades, eliminate incentive pay, broaden job flexibility, and ensure employment stability. Essentially, the sooner people are involved, the better.

Once the initial pilot stage has been completed, it is time to phase the suppliers into the implementation process. The suppliers' participation is essential to maximize the ability to economically respond to change throughout the entire manufacturing pipeline, as well as to implement the practice of purchasing by exception, which will be explained in greater detail in chapter 7. During the second phase, customers should also be brought on board so that the process of selling by exception can be initiated and the flow of orders into the factory can be smoothed.

To achieve a breakthrough success with JIT/TQC, *it is of the utmost importance that all of the essential pilot members listed above be included.* Suppose you are missing a representative from cost accounting. JIT/TQC then tends to become mere reorganization of the production floor rather than as a company-wide strategy that exposes and resolves constraints. Without widespread representation, JIT/TQC will likely result in nothing more than a satisfying level of production improvement. It won't drive changes through the rest of the company, and the continuous improvement aspects of the process are likely to be lost. It's not that you won't make progress. You'll probably make just enough progress for complacency to set in again. That's the danger. The downside, too, is that you risk never realizing the significant breakthroughs possible with when all functions are involved in JIT/TQC.

The implementation team should consist of approximately eight to twelve people. This is not to say, however, that it must be limited to that number. Tellabs had close to thirty people on its team. While a team of that size can become unwieldy, if people are interested in participating in the process, it's a good idea to include them. On the other hand, if you're thinking of trying to implement JIT/TQC with just two or three people, you will undoubtedly shortchange yourself. You just won't have the widespread base necessary to cover all the areas that JIT/TQC affects.

Once the implementation team is formed, its members must become thoroughly familiar with JIT/TQC. They must understand why JIT/TQC is needed and how to implement it. They must also be able to communicate to everyone in the company a consistent vision of the future, and the changes necessary to get there. This is not the time to stall. However, it is also not the time to rush ahead before everyone on the team has completely grasped the JIT/TQC philosophy and process. Nor should there be much activity until a common vision has been agreed upon.

Typically, the initial vision consists of beginning a pilot. (The need for a much longer range vision will be discussed in chapter 13.) Once the implementation team understands JIT/TQC, at least academically, it will be responsible for recommending the next steps.

TIME COMMITMENT

The truth is, no one ever has enough time to implement JIT/TQC. Whether or not a company ever begins depends on how it structures its priorities. JIT/TQC must be given a high priority if it is to achieve its breakthrough potential quickly, safely, and inexpensively. Therefore, each project competing for a company's resources should be formally evaluated, taking into consideration the following factors:

- company objectives
- potential improvements to quality, delivery, and cost
- resource requirements of time, money, manpower, and equipment.

Those projects that have the best cost/benefit ratio should receive top priority. Others should be postponed. If JIT/TQC is not at the top of the list, the company should wait. To attempt it at the wrong time will result in wasted resources and a poor probability of success. However, it is difficult to imagine a project that will yield more benefits faster and for less expense than JIT/TQC. Be sure that you make your comparison accurately.

If a "go" decision is reached, the implementation team takes on the *project* of implementing the JIT/TQC *process.* The implementation team stays together until JIT/TQC is firmly established throughout all company activities and has become a way of life. This usually takes between two to four years. Once a pilot project is implemented, it is not time to break up the team. Physically, the pilot may be in place, and everyone may be pleased by its progress, but converting the entire company, penetrating into the supplier and customer sections of the pipeline, and mentally settling into JIT/TQC as a way of life take a while. Keeping the implementation team together, even if some members change, helps ensure that this crucial integration step is completed.

It should be pointed out that being a member of the implementation team is time-consuming, but it is not a full-time job. Taking these key middle managers out of your process full-time would negatively affect the rest of your operations. However, some companies assign one full-time member to the implementation team, especially for the first pilot. This person can even be of lower rank than the other members, but he must be someone with good organizational, leadership, and communication skills.

Once the project is successfully under way in-house, the implementation team can lead the effort to motivate both suppliers and customers to implement JIT/TQC in their companies. Though the team may stimulate this conversion, introducing the whys and how-tos of the conversion project, it is still up to the suppliers and customers to take the initiative within their own companies. The implementation team has neither the time nor the authority to be actively involved in each of these company transformations. Team members may work closely with one or two supplier or customer pilots, but invariably, they will be too busy directing changes in their own company, and performing their own jobs to make this outside contact a full-time pursuit.

IMPLEMENTATION ORGANIZATION

The responsibility for the success or failure of implementing JIT/TQC does not begin and end with the middle managers and professionals on the implementation team (see figure 2.2). There are, of course, levels of responsibility that exist throughout the company structure. A senior-management steering committee has the overall duty of establishing policy, strategies, attitudes, and a vision for the entire company. However, when requested—and it will happen—it must

Figure 2.2
Implementation Levels of Responsibility

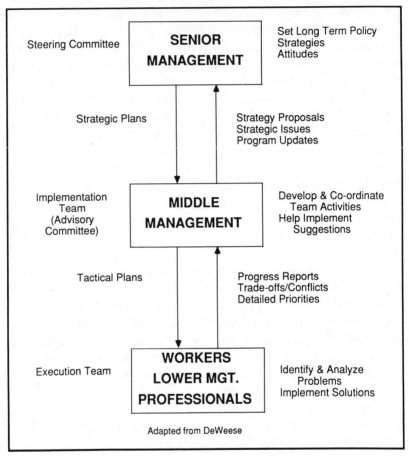

Adapted from DeWeese

change its own policies, strategies, attitudes, and vision to facilitate the implementation team and support its efforts.

It is up to the implementation team to develop the tactical plans. These consist of all the details on how to put JIT/TQC into place throughout the company. The tactical plans are then communicated to those who make up the *execution team*. These are first-line managers, operators on the production floor, programmers, material handlers, accountants, and manufacturing engineers.

It is up to the execution team to start the process of identifying and analyzing the problems that arise in the work areas as JIT/TQC is implemented. It is also responsible for finding solutions to those problems whenever possible. If there is a snag it cannot solve, this information is reported back to the implementation team. Typically, in the first pilot, the implementation team is actively involved in the execution team's activities. In subsequent stages, however, the execution team will report progress, priorities, problems, and trade-offs to the implementation team, which will prioritize the execution team's overall activities and resolve issues that it could not overcome. As progress is made, the implementation team must maintain a delicate balance between controlling the execution teams and allowing them to think and proceed on their own.

When constraints go beyond the authority of the implementation team—when obstacles arise that affect compensation, performance measures, regulatory agencies, union contracts, or long-term strategies and policies—the upper-management steering committee must set the agenda.

One complaint I all too frequently hear is that top management does not support the JIT/TQC effort. The first step toward remedying this situation is to re-examine the benefits, resources, and company objectives to make sure that JIT/TQC is what is needed. Normally it is, but its proponents must be certain. If the answer is yes, top management should be provided with an educational overview of JIT/TQC. Typically, at this stage, four to eight hours is adequate. The person conducting the education session should

- explain the philosophy and the process
- outline the changes that will occur and why
- document the benefits that can be expected and when
- establish the role of top management for the pilot and for converting the entire company.

For difficult meetings, it is particularly important that the instructor have broad hands-on experience. While the facts about JIT/TQC must be conveyed, it is also necessary to relieve the fears, doubts, and misunderstandings of the silent majority and of active opponents. The ideal instructor will be able to paint a vision of what can be achieved as well as to instill confidence and enthusiasm. We call this "bulletproofing." Approach this session wisely. You may not get another chance.

It is also extremely worthwhile to visit some successful JIT/TQC installations. Few people can doubt the power of this process once they have seen the working results with their own eyes. This is true for everyone, not just the skeptics. A note of caution, however: The first site to be visited by skeptical managers should be chosen carefully. It is also important in these instances to set realistic expectations prior to the tour.

In all probability, your first choice will be to visit a "famous" JIT/TQC site, especially if it's one that builds products similar to your own. You should be prepared, however, for the competition to refuse your request to view its operations. You should also be ready for skeptics to assert that your operations are unique, and that JIT/TQC won't work for you. In reality, you will be unique in many respects if you haven't yet made the changes necessary to support JIT/TQC.

Before touring other premises, you will also have to decide whether to visit a factory that is advanced in the JIT/TQC process—so that it may be difficult to relate to—or to visit one whose stage of development is closer to your own—and easier to find fault with. In either case, tours are a valuable part of the learning process. Ideally you will soon be conducting tours of your own pilot area; demonstrations of internal successes are the best kind.

If there is no top-management support for a JIT/TQC pilot, however, it does not mean that you can't make any progress, but it may require more work, take longer, and be more risky personally. This is why a champion of the cause is so critical. As we have previously seen, it is easier to apologize than it is to get permission. With this in mind, one strategy is to discreetly but quickly implement a pilot and use the results of the pilot to sell top management on further efforts. Without top-management support, however, it is very difficult to move beyond the pilot stage. It is particularly important in an unsupportive environment to make a fast and significant breakthrough in the pilot. Improvements that are anything less than breathtaking probably won't sell too well over other alternative actions.

EDUCATION

There are three primary tiers of education in the JIT/TQC implementation process (see figure 2.3). The first tier is designed for everyone, and is basically an overview of Just-in-Time and Total Quality Control. It covers most of the topics discussed in chapter 1. The process at this level should address what Just-in-Time and Total Quality Control are. It should cover the philosophy and especially the process. All the how-tos need not be explained, but everyone should understand how the process of JIT/TQC drives change and what their role in successfully implementing JIT/TQC is. If the company decides to go ahead with JIT/TQC, the second tier of education should involve middle to lower managers, the relevant professionals, and the implementation and execution teams. This level addresses the specific changes that will occur and how to make them, evaluating the impact of JIT/TQC on areas such as central stockrooms when materials are stored at the point of use, and noting what modifications will occur in order entry, production planning, and single-supplier sources.

Figure 2.3

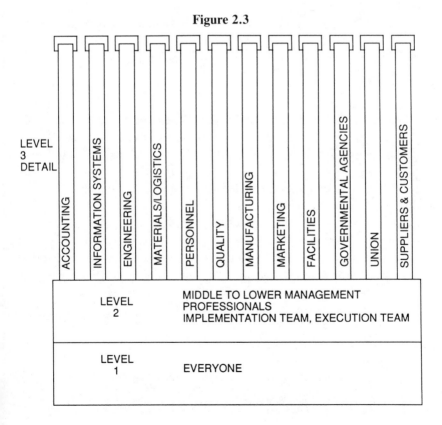

This second tier has an action-oriented agenda, highlighting the obstacles to implementation and explaining the proper alternatives for making the various changes. It covers the different techniques used to support JIT/TQC. At this level, it becomes clear why and how traditional work orders and purchase orders can be eliminated. It is also the time to learn how to properly plan the implementation process, including all the responsibilities and logistics that will be required.

The final education tier involves the departmental-level employees, that is, those employees actually doing the work in their respective areas. It is at this point that the implementation alternatives are selected and all the necessary changes are detailed. This level incorporates training in the mechanics of the new processes.

The need for education cannot be overemphasized. Successful companies have spent an average of forty hours per employee during the first eighteen months (more for the implementation team on education). JIT/TQC represents a new way of operating the business. We cannot expect people to enthusiastically turn from the familiar to the unfamiliar. Education is needed to make the unfamiliar familiar.

OUTSIDE GUIDANCE

The use of an *experienced* outside JIT/TQC expert is helpful during all phases of the implementation project. The outside expert may be an independent consultant or may reside elsewhere in your company. As we advanced in JIT/TQC at Hewlett-Packard, Fort Collins, we would lend out our "experts" to other divisions for up to ten days a year. Since the consulting was in addition to their normal jobs, we felt some limit on this outside activity was necessary.

Certainly, you are capable of learning on your own all that is required—the philosophy, processes, and mechanics of JIT/TQC are not that complex. But successfully implementing the required changes for a breakthrough during the brief time the "window of opportunity" is open can be very difficult. The role of an outside expert is to

- help establish the vision
- share personal experience
- share what others have done
- share what has worked
- share what has not worked

- share what might work
- assist in education and training
- expedite decision-making
- facilitate difficult meetings.

It does not take an army of outside people to do JIT/TQC, or to quickly achieve breakthrough results, if you follow the steps described in this book. Once the implementation team has attended a thorough implementation class, six to twelve man-days of consulting over the course of twelve months is frequently adequate to get a breakthrough pilot well established and serving as a model for complete conversion. In many instances, factories have been able to convert several areas during the first six to nine months and everything in twelve to twenty-four months. An army of people can construct the building you work in, but an army of consultants cannot change your mind-set—only you can do that. However, some instruction may accelerate the process. The role of the consultant is to help you understand and safely implement JIT/TQC, not to do it for you. It pays to remember this wise old saying. "Learn from the mistakes of others. You can never live long enough to make them all yourself."

When selecting outside guidance, look for hands-on experience. Look for someone who has been on the firing line and lived through the changes personally. Look for someone with experience in several functional areas. Look for a successful track record in JIT/TQC and for experience with Class A Manufacturing Resource Planning. Look for someone who can provide a balanced and objective approach to implementation. Look for someone who has the right chemistry with your upper management *and* with your factory workers. Make certain this is the same person you will work with after services are contracted. And finally, check references. Make phone calls to those references and visit them if necessary. Many people know how to spell JIT and TQC, but not many who offer to help you have actually done it themselves.

INSTITUTING CHANGE

Just as we at Hewlett-Packard initially couldn't believe that the methods of JIT/TQC were practical, there will be people who will balk at every new step forward. Their first response will invariably be "No way. It won't work here!" Demonstrate to them with a pilot that it does indeed work. When you show them the next change to be made, and they say, "Impractical," point out how someone else has made it work.

After four or five changes have been successfully implemented, people will be more hesitant to object. What you are trying to do is to make people realize that negative thinking is itself a constraint. There are difficult constraints and easy constraints; the job ahead of everyone is to think and find the way to eliminate them one by one.

Learning a new process is not always easy. As any teacher will tell you, patience and perseverance are key factors here. It has been shown that people must go through four different stages in their educational process in order to fully integrate what they have learned (see figure 2.4).

At Hewlett-Packard, prior to 1980 we were in stage one— incompetent and unconscious when it came to JIT/TQC. We didn't know what JIT/TQC was, let alone know how to implement it. When we entered the second stage, we didn't know how to do JIT/TQC, but we were con-

Figure 2.4
Stages of Change

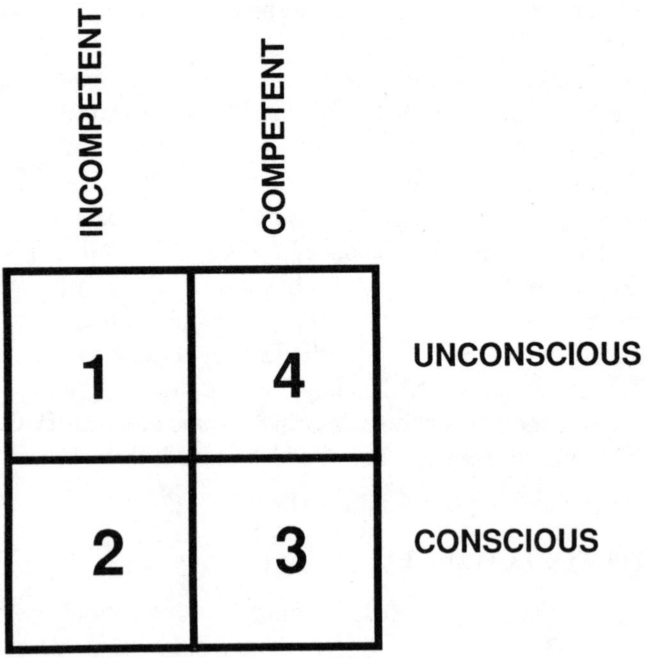

scious of the fact that our competitors were doing something differently. We were still incompetent, but we were at least conscious of our incompetence. In step three, we learned and practiced the JIT/TQC process. We struggled, and it took a lot of dedication and effort. We did JIT/TQC, but it took total concentration. We were consciously competent. It did not come naturally to us yet.

Now, after several years, a number of HP divisions, as well as many other companies, are entering into the fourth stage. Just-in-Time is becoming a way of life. They are not becoming complacent, but are unconsciously competent in driving continuous improvement.

MAKING CHANGE HAPPEN

How do we get people to change? In *In Search of Excellence,* Peters and Waterman say, "it is a matter of the *quantity* of the attention paid to the matter at hand rather than the *quality!*" The quality of the vision is important, of course, but communicating it once, no matter how eloquently, will not be sufficient to bring about change. If managers want JIT/TQC to become a reality, they can't just ask for the changes one time. They had better make sure that every time they open their mouths, with every action they take, they are reinforcing that JIT/TQC is a new and high priority. Then the changes will happen.

BUILDING TEAMWORK

The success of JIT/TQC, however, depends on more than a group of managers endlessly repeating that wasteful production practices must go. JIT/TQC works when all the various functions within a company together practice a process that forces changes to occur. The operative concepts here are practice, process, force, and team. We have already discussed the first three, now let us look at the fourth.

JIT/TQC establishes a continuous link of customer/supplier teams, involving all levels and all functions, and including all external suppliers and customers as well. It starts with the forming of the implementation team, and it continues throughout the company. In any environment, there are three primary ingredients to building a team:

1. exposure to different viewpoints
2. skilled group leadership
3. participation in the solution to common problems.

The most difficult problems exposed by the JIT/TQC process are cross-functional in nature. We are often weak when it comes to eliminating the root cause of our internal problems, but we are even worse when it comes to problems involving other organizations. Communication is required to eliminate cross-functional constraints. Communication requires teamwork. One person working alone is not enough. Without a combined effort, there is no way to achieve the breakthrough changes associated with JIT/TQC. But what if good teamwork does not already exist? Welcome to the club!

Some companies that began the JIT/TQC process believed they already had excellent teamwork. All learned that no matter how good the camaraderie was before JIT/TQC, there was a need for tremendous improvement. Typically, various groups discover that, while they are aware of each other, they operate independently in their decision-making. They find they are more accustomed to avoiding problems than working toward their elimination, particularly when the problems involve more than one organization. JIT/TQC links them together in a customer/supplier bond and forces them to learn how to communicate and work together in order to eliminate the root causes of their common problems.

The best way to build a team is perhaps to force a group of people together to solve a common problem. As the group works through the constraint together, they begin to develop an understanding of each member's needs and abilities. "When you've walked a mile in someone else's shoes," says Tellabs' Grace Pastiak, "you understand."

Teamwork becomes contagious in a JIT/TQC process. As production people begin working on solving the constraints on the factory floor, they see things that need to be communicated to the engineers. Today, at companies like Beckman and Tellabs, this direct communication is standard operating procedure between factory-floor workers and design engineers. In fact, it is not uncommon for design engineers to "come down" to the production floor to ask questions about upcoming designs or for production people to "go up" to design. Tellabs now builds its engineering prototypes in the manufacturing cell where the final product will eventually be built. As we will see later, this team approach is part of designing for manufacturability. And who knows, perhaps someday engineers will "go over" to production or vice versa.

Ultimately, this team mentality must permeate the company, from one group on the line to the next, from engineering to marketing, from production to finance. The team concept is at the heart of JIT/TQC. The JIT/TQC process simply exposes, prioritizes, and forces action on the next constraint. It's up to the teams of people to eliminate it.

BUILDING A COMMITMENT TO CHANGE

Creativity is thinking up new things. Innovation is putting those new things into action. Discussing change and actually changing are two distinct notions. Making change an active part of a company's overall plan means that those in charge must be receptive, considerate and committed. As with any behavioral attitude, there are right ways and wrong ways to foster change.

Rosabeth Moss Kanter of Goodmeasure, Inc. the author of *Change Masters,* came up with a powerful list of how to build a commitment to change. In parentheses I explain hew each of these relates to JIT/TQC.

1. Allow room for participation in the planning of change. (implementation team)
2. Allow room for choices within the overall decision to change. (education and open discussion of competitive pressures)
3. Provide a clear picture of the change, a "vision" with details about the new state of affairs. (vision statement)
4. Share information about plans for change to the fullest possible extent. (education and communications)
5. Take a small step first. Divide a big change into more manageable steps. (pilot projects)
6. Minimize surprises. It is important to give people advance warning about new requirements. (education, communications, and pilot)
7. Allow room for digestion of change requests. Give people a chance to become accustomed to the idea of change before making a commitment. (pilot)
8. Repeatedly demonstrate your own commitment to the change. As Peters and Waterman pointed out in *In Search of Excellence,* "Senior management's actions speak so loudly, we cannot hear their words." (active participation, education, and repetition, repetition, repetition)

9. Make standards and requirements clear. Let people know exactly what is expected of them in the change. (project checkpoints, performance measures)
10. Offer positive reinforcement for competence. People need to know they can make the change and that their efforts are appreciated. (public thank you, freedom to fail)
11. Look for and reward pioneers, innovators and early successes. These are models for the future. Acknowledging these efforts will make everyone take notice. (awards, recognition, bonuses and promotion)
12. Help people find or feel compensated for the extra time and energy the change requires. (awards, policy flexibility)
13. Avoid creating obvious "losers" from the change. But should they exist be honest about them as early as possible. (new vision, retraining, broader perspectives for a changing world)
14. Allow room for nostalgia and grief for the past. (empathy and understanding)
15. Create excitement about the future. (competitive potentials and celebrations)

As you get started with the implementation of JIT/TQC, it is unrealistic to think that everyone is going to be enthusiastic about the change. It is also unrealistic to think that everyone will do their fair share of the work. As in all ventures requiring change, you will find a few evangelists, a few atheists, and a majority of agnostics waiting to see which is the safe side. Be prepared for some people to drag their feet, but educate well, plan well, and implement a pilot quickly to keep fear from growing out of proportion. The point is, *if you want JIT/TQC to succeed in your factory, you have to be prepared and willing to do more than your fair share to get it implemented.*

SUMMARY

In this chapter, we have seen how to select the implementation team and establish the various responsibilities of its members. The importance of educating a multifunctional team for the pilot has been established. We have begun to see how the JIT/TQC process calls on the power of teamwork, and we have discussed how to build teams. Finally,

I have described how to lay a foundation for success with JIT/TQC by constructing a solid commitment to change. Once these concepts have been implemented into your process, you won't be able to go back. The positive, forward thrust of JIT/TQC will drive you to action. And that's the next step.

Chapter 3
Understanding Kanban

Inventory is time's shadow.
—**Robert Hall**

Historically, one of the worst sins in manufacturing has been to let a direct labor person run out of work. Management has been programmed to view this as a major error. Employees are expected to always be busy and never to be idle. Management's reactions have convinced employees, fearful of a layoff (even if it is for a few hours), that it is bad. In machine-intensive environments, letting an expensive piece of equipment shut down has been considered equally bad. As a result, inventory has become the price that is paid to support management's directive to keep producing.

Today, in relation to JIT/TQC, we often hear that it is acceptable to shut down the production line. It is okay if a direct labor person sits idle. In fact, with JIT/TQC, it is desirable to have excess machinery and equipment. Now, however, inventory is evil.

If we stop and look carefully at the situation, we can logically understand that performance measures are not like push buttons on a telephone with many lines. When you push one button down to activate a phone line, the others pop up and disengage. Today, we are pressing the inventory button. Idle labor used to be undesirable; now it is acceptable. Idle equipment used to be undesirable; now it is acceptable. Idle material (inventory) used to be desirable; now it is unacceptable. Idle material? Somehow idle material sounds bad, while inventory sounds desireable—yet they are the same thing.

The truth is, it is not a good practice to waste any of our resources. We should seek to minimize the total waste in the system, not overemphasize one element of the total. It is true, however, that in many companies, labor efficiency and equipment utilization have been over-emphasized for so long that the inventory resource has grown abnormally large. A focus on inventory is appropriate in these environments, yet an overemphasis on it is no more appropriate than our historical overemphasis on labor or equipment.

We should recognize that as we practice the "One Less at a Time" process, we will put a strain on various resources: machinery, labor, and material. In so doing, we run the risk of becoming inefficient in one of these areas for a short period of time. In fact, occasionally it may be necessary to shut down the production line, thereby idling both machinery and labor. Is this desirable? Of course not. It may be more desirable, however, than keeping one or both busy at the expense of adding inventory. Something is wrong if JIT/TQC causes us to shut down the line. If we are unable to resolve the problem in advance, shutting down the line may actually create less waste than if we had kept it busy. Keeping labor and equipment busy will result in an increase in the amount of wasteful inventory and slower velocities through the factory. It will also obscure the problem from view.

If we reach the point where the line must be shut down, we will definitely be forced to examine the constraint. It cannot remain hidden. We may discover that the product mix has changed, creating a balance problem on the line or between shops. There could be a quality problem that is causing one area to fall behind. If this is the case—and it often is—using good resources to make bad products is perhaps the ultimate waste.

When the pipeline is full, the last thing JIT/TQC calls for is more inventory. One of the problems with traditional labor-efficiency measures is that they assume the only constructive contribution a direct labor person can make is to build inventory. JIT/TQC refutes that premise. Direct labor people can help their supplier or customer operation. They can perform equipment and tool maintenance, do Total Quality Control, do housekeeping, attend education classes, train, cross-train, or help another department. I cannot remember a single occasion when we at Hewlett-Packard wasted a significant amount of time due to a line shutdown, because we always had something planned in that event. In fact, some of our improvement projects counted on occasional shutdowns to provide the time required to complete them.

Even if people must sit idle once in a while, it is preferable to producing more inventory than is necessary when the pipeline is full. If a piece of equipment can outpace its customer's rate of consumption, we must either slow it down or shut it down. We can shut it down once each year for a long period of time, to eliminate accumulated inventory, or we can shut it down for a short time each hour.

We cannot minimize total waste by continuing to optimize our labor and equipment resources at the expense of our inventory resource.

THE TECHNIQUE OF KANBAN

The technique that makes the JIT/TQC principles practical is called kanban (rhymes with bonbon). Loosely translated from the Japanese, kanban means visual record or card.[1] A kanban is an authorization to do your job, to produce or move inventory.

The kanban technique is similar to the process once used by the milkman as he delivered milk to a home. When the milkman arrived, he would immediately see how many empty milk bottles were left on the porch. Two empty containers authorized him deliver two full bottles. If there was one regular and one chocolate empty, he'd leave one regular and one chocolate milk. Those empty milk bottles were his authorization to leave more. No bottle, no milk. Without a traditional work order or traditional purchase order, the milkman knew simply by seeing the empty bottles exactly what he needed to leave.

Kanban works the same way, as a signal to replace what has been used. If the kanban authorization is present, you act. If it is not, you don't. Kanban is, therefore, a way of controlling inventory. As such, it is also an ideal method of exposing problems or opportunities for change.

The sum of all kanbans in the factory represents the diameter of the pipeline, or the high-water mark in the aquarium (see figure 3.1). When starting Just-in-Time, you don't just pull the plug and let the water run out of the aquarium. That would be courting certain disaster. You must empty it in a controlled manner, taking out a cup at a time. Kanban is that cup. The current level of inventory, or current number of

---

[1] It should be mentioned that the purpose of this book is to explain the philosophy and process of Just-in-Time and Total Quality Control. It is not intended as primer for Japanese words and expressions. Whenever possible I use the most familiar and descriptive English words available. One exception to this is kanban. It simply does not translate well into English.

Figure 3.1
Kanban Sets Upper Limit on Inventory

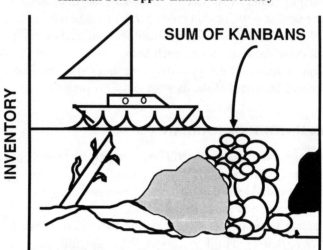

kanbans, is the level at which we know we can operate the factory. The question is, what stops us from operating with fewer kanbans? If we don't know, we find out by carefully removing a few kanbans. If we know the problem, we fix it and then remove a few kanbans to find the next constraint.

THE RULES

Each kanban signal has as its own charter; the license to act. Without that concrete token, nothing is authorized to be made, moved, or stored. This is one of the few hard-and-fast rules of JIT/TQC: No kanban, no production. As we have stated before, JIT/TQC makes use of visual controls. The kanban mechanism, in conjunction with workplace organization, makes visual controls both effective and efficient. Kanbans can come in all shapes, sizes, and materials, from squares taped to the floor, to pigeonholes, to cards, to returnable containers such as milk bottles.

Other rules associated with the kanban device are summarized in figure 3.2. These rules are simple but important. We will refer back to them as we progress through this chapter. The key point is to follow

Figure 3.2
Kanban Rules

NEVER EXCEED KANBAN CEILING

ALL MATERIAL KANBAN CONTROLLED

NEVER PASS ON A KNOWN DEFECT

FOLLOW FIFO IN THE KANBAN START QUEUE

REDUCE KANBANS TO EXPOSE PROBLEMS

CUSTOMER PULLS MAT'L FROM SUPPLIER

ONLY ACTIVE MAT'L ON WORK STATION

EVERYTHING HAS A PLACE/IN PLACE

---

these rules while continuing to improve quality, delivery, and cost—and not at their expense.

Here's how one company demonstrated this process to their people. First, they gathered a group of operators around a table in a conference room. The operators were told that they were initially going to simulate JIT/TQC and kanban. Each one had before him a number of different products the company made, as well as an information card stating what job he performed and how much time that job required. It was established that fifteen minutes of manufacturing time would represent one minute of simulation. If manufacturing process number one took thirty minutes, it could not be passed on to the next operation for two minutes during the demonstration.

During the first go-around, the operators simply simulated the environment currently on the shop floor and did not initiate kanban mechanics. Everyone kept busy, but inventory built up ahead of bottlenecks. The next time through the exercise, they followed the rules of kanban: no available kanban, no production. Although line imbalances led to some idle operations, the inventory ahead of bottlenecks and the queues stabilized. It did not take long for *everybody* around the table to see where the problems were. Line imbalances were apparent. It was impossible not to wonder why some operations were overloaded while others were idle.

A defect was arbitrarily placed at an intermediate work center. The operators had just been taught that one of the rules of Just-in-Time was *never pass on a known defect.* Suddenly the line stopped. The downstream work center was eventually unable to continue because its kanbans were empty. The upstream work center was also halted because the problem work center stopped. Workers at both centers were visually aware that they needed to come to the aid of the disabled work station to help analyze and solve the problem.

One of the great productivity leaps provided by kanban is that it makes problems visible. And if you make a problem visible to enough people, somebody will solve it. Throughout this book, I point out slogans or cliches that reinforce incorrect choices, such as "Don't rock the boat." There are some, however, that are apt. One proverb that applies accurately to JIT/TQC is "Necessity is the mother of invention." It is amazing how we achieve results when we *have to* put our minds together to solve a problem. Real breakthroughs come from the interaction of this critical mass of brainpower. It is when customer/supplier operations communicate about genuine opportunities that change takes place. Just-in-Time stimulates communication. Intelligence is randomly distributed throughout an organization; it exists everywhere. Once the company mind-set recognizes this resource, innovative change can begin to take place.

VISUAL FEEDBACK

When the McDonnell Douglas Computer Systems Division in Irvine, California, implemented JIT/TQC, the company quickly found it had a lot of excess work-in-process inventory in its circuitboard pipeline. It had no desire to replace this excess inventory as it was consumed, so it tagged each of the excess parts with a special start-up excess kanban tag. Every time a start-up tag made it to the end of the line, instead of being recirculated, it was removed from the system to prevent authorizing another part to be built. It was then "retired" to a wall as a display. Each tag was marked with a gold dollar sign, representing the money the organizations saved by operating with less inventory.

When JIT/TQC went on-line at MDCSD, the immediate savings from eliminating excess inventory was about $450,000. A year later, the firm had removed over $800,000 in work-in-process inventory. That is very significant when you consider that their previous manufacturing practices had held all $800,000 to be necessary inventory. The last $350,000 had been necessary when JIT/TQC was started, but with the continual improvements driven by JIT/TQC, it too became excess. The wall, covered with the removed kanban tags serves to remind everyone who walks past of the progress the company is making. It is also a constant motivator for continual improvement.

REINFORCING BEHAVIOR

Ed Davenport, from NCR's Orlando, Florida, division had been struggling with the need for kanban. Improving the scheduling side of the business wasn't a significant priority for his company. During the JIT/TQC implementation process, he attended a class on performance management, which dealt with how to get people to perform.

The basic premise of the class was that there are two primary ways to reinforce people's behavior, positively or negatively. Negative reinforcement got results, but it only brought people to a minimum acceptable level and no higher. After this point was reached, the results tended to decline over time until the company turned the heat up again.

Positive reinforcement was the only method that produced continued improvement over a long period of time. Before they could begin reinforcing certain behaviors, however, NCR had to figure out what measurements they wanted to use so that people could see how they were doing, and if they were doing the right thing. The class raised the question of what good measurements are. Davenport learned that *it is important to reinforce behavior and not just results,* that is, to reward people for trying the right things, even if they don't get the desired results with each attempt.

The management at NCR also had to ask itself, What kind of behavior do we want to reinforce on the production floor? "We couldn't come up with an answer." Davenport recalls. "Stay in your area. Work harder. These were useless. It was a big problem. We began talking about the kanban cards, and it suddenly dawned on us: reducing kanban cards was the behavior we wanted to positively reinforce." The kanban cards then became the means for driving the behavior rewards. Whenever a kanban card was removed, NCR, like McDonnell Douglas, celebrated it.

" 'One Less at a Time' and kanban helped us develop teamwork,"

Davenport said. "It dawned on me that kanbans were an excellent way to create positive reinforcement. At the same time they allowed us to prioritize our efforts. I finally understood why kanbans work. It isn't just a matter of scheduling; they got our people to do the right thing and in the right order."

THE MECHANICS OF KANBAN

As mentioned earlier, JIT/TQC encourages the use of visual controls. Therefore, it is usually best if we can see when our customer "purchases" our completed product. Pigeonholes and squares taped on the floor or work surface make excellent kanbans when inventory is stored within sight. Sometimes, however, we cannot see when our product is consumed by our customer. In this case, one of the best types of kanban is a returnable container or some other type of returnable material-handling device, such as a pallet or a cart. Another alternative is a card that is returned once the inventory has been consumed. In all instances, the "empty" kanban authorizes replenishment.

Tektronix used a returnable-container system between two of its factories when it first started JIT/TQC. Initially, the supply operation had 14,000 pieces in finished goods, and the customer had another 7,000 in its incoming stockroom inventory, for a total of 21,000 pieces. Tektronix decided to run the entire operation with six boxes containing 400 pieces each, for a total of 2,400. The boxes circulated from supplier to customer. When a box returned empty, it was refilled and sent back. This reduced Tektronix's finished-goods inventory by nearly 90 percent.

Had Tektronix used a card system, they could just as easily have sent back cards instead of boxes. Once the system was implemented, however, the status quo could not be maintained. Just-in-Time obligated Tektronix to continue to reduce the inventory between the customer and the supplier. What stopped them from operating with six boxes with 390 pieces in each, or five boxes with 400 in each? Nothing. And the process continues on.

When cards are used to represent a kanban, there are a number of ways to operate. Cards of two different colors can be used, one authorizing production and the other authorizing movement. Various cards might be developed not only for production and movement but for rework, restock, start-up excess, emergencies, and other operations requiring special instructions (see Appendix A). Just remember to keep it simple. Alternatively, a single card could serve to authorize all operations. No matter how many cards are used, the same rules of kanban apply. Every piece of material must be authorized by a kanban.

Yet another way to handle a kanban operation, particularly if the supplier is at a distance, is to use an electronic signal or kanban. It would appear on the surface that electronic kanbans are equal to if not better than the kanban card or returnable container. Experience has indicated, however, that the driver of continuous improvement, the forced customer/supplier interaction and the development of the thinking worker, is often lost when electronic kanbans are adopted. JIT/TQC is a very visual system, and that vision can be lost with electronic kanbans, particularly when the electronic authorization resembles the reports of more traditional systems. Often, however, electronic data interchange (EDI) is desirable, especially in order to communicate across great distances. In this case, great care must be taken to avoid loss of the visual-control feature of Just-in-Time, which focuses the supplier and customer on each other.

There is something about visual control that seems to force customer/supplier communications. In many traditional environments, a computer report provides the information used to initiate work activity. If something is questionable, we talk to planning or scheduling, or ignore it. Obviously, we cannot communicate with the computer. With JIT/TQC, however, we receive returnable kanbans directly from our customer. The customer receives product directly from us. If there is a problem, it is the norm, not the exception, for one production area to communicate directly with the other. In addition, it is up to the customer/supplier pair to communicate directly to learn how to reduce the kanbans in the pipeline.

In traditional environments, we perceive and act as if the computer or computer report is the customer. The focus is on the report. With JIT/TQC, the kanban physically links the supplier and customer together, forcing direct communications. The focus is on satisfying the customer's need.

In one instance where electronic communications was required, the customer company also used a board on which kanbans were hung on pegs. As the authorizations came back, rather than send the card to a supplier they hung it on the board and called the supplier to tell them the kanban was there. The supplier, who had a matching board, then took the corresponding card off and sent it through their production pipeline. Both the customer and the supplier were able to maintain the visual control systems, while using electronics to speed the process. Other companies fax diagrams showing empty kanban locations. One calls it "faxban"!

Technically, electronic kanbans should be an excellent alternative. We must remember, however, that we're dealing with people. Experience has shown that if we eliminate the visual control, there is a danger of losing the customer/supplier communication link and the driver of the thinking worker. The first question we must ask ourselves is, are electronic kanbans really necessary or are they just technologically appealing? If they are necessary, how can we minimize the side effects of this approach? Whenever possible, it is preferable to use visible kanban locations. Returnable containers are probably a close second choice, followed by cards. There is something inherently unifying about being able to touch, see, and know when a customer has consumed a product. It stimulates communication. It makes us focus on the customer rather than on a computer report.

BRAND-NAME KANBANS AND GENERIC KANBANS

By now it should be evident that the kanban methodology is very simple. Every product is authorized to exist by a kanban, and a kanban without a product authorizes the creation of a replacement product. Inherent in this kanban process are two questions: *what* to build and *when* to build it? Two basic types of kanbans—"brand-name" and "generic" kanbans—each answer these two questions by different means.

A brand-name kanban, the more familiar type, answers both questions at once. When we receive a free brand-name kanban, we are authorized to immediately ("when") build another identical item ("what"). Thus, as figure 3.3 illustrates, when a customer takes product A from the output queue of the fourth operator, that operator sees the empty kanban and is authorized to "pull" item A, his only choice, from the third operator's outbound queue. The pull process continues back to the raw materials inventory and ideally, eventually reaches all the way back to the external supplier's factory.

Figures 3.4 and 3.5 illustrate the same process for two and three

Figure 3.3
Brand Name Kanbans (1 Product)

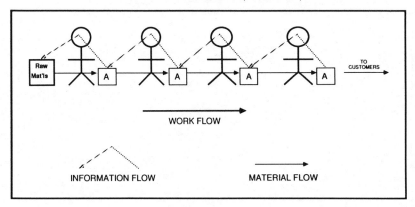

Figure 3.4
Brand Name Kanbans (2 Products)

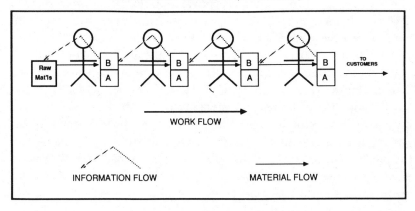

products, respectively. Here, the operator pulls the appropriate item from his supplier, enabling him to build an identical item to replace what the customer pulled.

What happens, however, if we have hundreds of items? Theoretically, we could use brand name kanbans, but in practice they quickly become impractical in high-product-variety environments. Or what happens if we do not immediately need an identical item, but do need a different one? This is when generic kanbans come into play. They work well in

Figure 3.5
Brand Name Kanbans (3 Products)

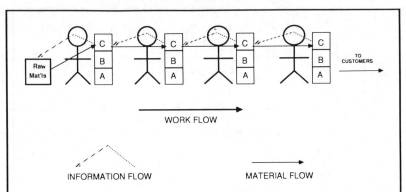

situations where the product variety is high, volumes are low, and/or the demand is unstable and intermittent.

A generic kanban authorizes production to begin immediately ("when"), but it does not provide specific information regarding what to build. Often the generic kanban will authorize production of an item within a family of parts but will not specify the item or its options.

Let's walk through an example beginning with brand-name kanbans and moving to generic. At Hewlett-Packard we had seven different flavors of keyboards for one of our engineering-workstation computers. We made one each for the United States, France, Germany, Scandinavia, Africa, and Japan as well as an ASCII version. We initially authorized the production of four of each keyboard type, so that we had twenty-eight pigeonholes. Just-in-Time, however, requires that you make shipments with one less kanban. The question was, which kanban are we going to reduce? (See figure 3.6.)

We looked at the production figures, and saw that we didn't sell many keyboards to Africa. We eliminated one from that category, bringing the total down to twenty-seven, and then repeated the process. Our next lowest-sales were to Scandinavia, so we took one from there, and then continued down the line. Pretty soon, we were down to twenty-one pieces. We repeated the process, reducing them to fourteen, and then underwent the procedure again, finally bringing the total number of pieces down to seven.

Figure 3.6
Kanban Transformation

KEYBOARD VARIETIES

USA	ASCII	FRANCE	GERMANY	UK	SCAN'DV	AFRICA

Just-in-Time says to repeat that process again. But how could we? If we don't have one of everything, how can we give good customer service? We had just *one* of everything. Remember, Just-in-Time only points out the opportunity. It's up to you to rise to the challenge. The constraint in the system was that we couldn't figure out how to get less than one of everything. The solution was to switch to *generic* kanbans.

Instead of having seven brand-name kanbans authorizing us to build each specific keyboard type, we progressed to four generic keyboard kanbans. But when a kanban card returned authorizing production of another keyboard, how did we know which one we were to build? We had seven different choices. The answer is provided by the final assembly schedule, the Master Production Schedule, or, ideally, the next immediately shippable customer order. The generic kanban is the authorization of *when* to build; the schedule or customer order specifies *what* to build. By looking at the next shippable customer order and performing a simple, and often mental, explosion through the bills of material, we could determine which keyboard to build for the next shippable customer order. In this case, we began the generic approach with four cards authorizing four keyboards of any flavor. The actual sequence of the four pieces authorized to be produced depends on the prioritized sequence of customer orders or on a final assembly schedule.

Figure 3.7
Kanban Alternatives—Brand Name and Generic

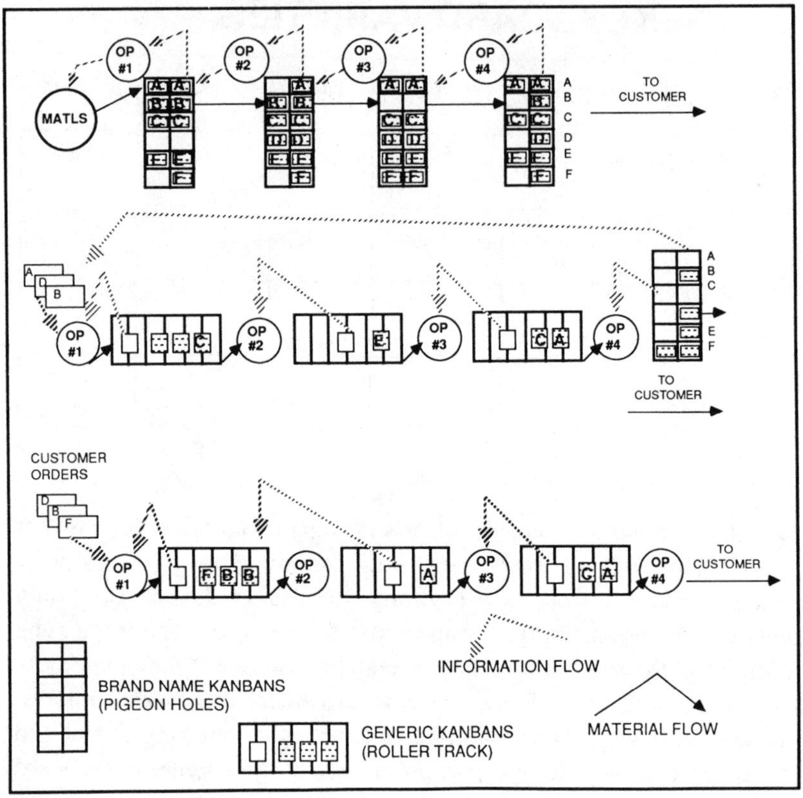

Figure 3.7 illustrates a possible transition from brand-name to generic kanban control. The first row shows brand-name kanbans (pigeonholes) cascading back through the process steps. The pull process here works in exactly the same way as the one described for Figures 3.3, 3.4, and 3.5. Figure 3.7 shows forty-eight kanban locations.

Row two shows brand-name kanban locations at the finished product stock point after the last operation. When a customer pulls a product from finished goods, a kanban signal is sent back to the first operator. When the first operator sees that a generic kanban space is available in the manufacturing pipeline, he is authorized to initiate production of the product indicated on the kanban card. The card is brand-name, as are the pigeonholes in finished goods. The spaces in the manufacturing pipeline, represented graphically by a roller track, are generic. Any combination of four of the six available product types could be in the squares between operators one and two. The figure shows twenty-one inventory locations authorized by either brand-name or generic kanbans.

The third row shows no finished goods and only generic kanbans in the pipeline. Only nine units are allowed to be in process. When operator two pulls a unit from the roller track between operations one and two, a space will empty on the track. That empty generic kanban space authorizes operator one to begin production; what he begins to produce is determined by the next shippable order in front of him. The figure shows nine kanban locations, all generic. The totally generic process allows for greater flexibility, less inventory, and faster response time.

ENGINEERING CHANGES

Engineering changes are relatively easy to interject into a Just-in-Time system. You have to know when you want to make the change, but once a time has been established, the process is quite simple. When a kanban card[2] for the changed part is returned for replenishment, it simply has to be intercepted so that instructions for incorporating the engineering change can be attached. When pigeonholes or squares are used, the location can be flagged or blocked, so that when the customer goes to the kanban location to retrieve the next part, or when the supplier initiates production to replenish it, he is alerted that a change is being initiated. A note in the storage location can also trigger a change once that material has been consumed. Color-coded kanbans can also indicate a revision. Once all cards are of the new color, the pipeline has been purged of previous versions of the product.

Engineering-change procedures for Just-in-Time are normally simple. However, it is important to carefully document the procedures and train workers regarding them; otherwise mistakes are certain to occur. Traditionally, a change is entered into the bills of material, and a new work order generates the picking list that instructs the material handler

---

[2] Throughout the book I often use the term "kanban cards" to refer to kanbans generally. Kanbans, of course, can take any number of forms.

in the stockroom to issue the new material. If the engineering change is not communicated to production, workers may not know what to do with the new material. A fail-safe mechanism of sorts exists, because it prompts workers to stop and ask questions. With Just-in-Time, that checkpoint will not exist. In a JIT environment, the new material may already be stored at the point of use, but the production workers may not have been instructed to use it. Or, the new material may not be at the point of use and the operator may not know that it should be. Hence, it is critical that the people in the production areas be informed of the production changes and receive the appropriate documentation and materials before the change is supposed to take effect. Actually, this is true in any environment; it is just more crucial under Just-in-Time.

As stated in chapter 1, *what's important with JIT/TQC is not that you repeat your product but that you repeat your processes.* Generic kanbans allow you to build an infinite variety of products through a limited set of repeating processes. It doesn't matter which flavor or color comes next; the generic kanban simply indicates when to build it. The customer order (or schedule) tells which one to build.

What happens, though, if we cannot economically manufacture one at a time? What if economics dictates we use a lot size? When we group orders into an economic lot or periodic lot, we must work to reduce the lot size or the time element, to expose the constraints to our ability to respond. Lot size directly affects the amount of inventory and, therefore, the number of kanbans we will have in the manufacturing pipeline. Because we do not want to begin replenishment production until we accumulate enough kanbans to reach a lot size, more inventory—and therefore more kanbans—is required to compensate, resulting in slower velocities and a more uneven flow throughout the pipeline. Until we can economically reduce our lot sizes by reducing setup times, larger lots will also cause delays prior to entry into the manufacturing pipeline. This will result in longer throughput times. The process of reducing setup times will be discussed in greater detail in chapter 5.

At this point in the implementation process, it is important first to establish the kanban method best suited to our particular production environment—brand-name for higher-volume/lower-mix and generic for lower-volume/higher-mix situations. Most companies make extensive use of both types of kanbans.

Eventually, the driving mechanisms of JIT/TQC will lead in the direction of smaller lot sizes, less lumpiness, and higher velocities. JIT/TQC will also draw us toward generic kanbans, since these result in less inventory and greater flexibility. Whether it is ever necessary in high-volume/low-mix environments to adopt generic kanbans is debatable, but we will be drawn in this direction.

Whichever kanban type we choose, kanban will set the ceiling, the upper limit, on all our inventory. Total inventory cannot be greater than the sum of all kanbans. By introducing the kanban methodology, we place a cap on the number of materials between a customer and a supplier. This is the case whether the customer/supplier relationship exists inside the factory or between the factory and an outside supplier or customer. The job of each customer/supplier pair is to continue to economically make shipments with "One Less at a Time" in their pipeline segment. We then expand the process to include the next section of the pipeline, continuing on until the entire manufacturing and distribution pipeline is connected. The questions we must continually ask ourselves are, Why can't we economically operate with one less? What is the constraint? Kanban allows each customer/supplier link to carefully lower inventory, as each exposes constraints and tracks data to analyze their cause.

By reducing inventory and solving the problems that arise, we quickly shorten throughput times. Things begin to move much faster. As Professor Robert Hall says, "Inventory is time's shadow." An abundance of inventory is only a cover for problems. It does nothing to aid a company's inherent flexibility. Flexibility comes with the ability to achieve higher velocities. Every time a kanban is removed, the velocity of the process picks up.

ESTABLISHING KANBAN CEILINGS

As demonstrated earlier, kanbans facilitate our use of visual controls by enabling us to establish a visible ceiling on the amount of work a supplying operation is allowed to get ahead of its following consumer operation. That is, we can visually indicate the amount of time one work center is allowed to get ahead of another. When each product type flowing through a series of production processes requires a relatively consistent amount of time, the kanban ceiling can be expressed in terms of a maximum number of pieces. When products vary in work content, however, we must establish a kanban unit of measure that represents a consistent amount of time. For example, in a sheet-metal area, a bracket may require substantially more work than a side panel. But if, for example, a supplier never places more than one hour's work on a pallet, we can use the pallet as the kanban. Each pallet visually represents up to one hour's work. In this instance, the pallets are generic kanbans, because they may contain a variety of products.

Theoretically, a kanban could also represent an entire operation, allowing us to limit the number of jobs one work center can complete in advance of customer need. In some pharmaceutical and blending operations, for example, the amount of work does not vary greatly according to the size of the batch, and the number of "jobs" in queue may serve as a good kanban ceiling. But where jobs vary considerably in work content, the number of jobs cannot be used to establish a consistent kanban ceiling.

Whatever a company's particular circumstances, the objective when establishing a kanban ceiling is to *keep it simple, keep it visual, and keep it consistent*. General guidelines for how to calculate the correct number of kanbans for a given environment can be found in Appendix A.

SPECIAL APPLICATIONS OF KANBAN

Though in most cases kanban is a highly efficient process, there are some special considerations that need to be taken into account, especially when it comes to very intermittent requirements. If we have products that are needed just twice a year, we can still use kanban: We'd build the product, the card would come back, and we'd be authorized to build another. The problem surfaces when that newly authorized product ends up sitting on the shelf for the next six months. One solution would be to have someone intercept the kanban card on its way back, and then hold it for five months before returning it to the pipeline. But that's a rather awkward process. It would be better to use a generic kanban approach. In this way, we could limit the number of products, and only the products that were shippable would move through the pipeline.

However, in environments where one portion of the factory feeds another and both have relatively long lead times, the generic method is difficult, because by the time we complete the lengthy production processes, the product need may change. In these environments, the supplier portion of the factory will often maintain a completed inventory of its finished products. Brand-name kanbans are usually used for those items that have a more stable consumption. For those items that are needed only intermittently, a traditional Manufacturing Resource Planning work order is required to authorize production. However, generic kanbans are still used to limit the *amount* of inventory in the pipeline, regardless of the type of authorization. Brand-name products move through the generic openings in the pipeline and end up in brand-name inventory locations. Products that are triggered by a work order also flow through the generic openings in the pipeline but wind up in a generic inventory position at the end, ready for consumption.

In some environments, sudden surges in consumption occur; others experience severe seasonality of demand. A company that makes telephone-switching equipment might experience a sudden surge. Ninety percent of their customers may order less than twenty-five trunk lines, each of which requires a specific circuit board. There might be occasions, however, when a customer would order 100 lines. One undesirable way to handle surges is to carry enough inventory to cover the worst possible situation. To solve this problem we could use a combination of alternatives: brand-name kanbans (to cover the typical unevenness of customer orders), generic kanbans for more flexible capacity, and a requirement that abnormal orders receive longer leadtimes. In these situations, inventory may be necessary, but it is still wasteful and it should be minimized. We certainly do not want to carry inventory all the time simply to handle the occasional exceptional demand.

In environments where severe seasonality occurs, inventory is used more frequently. Flexibility of products and processes is helpful, but it is often woefully inadequate to meet the increased demand itself. Building inventory may be wasteful, but it remains necessary until we can smooth customer orders. For example, when agricultural products are used as raw materials, storing inventory is wasteful, but until we learn how to harvest corn or wheat throughout the year, we will have no alternative.

RULES OF KANBAN

Earlier, we learned three basic rules of Just-in-Time. Now that we have a better understanding of the kanban system, we will elaborate on them and examine a few more.

1. Make or move material only when you have a kanban authorization.

If you calculate a ceiling of 1,000 pieces in the production pipeline, then that quantity should never be exceeded. It is important to maintain the integrity of this ceiling. Sometimes, however, companies become very sloppy in how they use kanbans. If they want a few extras, they make a few extras. That is very dangerous; like work orders, kanbans provide a tight control system. A company should be using either work orders or kanbans correctly. To get rid of work orders and not follow the rules of kanban is asking for trouble. It is essential never to exceed the established kanban ceiling. This ceiling allows kanban to expose constraints to higher velocities while maintaining control.

There is one exception to this rule. During the pilot, when all the material from the stockroom is stored at the point of use but is still reordered from the external supplier using traditional purchase orders, that material will not initially be under kanban control. Later, as we authorize supplier shipments via kanbans, a ceiling or allowable inventory will exist.

2. Follow First in First out (FIFO).

The first kanban authorization that comes (back or the first set to add up to a lot size) is the first one that reenters the process.

Where lot sizing still occurs, production is authorized to begin whenever the lot size is reached. Lots for various products should be processed in the sequence in which they are reached. But where lots for a family are run periodically, all available kanbans for the group should be collected and run consistently as scheduled.

If you are incapable of manufacturing the highest-priority kanban due, for example, to material shortages, cross-training, or equipment problems, then you need to select the first job in the queue that you are capable of doing. The authorized product that could not be made remains at the front of the queue, automatically retaining the highest priority until it can be produced. Arbitrarily jumping to a later job in the queue will cause problems. As we reduce the inventory in the pipeline, we reach a point where not enough inventory remains to allow distortion of the priority by days or hours. If we do not get around to doing the first one in the queue for four hours, we could end up with a stock shortage because the system may no longer have four hours of slack in it.

3. Never pass on a known defect.

The objective is to make-high quality, cost-effective products in a responsive manner, not simply to move material from one operation to the next. If a product is known to be defective, it cannot move on, and until is is repaired or scrapped, it occupies an authorized kanban location in the pipeline. If a rework location exists, outside the normal production pipeline, the product can be moved to that location, but the number of items in rework should also be under kanban control.

If a situation arises where a particular part is needed but will not be available for a number of days, it is perfectly acceptable to add this part on later. You can define your process in any way that makes sense. If it is practical to add a part in operation ten instead of operation one, you may. However, with Just-in-Time, the throughput time is so short that this is often a wasted effort. If, prior to Just-in-Time, your throughput time was ten days, conceivably you could have continued to build without the part for a week or more, quickly adding the part when it came in. Under Just-in-Time, however, if your throughput time is reduced to two days, you can change the process only enough to delay your agony by a few hours. Usually, with Just-in-Time there's no real advantage to adding a part later on, because only a relatively short period of time is gained.

4. Reduce kanbans to expose problems.

While continuing to make shipments, One Less at a Time requires that we reduce the total number of kanbans in the pipeline one at a time in order to isolate what is constraining a faster throughput. Each time a constraint is identified and resolved, we repeat the process, gradually achieving higher velocities and an improved ability to respond.

Some of the constraints to higher velocities come from outside our factory walls. As we will show in chapter 7, however, it is best to learn how to do the "One Less at a Time" process at our own company first, and then progress to suppliers and customers. It is important that we understand the process before we expect someone else to use it.

Nevertheless, once we have streamlined our internal pipeline segment, accelerated our velocities, and simplified our processes, we often discover significant problems with the segment of the pipeline between our suppliers and us. For many, there are also problems between us and our key customers. At this phase, the big gains to be made are external. JIT/TQC will link the internal section of the pipeline with the external supplier; then it will link back through the supplier's operation to the supplier's supplier. The fact is, the pipeline keeps expanding, link after link, from the earth to the final consumer.

Part of the reduction process occurs entirely within our own area of control, but part must also involve the supplier and the customer. Our interactions have an impact on the amount of inventory in the pipeline. Reducing the inventory will expose constraints that require communications and changes on the part of both the customer and the supplier.

It is important to realize, however, that removing kanbans is a one-way process: Once they come out, we give up the right to put them back in. Discuss your desire to lower the kanban level with the appropriate work groups; if it seems feasible, cautiously take one out. If there are no problems, do it again. When a constraint surfaces, work around it until a solution is found. Don't put inventory back in to hide the problem. Force constructive thought at *all* levels to eliminate it.

5. The customer pulls material from the supplier.

It generally works out best if the customer pulls his material from the supplying operation. It's very visual, and what needs to be replaced will be immediately visible. However, this outbound-queue control may not work well if a large number of operations or machines are feeding the same operation or piece of equipment. In this case, it may be better to put an inbound-queue control in front of this bottleneck area. When the input queue is nearly full, a yellow caution light will signal the feeding operations to slow their rate of input. These operations might then work on the items in their own queues that do not require the bottleneck operation. If that is not possible, they may have to shift their resources around.

If the input queue is full, a red light will prevent any more work that requires the bottleneck operation from being done. Once the red light goes off, indicating that the input queue has been reduced, the production feeding this operation can resume. Of course, the signal lights discussed here can be either actual physical objects or, if the input queue is visible to all feeding operations, imaginary devices. This kanban process applies equally well to both manufactured products and processed paperwork.

In some environments where we wish to utilize kanban, however, we may be unable to shut off our supplier shipments. For example, if we decide to use kanbans in the incoming-materials receiving/inspection area, we cannot easily stop shipments that are already en route. Similarly, if we want to use kanban in the customer repair area, we cannot control customer returns. In these instances, when we reach a kanban ceiling, we do not shut off the incoming product, but rather shift our resources to the operation that is falling behind.

6. Only active material is allowed at the workstation.

The work center is not a general-purpose storage location. At this point in the pilot project, the storage location for kanbans has already been defined. By setting a time limit on the amount of work allowed at a given station—ideally one kanban—we prevent the workers from picking up a day's work at the kanban shelf, taking it back to their area and then working on it for the next eight hours. However, for various reasons, it might be impractical for workers to go to a storage area for every single kanban. If so, try never to have more than one hour's work at the work station at a time. Material should be moved at least every hour. With JIT/TQC we want smaller batches to level the load throughout the factory. By forcing hourly movement we can minimize the waves of work going through the factory. Of course, in some environments movement occurs continuously.

It is also important to enforce the rule that everything has a place. The best example for this might be an auto mechanic's garage, where there is a pegboard with a shadow of each tool that belongs there. That is the level of organization we are seeking with Just-in-Time.

SILVER BULLET EXCEPTIONS

Even though the rule states that we should never exceed the kanban ceiling, the truth is, this process is not always practical. At times we may find that we *have* to exceed the kanban limits. It is for this reason that I think an exception clause is appropriate. Just-in-Time rule number one is, *Never exceed a kanban ceiling.* We might find ourselves in a position, though, where we temporarily need a higher ceiling to make shipments (even when seasonality is not a factor). After all, our job *is* to make shipments. The important thing to remember is that JIT/TQC is the tool, not the answer.

When I was at Hewlett-Packard, I was once called out of a meeting by some people from one of my production areas, who informed me that the line was running out of a part. These soon-to-be-missing parts were required for the final operation. I was told they would run out at 10 a.m. that morning and wouldn't get any more until 10 a.m. the following day. Their solution, which was technically correct, was to shut the line down. I told them to wait a minute. We had only three days to the end of the month, and if we shut the line down, we would miss our monthly shipment plan because we did would have enough time to recover.

The workers reminded me that Just-in-Time says you cannot pass on a known defect. The reality was, the product couldn't be shipped without the part. I suggested that maybe we should build ahead. Their reaction was that we'd be violating the rules of kanban and JIT/TQC. I still wanted to make shipments, however, and we couldn't if we stopped the line.

After discussing the alternatives, I decided to authorize twenty extra kanbans in process to cover us until the part arrived. That allowed us to set aside twenty units without the part. Authorizing these extra kanbans required the assent of two people, the person in charge of production and the person responsible for the problem. We authorized twenty extra units, but not one more.

There is a danger here. If you do this every Friday and three times at the end of each month, you're just kidding yourself. You can label what you're doing Just-in-Time if you want to, but it's not. Every time a problem comes up and you use inventory to make it go away, you are removing constraints with inventory rather than correcting the root cause of the problem. By doing so you are defeating all you have worked for with JIT/TQC. In this instance, these people had been on JIT/TQC for only three days, and I destroyed my credibility with them. We did make shipments, and, fortunately, it didn't happen again. However, it took me six months to re-establish my credibility.

Another line ran into a similar problem. The people on the line wanted to interject more units into the system. This time, I took the other side of the argument by saying that the interjection of inventory simply covered problems. In this case, the line workers had been practicing JIT/TQC for a year and a half. They explained that during the last twelve months they had used emergency kanbans only four times, and that they lasted in the system an average of six hours. I acquiesced.

I have come to the conclusion that there are times during the course of the year, when for business reasons, it may be necessary to exceed the established kanban ceiling. However, under no circumstances is it acceptable to exceed the level without formal authorization of emergency kanbans. What I tell people today is, "I'll give you a six shooter with six silver bullets. I can believe that six times during a twelve-month period you may need to exceed the kanban ceiling you have set." But if you continue to shoot a couple of bullets at each month's end, you will soon be out of bullets. You will also be kidding yourself if you think that you are doing JIT/TQC. When you are shooting silver bullets as if they are coming out of a machine gun, you are doing business the same old way, and not forcing problem-solving the JIT/TQC way.

SUMMARY

It is important to remember that kanbans are bad, not good. Kanbans authorize inventory to exist, and inventory is waste and masks waste. We can unleash the power of continuous improvement by constantly making cost-effective, higher-quality shipments with "One Less" kanban in the pipeline. Once we begin to have difficulty in removing kanbans without negatively impacting quality, delivery, or cost, we have reached a constraint. The constraint is clear to all and prioritized for action. The constraint is an opportunity to become more competitive if we are smart enough to overcome it or economically work around it.

Facing constraints is a nightmare for many managers. We would rather avoid problems than face up to them or run the risk of stopping the line. But JIT/TQC is not about stopping the line. It is about recognizing the constraints to higher velocities, making those constraints visible to a large number of problem-solvers, and forcing action toward solutions. JIT/TQC places us, uncomfortably, between a rock and an opportunity. The "One Less at a Time" process is relatively straightforward. The kanban mechanism is relatively simple. The difficulty lies in emotionally rising to the challenge and economically eliminating kanbans.

Throughout this chapter I have detailed the rules and mechanisms of kanban. I have demonstrated its simplicity, its usefulness as a visual control, and its ability to make the "One Less at a Time" process practical. I have also shown how kanban sets a ceiling on inventory and then allows each customer/supplier pair to lower it. And, as McDonnell Douglas Computer Systems' wall display of removed kanbans illustrates, the system provides an excellent feedback mechanism.

As we will see, every area of the company can use Just-in-Time to drive continuous improvements. Changes to every functional area will result as constraints are exposed by practicing JIT/TQC in production. Waste, however, can also be uncovered directly in each functional area with the "One Less at a Time" process. Engineering documentation can set limits on the number of changes allowed between one process step and another. Order entry can set limits on orders in various queues. Information systems can use the concepts of checklists and setup reduction in the computer room. And as we will see in chapter 11, Total Quality Control is universally applicable. Only when everyone in the company begins to think in terms of exposing and eliminating waste will JIT/TQC become a way of life in the company.

Chapter 4

Restructuring the Shop Floor

All good ideas ultimately degenerate into hard work.
—Eric Hoffer

SELECTING A PILOT

Now that we have an understanding of the philosophy and process of Just-in-Time/Total Quality Control, it is time to put them into practice. The first step is to select a pilot. There are a number of important reasons for starting Just-in-Time on a smaller scale rather than attacking the whole process at once. First, except in the smallest of factories, the magnitude of change involved in converting an entire factory all at once could be overwhelming. Second, by initiating a pilot, you are able to verify the usefulness for your factory of the JIT/TQC process. You will also maximize your ability to maintain control while making changes. In addition, starting a controlled pilot allows you to maximize your chances for success. Many of the difficulties that will surface in this controlled environment can be avoided later by applying the lessons learned in the pilot. Finally, a pilot can actually accelerate the whole factory conversion. Logical arguments alone will not convince people of value of JIT/TQC. The pilot gives proof of performance.

How do you go about choosing a pilot? We often hear that Just-in-Time is best suited for "repetitive manufacturing," which implies that you should choose a high-volume/low-mix product. And since you want to be careful, you will probably want to pick a product that is somewhat stable, as opposed to, for instance, choosing a new product, which might undergo numerous engineering changes, have a volatile forecast and experience uneven sales. If this is your reasoning, you will find yourself seeking a high-volume/low-mix, mature product that requires no changes. The only trouble with this approach is that you may die waiting for such a thing to come along in your company. If you don't have such a product in your facility does that mean you can't do Just-in-Time? Of course not. Just pick an existing product. The question is, which one?

There are a number of different ways to select a pilot area. One method is to choose a product line. This selection doesn't necessarily have to do with volume or stability, though they are worthy of consideration. It is most important to pick a pilot from which you're going to learn something. It need not be the simplest product you can find. However, it should be relevant to the bulk of the business and large enough so that when you finish the pilot, people will notice, even if this makes the process more difficult.

Occasionally, people pick a pilot area that is completely different from the rest of their operations. They choose this product or process because JIT/TQC will be simple to implement with it, and they want to maximize their chances of success. The problem is that even if they do implement the pilot successfully, they won't learn much about how to apply the JIT/TQC principles to the rest of their business. Setting your sights too low will elicit little more than a yawn from observers. The results demonstrated won't pass the "so what" test.

The pilot also must be large enough so that if you run into trouble and expose a constraint, people will get excited and move to correct it, because the consequences of that constraint are going to be felt. However, the pilot should not be so large that you could bring the company to its knees. If you get into trouble, you should be able to use brute force to shove your way out. That doesn't mean it's going to be easy to get out, but you will eventually get out.

The pilot should comprise three or more kanban links. One cell feeds another, which feeds another and another. Multiple links are vital to convey a sense of the rhythm and cadence of Just-in-Time. They may consist of vertical links across functional areas for a product line or come from conversion of an entire functional area. The important point is that the *pull* of Just-in-Time must be demonstrated across several work groups.

If a company has a product line and a functional area that both contain three to four linkages and represent a meaningful part of the business, the pilot choice could go either way. Frequently a product line is chosen. The second pilot may also be a product line. With the third step, however, one of the main functional areas is often converted in its entirety. The key is to decide where the most will be learned while obtaining the greatest benefits for the fewest resources.

When Beckman Instruments entered its pilot-selection process, it took what some would call a courageous step. Originally, Beckman planned to choose more mature and stable product for its first pilot. After we had finished talking, however, Beckman changed their plans and selected a complex new product that had just come out of the design lab. They concluded that JIT/TQC was actually a better way to introduce a new product, because it would maximize their ability to respond. Of course it was more difficult to do the pilot, because there were more unknowns and changes. Beckman understood that they weren't in business to do JIT/TQC, but to serve the customer with higher quality, lower cost, and more responsive shipments. They figured that when constraints arose they would get quick attention. Ultimately, their choice was for the good of the company.

Tektronix's Lab Instruments division began the process even further back than Beckman, initiating a Just-in-Time pilot at the design inception stage. It took about two years for the product to progress from design to implementation. Although this process was successful For Tektronix, it is not generally recommended. Usually, there's more to be gained by picking an existing product line and implementing Just-in-Time, while simultaneously working on the design process for the next generation. This way, both tasks are accomplished, and the results of the pilot are visible in a shorter period of time.

Remember, the pilot should be the lead project for any other improvement activities involving all functional areas. Don't set your sights too low. You will never have a better opportunity to sell a breakthrough change than you do in the pilot phase. This is, after all, a model for the future. An impressive success here will go a long way toward helping you sell the concept throughout all other areas later. And don't limit the pilot changes to the shop floor. Modifications in the support areas and information systems are at least as important and as difficult as changes in production. Don't be afraid of attacking difficult areas. It is important to perform the difficult tasks in the safe and controlled environment of the pilot. Don't save them until the last. Study the changes and alternatives, then commit to action. Do not succumb to "paralysis by analysis." Get started and learn as you practice—that is why you are doing a pilot. The biggest mistake a company can make, of course, is never starting at all.

BREAKTHROUGH PILOT SPECIFICATIONS

The breakthrough pilot specifications discussed in this section were developed through hands-on experience at Hewlett-Packard and through working with client companies. These criteria are designed to yield breakthrough results, not to minimize change or to create marginal improvements by adapting JIT/TQC to fit existing processes and policies. They will involve several functional areas in JIT/TQC from the beginning, because all of the constraints to higher velocities do not lie exclusively within manufacturing. These specifications were formulated to help you solve the most difficult and emotional constraints within the safety and controlled environment of a pilot, not postpone the tough issues until the end. They are designed to be executed quickly, before the opportunity to change disappears. And, finally, they were developed to make you competitive, not necessarily to be easy.

The criteria are shown in figure 4.1 and discussed below. Remember, they apply only to the pilot area, not to converting the entire factory all at once. Details on how to implement these required changes will, of course, be contained in the appropriate chapters throughout the rest of the book.

1. Work orders will be eliminated. Work orders will not be used to authorize production or to trigger material replenishments from the stockroom or from other areas within the scope of the pilot. They also will not be used to collect labor or track material. They will be gone. We cannot afford to let the cost of paperwork rise as lot sizes shrink. We cannot afford the delays of paperwork as we attempt to improve responsiveness.

A top-level work order may remain if it is equal to the customer order or a master-scheduled item. Technically, it is still wasteful to have a redundant document, but during the pilot, retaining the top-level work order is sometimes expedient.

This change will require the efforts of production, production planning, production control, and information systems.

Figure 4.1
Breakthrough Pilot Specifications

```
KANBAN CONTROLS FOR

   EXECUTION
   MATERIAL REPLENISHMENT

NO WORK ORDERS FOR

   PRODUCTION AUTHORIZATION
   MATERIAL REPLENISHMENT
   TRACKING LABOR & MATERIAL
   PLANNING (OK FOR MPS & PLANNED
      ORDERS INTERNAL TO MRP)

LABOR COLLECTION BY EXCEPTION

MATERIAL STORED AT POINT OF USE

TQC STARTED WITHIN 30 DAYS

PRACTICE "ONE LESS" TO UNLEASH THE
POWER OF CONTINUOUS IMPROVEMENT
```

2. Kanban will control and authorize. When we eliminate work orders, we eliminate a shop-floor control mechanism. Kanban will now serve to control the inventory in the manufacturing pipeline. It will be used to authorize all production and all material replenishments within the scope of the pilot, including replenishments from the stockroom if still required.

This change will require the efforts of production, production planning, production control and information systems.

3. Labor will be collected by exception. Since there will be no work orders, labor-collection procedures must change for most companies. Also, as lot sizes decrease, the number of labor-collection transactions and corrections to them will increase unless changes are made. Consequently, only labor exceptions will be reported. The remaining time will be charged to work produced by the cell. This will be the case whether

one product or a large variety of products is produced by the same group of workers.

Those companies that track labor to the work order, part number, and operation level tend to have the most difficulty with this criterion. Those that currently do not track labor to the work order should have less difficulty.

This change will require the efforts of production, production control, cost accounting, and information systems. This criterion is contractually more difficult with government-contract and other regulated environments, although it is still possible.

4. Inventory will be stored at the point of use. Material used by the pilot area will be stored at the point of use. The only material to be held in the main stockroom will be the overflow portion that does not fit near the point of use. The primary stockroom will be known as the point-of-use storage area. The former main stockroom will now be considered the overflow stockroom. This criterion is already the norm for many companies that deal with metals, rolls of paper, or large bulk ingredients.

This change will require the efforts of production, production control, stockroom, manufacturing engineering, and information systems.

5. Total Quality Control will be used to solve problems. Basic problem-solving skills should be employed within days of turning on the pilot. Later, more rigorous, statistically based tools should also appear where appropriate. Problem-solving, not problem masking, will quickly become the norm. This change will require the efforts of the quality department and each area of the implementation team.

6. Unleash the power of continuous improvement. Gently reduce the number of kanbans to expose constraints to higher velocities, and to prioritize and force actions.

A number of changes will be required. Most are not technically difficult, but many are emotionally challenging. One of the best ways to make the factory population comfortable with the impending changes is to let them quickly see an operating breakthrough pilot. Helping people to accept all of the changes necessary and to learn new jobs requires the efforts of the personnel or human resources department.

Because the pilot serves as a model for the future, many companies incorporate difficult changes on the first day the pilot is turned on. Recognizing that most day-to-day activities will fall under the responsibility of the cell members, a number of companies begin the pilot with the understanding that the cell members are now responsible for routine housekeeping, routine equipment servicing, and routine maintenance.

Even more emotional changes may be tested in the pilot. One company in Chicago and another in the United Kingdom stopped incentive pay for the cell members the day the JIT/TQC pilot began. Management first explained why incentive pay was difficult in a JIT/TQC environment and promised that they would attempt to pay individual cell members about the same amount as they had earned in the past. Then they asked for volunteers for the pilot. The company used the program to learn how to motivate people without giving incentive pay. Another company stopped paying those that volunteered to be in the pilot bonuses for their improvement ideas, and another modified seniority benefits.

Only about 120 calendar days should elapse from the day the implementation team completes an in-depth implementation course until the day the pilot incorporating the above criteria is turned on. Some companies move much faster; others take longer. One major pilot area for one company took 140 days, while their sister division studied JIT/TQC for eighteen months. The breakthrough criteria do entail a lot of work and emotional change, but not so much that a pilot can't be implemented within 120 days.

MOVE QUICKLY

Rapid progress is essential. When you are planning a change and you get the broad-based commitment necessary to make it happen, unless you're a very unusual company the green light isn't going to stay on very long. Before you know it, you'll be too busy to do a pilot, things will be too slow to initiate a pilot, or you'll find that one of the champions has been promoted or has left. There are many factors that can cause that light of opportunity go out. Your chances for successfully pulling off a pilot using this breakthrough approach begin to drop off after 120 days.

If you see your pilot taking much longer, you should ask why. Something is wrong. If you find there are always good reasons for delaying implementation, something is still probably wrong. The truth is, everyone is too busy to implement JIT/TQC. No manager stands up and asks for more work. Everyone has too much to do as it is.

McDonnell Douglas Computer Systems was extremely busy when it implemented JIT/TQC. In addition to its southern California factory, it had a similar-sized factory in northern California that had to be closed and consolidated into the southern California facility, nearly doubling its size. All this was accomplished just as the firm was in the middle of trying to implement Just-in-Time. McDonnell Douglas proceeded with JIT/TQC anyway. Why? Because they felt if they waited six months, things would not be that much better. If they had waited a year, they might never have gotten the opportunity again. Finding the time to implement is a matter of priority. You must decide how important JIT/TQC is in relation to the other demands on your time. In order to do JIT/TQC, you have to make it an "A" priority. If you can't make it an "A" priority, you had better wait until you can. Otherwise, you're going to take up a lot of time, frustrate yourself, and get nowhere.

It is also advisable to avoid spending a lot of out-of-pocket money during the pilot. Other than the cost of education, there should be little expense in getting started. Don't buy a lot of new equipment or implement expensive new factory-floor layouts for the pilot. If it's a matter of sliding work tables around to reconfigure the flow, that is acceptable. Otherwise, practice a while with JIT/TQC before investing large sums in equipment or new factory plans. Let JIT/TQC direct and prioritize how you spend your budget.

If your entire operation is based around heavy machinery and distance is a constraint, you will require a higher number of kanbans to cover the layout problem. The extra kanbans mean that distance is a problem. First learn how you operate with Just-in-Time for a while, and then you'll learn how to redesign the layout. If you modify the layout before you start, you'll almost certainly have to change it again anyway. As your inventory drops, you won't need the same amount of distance between the work areas. Just-in-Time constantly drives change and that change will continually lead to refinements in layout, even where heavy machinery is a factor.

Besides, you don't have time in 120 days to spend a lot of money! The criteria listed above, when applied properly, have *always* resulted in a major breakthrough in manufacturing quality, delivery, and cost. The criteria represent some of the most serious stumbling blocks to sustained success. They must be addressed in the pilot so that the continuous improvement process will be less likely to stall once changes are required in nonmanufacturing areas.

Figure 4.2
Production Layout Alternatives

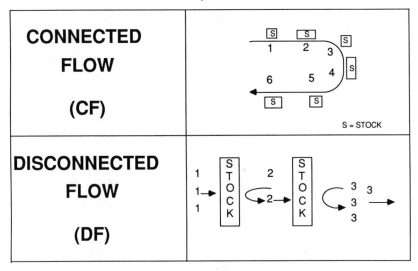

CONNECTED FLOW (CF)	

S = STOCK

| DISCONNECTED FLOW (DF) | |

MATERIAL-FLOW CONSIDERATIONS

As we address the issue of material-flow considerations, we encounter the idea of "repetitive manufacturing" once again. "Repetitive manufacturing" is a loose term. Many companies think it applies only to high-volume/low-mix products. While it is true that some of the first companies to do Just-in-Time well were those with a high volume/low mix, the term also applies to the job shop. Actually, better terms for high volume/low mix and low volume/high mix are *connected flow* and *disconnected flow* (used by professors Hayes and Wheelwright). (see figure 4.2.)

"Connected flow" is used to describe the assembly line, while "disconnected flow" refers to a setup composed of individual workbenches or machines—the job shop. Just-in-Time applies to both situations. In fact, a strong case can be made that there is more to be gained from doing JIT/TQC in a job shop, because the environment is more complicated. The more we can do to simplify the process, the more we are going to gain. Again, the important point is not that you repeatedly build identical products but that you repeat your processes. If

Figure 4.3
Production Layout Characteristics

CONSIDERATIONS	CONNECTED (Assembly line)	DISCONNECTED (Job shop)
LINE BALANCE	Equal Times	Different Times
ROUTINGS	Fixed	Variable
WORK STATIONS	Dedicated	Generic
OPERATIONS	Linked	Decoupled
PROCESS	Product Dependent	Product Independent
EXPANSION	Replicate, Re-engr.	Add Work Station
FLOW	Simple, Rapid	Complex, Unclear
TRANSFER LOT	Container → One	Batch → One
THRUPUT TIME	Shorter	Longer
TRAINING	Operation	Area
SETUP	Few	More
MATERIAL STORAGE	At Position	Off Position
SCHEDULING	Rate Based	Lot Based
DISTANCES	Short	Long
FLEXIBILITY	Less	More

your processes repeat, even if the products and routings vary, Just-in-Time applies.

Connected flows can exist in an unlimited number of configurations, including the traditional straight assembly line and the U-shaped line. No matter what the shape, however, there are certain characteristics that must exist before a connected flow (assembly line) is valid (see figure 4.3). If you are unable to meet the connected-flow restrictions, then a disconnected-flow process should be adopted. You should be aware, however, that even if you start with a disconnected-flow configuration, Just-in-Time will take you toward a connected flow process. Every time the disconnected flow is simplified, every time one kanban is removed, you move closer to a connected flow.

A traditional, functional department provides an example of a disconnected-flow process. While it is a very flexible environment, it does not move material as efficiently as an assembly line.

To change over from a traditional job-shop/batch-production environment to a Just-in-Time disconnected-flow approach, a company could use a closed-loop transporter for material handling, with a carousel at the head of the transporter for material storage and/or WIP storage. Another possibility is to adopt a progressive-assembly carousel, which maximizes flexibility. Both the transporter and the progressive carousel are intriguing, but in practice they seem to have limited applications. In many instances where one of these is workable, a simpler, less expensive, more flexible, and equally effective alternative can be found.

It is important to recognize that it is not intrinsically wrong to use transporters, carousels, conveyors, or storage-retrieval systems in a JIT/TQC environment. However, it is inconsistent with the goal of reducing the waste of transportation and storage while maximizing flexibility. In some narrow areas of application these types of equipment are very useful, as long as they help minimize waste and maximize flexibility, rather than inhibit it. A good JIT/TQC rule of thumb is to *keep it simple!*

Basically, we have a choice of a connected flow or a disconnected flow, with an infinite number of possible configurations and hybrids. It is not unusual to find one portion of a factory using connected flow, while another uses disconnected flow. The question is, how do we go about determining the proper layout?

DETERMINING THE PROPER LAYOUT

The first step in analyzing the layout of an operation is to document the flow of the product through the various pilot process steps while noting the important characteristics of each process. One company found it had forty-two products traveling through thirty-five separate process flows. Charts similar to the one in figure 4.4 were drawn up and revealed that the flows were incredibly complex. The important next step was to understand the reasons why the flows differed. As the company documented and challenged its processes, it was able to simplify them, reducing the number of flows to six. At this point the firm went ahead and implemented some of its layout changes.

Once we understand our product flows, we need to compile some basic information about the processes. For each product and process we should gather the following data:

- setup times/job
- run times/piece

Figure 4.4
Process Flow

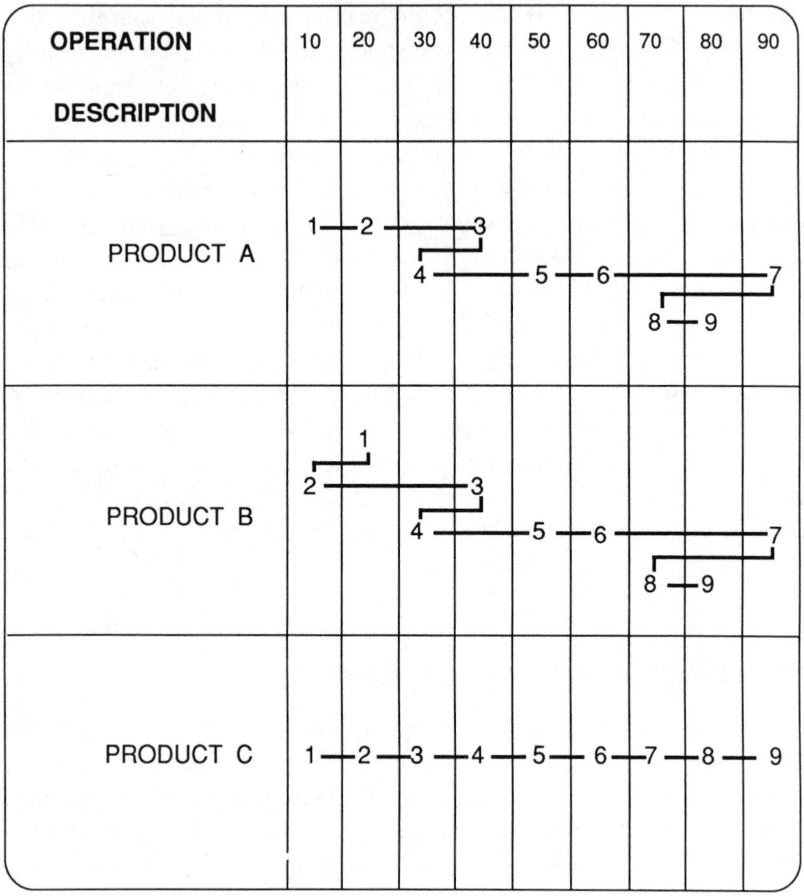
OPERATION
DESCRIPTION
10
20
30
40
50
60
70
80
90
PRODUCT A
1—2—3
4—5—6—7
8—9
PRODUCT B
1
2—3
4—5—6—7
8—9
PRODUCT C
1—2—3—4—5—6—7—8—9

- aging characteristics (cure, stress, dry bake, etc.) and time/piece
- batch size requirements if any
- number of shifts each operation is available
- external processes in flow
- capacity of bottleneck and near bottleneck areas
- units in process and complete
- units in rework
- units in stock

- time in queue from completion of one operation to start of next
- other unique characteristics

Any special conditions should also be noted, such as "Due to nature of equipment, up to eight units can be tested simultaneously just as quickly as one," or "Batch must be at least 50 gallons and no more than 300 gallons but run time is not affected."

The *setup-time* information should show the average setup time expected at the turn-on of the pilot, as well as the minimum lot size that can reasonably and economically be tolerated, as this will directly affect the number of kanbans in the pipeline.

For each product, the *run time* required for each step must be determined. Normally, understanding the average actual tact time[1] at each process step for each product is sufficient. This number excludes setups amortization and queue times. For example, if the production rate at a specific dedicated operation averages 100 of a given product per day, the tact time is 4.2 minutes [(7 hrs./shift × 60 min./hr) / (100 units/shift) = 4.2 min./unit]. For shared equipment, the tact time will need to be calculated based on the units produced during the time the equipment was in use on the product in question. Again, it is usually not necessary to be absolutely precise at lower volumes, but of course, greater accuracy is required when producing 100,000 units per day than at 10 per day. In addition, in the early stages of JIT/TQC, the run times are frequently insignificant to the queue times.

In other words, to begin JIT/TQC, it is usually *not* necessary to conduct laborious time studies to document each hand movement and identify times to the fractional second. We are just looking for a place to start. Changes and improvements will occur as soon as JIT/TQC is

---

[1] Some confusion exists about the terms "tact time," "cycle time," and "throughput time." Tact time is the time required between successive units of end product existing at a production operation. Throughput time is the average time from when material enters a production facility or area until it exits. This is the average actual manufacturing lead time. Cycle time is sometimes considered a synonym for tact time and for throughput time, depending on the scope of production being considered. The American Production and Inventory Control Society, at the time of this publication, uses cycle time as an equivalent for tact time in its Just-in-Time certification exams. Electronics manufacturers typically use cycle time as a synonym for throughput time. In this book I will avoid using the term "cycle time" since its meaning is not specific enough.

implemented. If we invest too heavily in the documentation of every movement, those who did the study or paid for the analysis may be reluctant to change the processes for fear that their work will become obsolete. To improve and standardize production processes, detailed analysis may be useful. However, if JIT/TQC is in place, the operators themselves should be intimately involved in the analysis.

Test times follow the same analysis logic as do run times. In essence, routine tests and inspection are treated as any other process step. They may be wasteful, but if they are a normal part of the process, they must be counted as such.

It is important to consider any significant times required for drying, curing, baking, aging, burn-in, run-in, or environmental-stress screening of the product. If the process is performed in batch, challenge it to see if the equipment or process actually requires a certain batch size in order to function properly. Do we batch simply because of tradition? Can we start to remove some items from the process without affecting others?

Document the number of *shifts* each operation is available. If a supplier operation produces only on the first shift, but the customer operation produces on two, the first shift must have enough kanbans in its output queue to keep the customer's first and second shifts busy.

Where an *external process* lies within the scope of the pilot, it will be necessary to document those process steps as well. The external processes will most likely need to become a part of the JIT/TQC pilot. For example, when the output of a process step must be sent outside for plating and then returned for completion, a rhythmic and predictable schedule must be established with the external plating shop. Essentially, we want to understand these operations so that we can intelligently buy a piece of the plater's capacity at known intervals and determine the number of kanbans required in the pipeline.

We should also determine the capacity per shift of each *bottleneck* and *near bottleneck operation*. Where bottlenecks exist, we are likely to have more kanbans in front of the bottleneck to minimize the number of interruptions not only to it but also to supply and customer areas. Are extra kanbans wasteful? They certainly are. All kanbans are wasteful. Our job is to make shipments with "One Less" kanban in the pipeline. However, to satisfy the "make shipments" portion of our job, we must be careful with bottleneck areas. Information on secondary bottleneck areas is useful too, because as we make improvements to the bottleneck process, the bottleneck areas often change.

Next, we need to determine the average time each item will spend in *queue* between operations, ideally when conditions are slightly worse than normal. We are looking for the inventory level that will cover problems most of the time. Experience will usually provide this number. Elaborate statistical calculations of standard deviations are normally not necessary. In fact, we could start our kanban levels a little high and arrive at the same number experimentally. Under most circumstances, this is actually faster than gathering the data and calculating it statistically, but if data exists, use it.

We need this queue information for the current layout and for the proposed new layout. If we know the total number of units in the pipeline and the total output per day, we can easily determine the throughput time. (Remember, where pieces are not a consistent representation of time, you will need to use hours in the pipeline and hours produced per day.) We should also know the approximate queue times that exist after each operation. When actually setting kanban limits, we may let the sum of each outbound queue be larger than the total number allowed in the pipeline. For example, we may control the total number of pallets in the pipeline but allow some leeway between each process step. Then, by using generic in-process kanban locations and recirculating brand name or generic kanban cards, we can control the total in process.

When only a portion of a shop's output is to be converted to JIT/TQC, it is still important to consider the queue times for all products in order to determine the average time in queue between the completion of one operation and the start of the next.

Finally, we need information about the requirements per day of the product or product family. We also must know about the number of units in production and rework. Rework should not provide a limitless escape from the JIT/TQC process.

Once all the above information has been obtained, it is useful to prepare a process flow chart of the operations (see figure 4.5) and note the kanban levels between operations and in total.

GROUP TECHNOLOGY

Once you understand the various flows, it is time to examine group technology. This process allows you to analyze different types of pro-

Figure 4.5
Process Flow

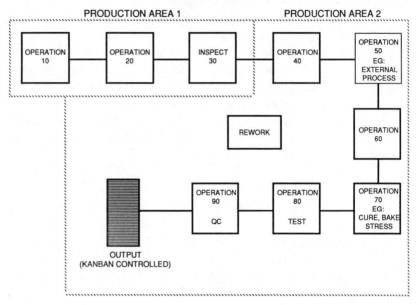

cesses and equipment so that they can be arranged into a cell. By doing this, you minimize distance and throughput time while still maintaining high utilization of equipment. Tellabs was able to shrink its pilot production line from an area covering 7,500 square feet of factory space to three cells of 500 square feet each, an 80 percent reduction.

In production we have traditionally tended to group machines of a like type together, placing all the sheet-metal shears in one section, the punches in another, and the breaks in a third. This was probably very practical when machines were powered by belts connected to a common drive shaft turned by a waterwheel in the creek outside. That restriction is gone today, and we have the option of arranging equipment as we choose. Today's restrictions have less to do with physical constraints than with inflexible organizations, workers, and layouts.

Adopting a group- or cellular-technology approach, we might rearrange equipment into "work centers," each containing one shear, one punch, and one break. Group/cellular technology can be very efficient for families of parts, allowing for rapid transfer of small lots of material from one machine to another, rather than requiring larger batches to be transported from one work center to another.

According to an article in the *Harvard Business Review* by professors Nancy Hyer and Urban Wemmerlov, the aim of group technology is "to capitalize on similarities in recurring tasks." They see this taking place in three ways:

1. performing similar activities together
2. standardizing closely related activities
3. efficiently storing and retrieving information related to recurring problems.

When we relate these ideas to the grouping of parts, we find that they have two primary applications. The simplest, useful to a job shop, is to sequence similar parts on a machine. We will see an example of how NCR handled this technique in chapter 5. The second, more advanced application has to do with the creation of manufacturing cells. The Harris Company reorganized its integrated-circuit assembly area from a traditional, functional layout to one utilizing group technology (see figure 4.6). The changes helped achieve a 50 percent reduction in inventory and a 20 percent improvement in yield.

LAYOUT CONSIDERATIONS

Now that we have a handle on the process flows, process characteristics, and kanban inventory requirements for the pilot, we must construct a new layout. When designing a new layout, whether it is a connected- or disconnected-flow configuration, there are a number of factors that you need to consider. First, you want to minimize movement. Movement is waste, and shrinking the distances involved will reduce this factor. Second, as the distances are shortened, handling is also reduced. It is much easier to lift and pass one small part than to move a large box with hundreds of parts.

Next, you need to maximize visibility. Just-in-Time is a highly visual process. If possible, the layout should enable the supplier to see his output kanban and the customer to see his supplier's kanban. It should also facilitate supplier/customer communications, since their feedback will help you determine how to continue making shipments "One Less

Figure 4.6
Group Technology Cell

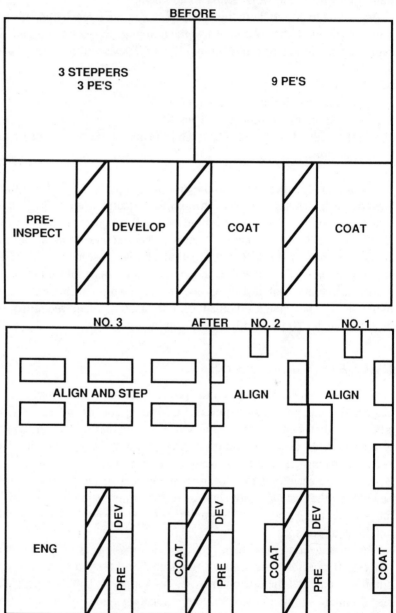

at a Time" and thereby reduce the inventory between them. The layout should be simple and flexible, providing for efficient utilization of equipment and resources. Naturally, it should be safe. Finally, it should be orderly. Housekeeping is of critical importance in a Just-in-Time environment. Very often, one of the first things that must be done is to remove of all unnecessary and inactive materials, tools, and equipment at the work positions. *Everything should have a place and be in its place.* Orderliness is necessary to ensure that visual controls keep Just-in-Time effective and simple. (A checklist is given in chapter 11.)

The layout must also maximize kanban discipline. It should be instantly obvious when an item without a kanban authorization exists. Workers should be able to visibly verify with a single glance whether a given piece has a kanban authorization.

In designing the layout, simulate as far as is practical through the "One Less at a Time" process on paper by soliciting input from everyone who can contribute. Then physically incorporate as many of the changes as possible into a new layout, keeping the modifications inexpensive and rapid. It is important to remember that there is no ideal layout for JIT/TQC; there are just those that are right for the moment. Continuous improvements will drive continuous layout changes.

EQUIPMENT SELECTION

Just-in-Time also requires a new approach to equipment selection. The type of equipment you choose will depend substantially on whether you are using a connected or disconnected flow. With connected flow, you may be able to use a dedicated piece of equipment or even multiple copies of small machines. With disconnected flow, you will probably need to select more general-purpose machines. Unfortunately, in most instances, using general-purpose equipment means having to do setups. Try to find flexible equipment that can be set up quickly. Equipment manufacturers are beginning to understand the importance of fast setups, and new equipment is slowly becoming more efficient in this respect.

It should be noted that implementing Just-in-Time does not require a company to buy new equipment. However, if you do find yourself struggling with existing equipment, and it is economically justifiable to replace it, be sure to consider the need for faster setups and balanced flow in addition to evaluating technological features.

SHARING COMMON EQUIPMENT

During the transition from batch production to full Just-in-Time production, it is common to have to share some pieces of equipment. There are different ways to do this. One approach is to alternate jobs, running a batch job and then running whatever Just-in-Time jobs are waiting. A problem may arise with this method, however, if the batch runs are extremely long, since the shorter Just-in-Time jobs could have to wait a long time before they can be run. In this case you have to either run larger Just-in-Time lots, because you can't use the machine as frequently as you would like, or break up a few extremely long batch jobs to accommodate the Just-in-Time pilot.

When there is no significant setup involved, some companies are able to manage equipment sharing by performing a "time slice." Every hour on the hour, they interrupt whatever batch jobs they have been running and do whatever Just-in-Time work is present. They may run Just-in-Time jobs from 2:00 to 2:15 and then from 3:00 to 3:15. A time slice is feasible only if no major setup is required.

One technique, used by Tellabs, is to run Just-in-Time by shift. Tellabs' first pilot took place on the third shift, and during that period the entire factory performed Just-in-Time work. It allowed them to postpone having to share common equipment. Nonetheless, before a Just-in-Time implementation has been completed, almost everybody is going to have to learn how to share common equipment.

Another way to deal with equipment limitations is simply to dedicate some equipment. If you have enough pieces, group-technology analysis may enable you to dedicate some of them to the Just-in-Time process, while the reset can serve for batch. Again, you don't have to share them, just dedicate them.

MATERIAL STORAGE AT THE POINT OF USE

As we have already learned, putting inventory at the point of use minimizes handling and reduces response time. With connected-flow in place, there is a reasonable chance that all material can be stored at the point of use. Turning to figure 4.2, we see that at any one position, storage space for only one-sixth of the total material may be required.

With disconnected flow, there is typically more product variety going through the production steps. Storing a portion of the material for all the products at each work station is often impractical. If all required material cannot be stored at the point of use, it should be kept as close as practical. The disadvantage is one extra handling step, which forces the worker to get the material instead of simply reaching into the bin of stock stored at the work position.

One way to minimize this extra handling step is to keep a transportable sub-stockroom in a tray or cart so that the worker can retrieve material for the work position in a matter of seconds. As a rule of thumb, in most disconnected-flow environments material should be able to be exchanged from one product to another in sixty seconds or less. In many environments, this step takes only fifteen seconds. Wherever a disconnected flow exists, the goal is to insure that material changeovers are not a limiting factor. For this reason, pieces are issued out to the sub-stockroom not in synchronized kits, but separately in reasonable quantities.

During the initial Just-in-Time conversion, you want to store some of every routinely needed material at the point of use. Ideally, 100 percent of the material for some items can be placed on the line. However, in most factories there is too much material to store everything at the point of use in the beginning. Also, you really shouldn't put everything on the floor until you can demonstrate control. It's definitely easier to gain control with a limited quantity.

It is virtually impossible to determine how much material to relocate from the stockroom to the point of use by looking at a list of part numbers. The best method involves a team of people and physical contact with each item. The team should consist of a production scheduler with usage information, a stockroom attendant, and someone from the production area. The three will then walk through the stockroom. As they encounter each item to be relocated, they will examine the supplier package size to see if it can be moved to the line without being opened. They will then examine the size of the material or package and make a balanced decision. Hopefully, a supplier package multiple can be selected that will

- economically utilize storage space and facilitate inventory accuracy on the line

- minimize material handling and counting in the stockroom
- be consistent with projected usage
- be consistent with plans for direct supplier deliveries to the point of use

When the team reaches its decision, a storage bin, pallet, or shelf label is prepared and a replenishment kanban is completed. Prior to implementation of the pilot, the physical material-storage locations are established on the line. Then, just prior to cutover, the kanbans are submitted to initiate the transfer of material.

It is unlikely that all the material will fit at the point of use when you are starting Just-in-Time. As mentioned earlier, some of the material will be held back in the locked stockroom. The difference here is that the point of use is now considered the primary stockroom. What is held back is in the *overflow* stockroom. Naturally, it's not desirable to have an overflow stockroom, and you will want to eliminate it eventually.

Once you have demonstrated control, you will want to put all unique parts at the point of use. If it's still not physically possible to do so, determine the delivery frequency of the material (for example, two weeks) and try to place the corresponding quantity at the point of use. If that is still too much, put as much as you can and inform purchasing of the amount (for example, five days). Now purchasing knows that if they can economically achieve weekly deliveries, the waste inherent in the traditional stockroom activities will be eliminated. Even if incoming inspection is still required, at least the overflow area can be bypassed.

In the final stage of this process, all material is stored at the point of use. It comes directly from the supplier to the line. Record accuracy procedures and how to figure inventory deduction calculations will be covered in chapter 9.

IMPACT ON FACILITIES

As you progress with Just-in-Time, storing material at the point of use can have a major impact on the physical plant itself. With Just-in-Time, material is distributed throughout the facility. Eventually, most companies will no longer need a central stockroom, much less one with automated storage-and-retrieval capabilities.

One of my client companies owned one of the world's largest private automatic-storage-and-retrieval warehouses. Manufacturing Resource Planning, Just-in-Time, and Total Quality Control are making it obsolete. As fewer and fewer parts have been stored in the facility, the allocated cost per transaction has risen proportionally. Managers at various manufacturing sites quickly realized that it would be wise to avoid being the one with the last transaction, because it was going to be very expensive! Today a large portion of the warehouse is subleased to an offshore manufacturer of tennis shoes.

In addition, as your factory starts receiving more frequent deliveries, it may be necessary to establish traffic patterns on the plant site. You may also want to receive material at more than one location, so the deliveries can be closer to each point of use. The point is to minimize the wastes of handling and distance as the number of receipts increases.

JIT/TQC's drive for continuous improvements calls for reduction of these wastes and leads to a continually evolving factory layout. The problem of factory design reminds me of that frustrating child's puzzle where you try to rearrange the squares in order, but there's only one empty space. When you move one square, all the rest have to move. The same is true for most major factory re-layouts. They are not only difficult, they are also expensive and take a lot of planning. Yet Just-in-Time continues to drive the system toward more flexibility. Like most changes initiated by Just-in-Time, this one requires concentrated effort.

Initially, you should at least maximize your ability to rearrange within certain territorial boundaries, such as a cell. This might include everything from moving shelves to rearranging machinery. One solution is to put power drops on flexible conduits so that equipment can be moved in any direction desired within a certain radius. At Tellabs, everything is being put on wheels. In other facilities large, heavy machines are being placed on steel plates so that a tractor can relocate them relatively easily.

The need for more flexibility will also affect the bureaucracy involved in making change. As stated above, manufacturing needs the flexibility and freedom to make small layout changes within its own territory, and should be able to do so without going through long approval cycles. Similarly, design should be allowed to make some changes locally. Since there is no such thing as "the" layout under Just-in-Time, only what's correct for the moment, it is essential to loosen the red tape restricting changes. For some, this will also have an impact on unionized job categories and responsibilities.

It is not unusual for Just-in-Time to result in factory-floor space savings of 50 percent or more. This alone will affect facilities planning dramatically. It is also not unusual for managers to attempt to keep their excess space by giving excuses such as "we already own the space, so there will be no real savings anyway." Of course, the savings won't actually be realized by the company until a lease is canceled, or new expenditures are avoided, but we reach that point by saving a few square feet at a time. In situations where space charges are allocated to the respective department managers, the motivation to save space is provided by reducing the allocation as usable space is saved. Eventually, enough space should be saved on which to capitalize.

AUTOMATION

As the number of kanbans in the pipeline begins to decrease, the velocity increases. There comes a point, however, when some sort of mechanical assistance may be required before further reductions can be realized. JIT/TQC makes it very clear when and where automation belongs. For example, say we have two machines performing two consecutive operations on long coils of steel. After the first operation, the coils are collected and moved to the next operation. If we are practicing JIT/TQC, we are learning how to operate with "One Less" coil in the pipeline. Eventually, we will be left with only one coil between operations. At that point, it becomes obvious that we should link the two machines together and feed the coil directly from the first machine into the second. If the first machine gets ahead, the strip of coil between the two machines will sag. This sag will activate a switch, which might either momentarily shut down the first machine and/or turn on the second. If the coil becomes too taut, it will shut off the second machine and/or turn on the first. By setting a ceiling on inventory using kanbans, we are setting limit switches on our processes. Each time we remove one kanban from the pipeline, we get one step closer to automation. We may never reach that point in some environments, but we still gain from accelerating and simplifying the processes.

Once your processes have been simplified, you may find that a human is actually able to do the job more flexibly and economically than a robot. Those situations where that is not the case, however, become painfully obvious. Generally, companies that automate prior to implementing Just-in-Time spend more money and spend it in different areas than they would if they automated after Just-in-Time. (All generalizations, of course, are accurate only some of the time, including this one.)

At Hewlett-Packard in Fort Collins, as lot sizes on circuitboard assemblies were driven down, setups became more of a constraint. It got to the point where it was hard to go any lower without automation. Just-in-Time eventually led them to automate a portion of the process which will enable them to make one board at a time, anytime, with virtually no setup of equipment.

Hewlett-Packard accomplished this by first dedicating some of its front-end equipment to insert only higher-volume components. That left a large number of individual components that were used in low volume on various boards. The next step was to construct a robot to be placed in front of a highly compacted bank of available components. While a person would be incapable of accurately reaching into that sort of matrix and pulling out the right part every time, HP found that a robot was very accurate. With Just-inTime, it becomes very clear where robotics belong.

While there are those who insist that having "islands of automation" is undesirable, this need not be the case. With Just-in-Time, we constantly strive for higher velocities while improving quality, delivery, dependability/flexibility, and cost. A "lights-out," fully automated factory does not necessarily achieve these objectives. A more cost-effective, typically more successful, and at least equally expedient approach to automation involves simplifying and accelerating the existing processes and then using automation at those points where humans are less capable of delivering the quality, flexibility and cost required. Others use automation to enhance the quality of work life by applying robotics in situations that are too dirty, too dangerous, or very demeaning to humans. There is nothing wrong with a customer/supplier relationship between a robot and a human. In fact, creating "islands of automation" may be the best way to progress toward automation, when those islands that require automation are correctly identified.

START-UP AUDIT

Once you have Just-in-Time running, it is a good idea for someone on the implementation team to tour each Just-in-Time area on a daily basis.

This practice is commonly known as MBWA—Management by Walking Around. The tour should normally take only five to fifteen minutes. The implementation team should listen and observe, then compare notes, looking for trends and common problems. They should then make any adjustments they find necessary. McDonnell Douglas Computer Systems Division followed this procedure with great success. They found that it helped to keep management aware of constraints and to leverage efforts on common constraints.

One direct-labor employee who had been with McDonnell Douglas for many years, volunteered that, while she had seen many new ideas come and go, Just-in-Time definitely looked as if it would stay. The factory was running more efficiently than ever before in her career. And better still, for her, Just-in-Time had provided the workers an opportunity to be heard and had forced everyone to take action to resolve problems.

SUMMARY

In this chapter I have covered the installation of Just-in-Time on the shop floor, diagramming the steps by which to establish a pilot and outlining material-flow considerations. Now it's time to examine a specific technique to help you apply "One Less at a Time" to decrease your lot sizes. In chapter 5, I will describe the process for reducing and eliminating setup times.

Chapter 5
Reducing and Avoiding Setups

The key problem is not diversified low-volume production but multiple setups and small lots.

—Shigeo Shingo

In many industries, as we go through the Just-inTime/Total Quality Control process of "One Less at a Time," one of the first major constraints we encounter is long setup times. Setups are often so long and so difficult that it is virtually impossible to reduce lot sizes economically without making an initial major breakthrough in this area.

We have seen a lot of impressive results from companies that have made substantial throughput-time, work-in-process, and factory space reductions. Often the numbers they cite seem unbelievable. There are companies that have lowered their setup times on particular machines from several hours to just a few minutes or even seconds. These results were obtained by following the same JIT/TQC process, progressing "One minute Less at a Time."

There is no *one* change that's going to take us from an eight-hour setup to a setup of two minutes. Like other manufacturing aspects challenged by JIT/TQC, setup times are reduced by means of a continual and relentless process. You take out a minute here, two minutes there, and five seconds over there. You get dramatic setup reductions by taking one step at a time. But you do get them.

THE SMED APPROACH

Much of the credit for the techniques and insights developed to reduce setup times goes to Shigeo Shingo, of Japan, who created a scientific system for reducing setup times and set the objective of SMED, or Single-Minute Exchange of Dies. This translates into setups that take less than ten minutes, or single-digit setups. Shingo isolated multiple setups and small lots as the key obstacles to cutting back setup times. Solving that constraint is a primary objective of JIT/TQC in environments where setup times are a major factor. In order to obtain the benefits that come from higher velocities, we have to learn how to reduce our setup times to produce smaller lot sizes economically.

The aim of setup-time reductions is to improve our manufacturing competitiveness by placing ourselves in a position to build exactly what is sold, as opposed to what should have been sold. The faster the throughput time, the closer we get to meeting the actual demand. In order to respond to change economically, we need frequent access to equipment without the added cost of long setups. If we go from two hours to two minutes on a setup, it is definitely going to provide us with better responsiveness to market changes, without increasing costs. Reduction of setup times, and the resulting decrease in throughput time, will also produce more immediate feedback on quality problems and allow us to reduce inventories.

Most companies use the benefit of setup-time reduction as a means to convert their runs into smaller lot sizes. But there is another reason for reducing setup times, and that is to give us more capacity on a bottleneck piece of equipment. If a machine is utilized to a great extent, reducing its setup time will free up more time for production. Both strategies are correct. Which one you choose depends on your particular situation.

ECONOMIC ORDER QUANTITY

The traditional batch-production scheme is to balance setup expense with the cost of carrying material in inventory. But why would we want to balance these two elements? Setups are wasteful; they add no value. Inventory-carrying costs are also wasteful. There's no value in carrying inventory. It would be more logical to eliminate both than to try to keep them in equilibrium.

In order to better understand this point, let us take a brief look at the logic that went into the construction of the economic order quantity (EOQ). The formula for determining economic order quantity has a number of variations, but basically the EOQ is equal to the square root of two times the estimated annual requirements for the part times the setup cost of the part, divided by its inventory holding cost times the piece cost (see figure 5.1). Essentially, this formula balances the setup costs and the inventory-carrying costs by calculating the lowest economic order quantity.

While the concept behind this formula may be correct, there is an enormous blind spot in our application of the logic. The main variable in this equation was believed to be the annual usage. The 2 is, obviously, a fixed number, and setup cost and all other elements of the operation were also assumed to be fairly fixed. Well, we have discovered that with appropriate analysis we can make dramatic decreases in setup costs. As it turns out, setup cost is one of the most variable items in the EOQ equation.

Traditionally, the way we've gotten around long setup times and high setup costs has been to produce large lot sizes. This does nothing to actually reduce setup times; rather it amortizes those long setup times over the size of the lot. Another practice has been to combine similar lots. This also does not reduce setup times; it avoids them. Setup avoidance is a useful strategy as long as we're not building products we don't need. However, if we combine lots to build something we can't use right away, then all we're doing is trading setup cost for inventory costs. In this section we will concentrate on the process of reducing the actual setup time.

THE NEED FOR SMALL LOT SIZES

Advantages of Larger Lot Sizes

Before we attack setup time reduction, however, let's see why companies thought larger lot sizes were a good idea.

1. A larger lot size amortizes the fixed setup time over more pieces.
2. Inventory helps us level overloads through the factory.
3. We can insulate problems with inventory.
4. We can use inventory to cover uncertain demand.

Figure 5.1
EOQ Formula

$$EOQ = \sqrt{\frac{2\,(EAR)\,SU}{I\,(STD\ COST)}}$$

EAR = ESTIMATED ANNUAL REQUIREMENT
SU = SETUP COST
I = INVENTORY CARRYING COST
STD COST = COST OF THE PART AT STANDARD

Notice that all the advantages are based on the belief that inventory is desirable, which is pre-JIT/TQC logic. Inventory may be desirable, but it is still wasteful. The question is, what can we change to eliminate the need for some of the waste? The answer is to reduce and avoid setup times.

Advantages of Smaller Lot Sizes

As we learn how to economically manufacture "One Less at a Time," smaller lots will allow us to:
1. Improve our costs by
   a. increasing the return on inventory assets
   b. increasing the return on the total asset base
   c. reducing our exposure to scrap and rework
   d. allowing lower volumes to break even
2. Improve our quality by
   a. quickening feedback on quality problems
   b. speeding the phase-in of an engineering change
3. Improve our delivery responsiveness by
   a. decreasing manufacturing lead times

b. increasing the frequency of access to equipment
c. improving product-mix flexibility

In other words, smaller lots help us to improve our ability to respond to change economically. The challenge is to achieve smaller lot production in a cost-effective manner. Let us see how that is accomplished.

SETUP-REDUCTION PROJECT

Setup reduction is a process. The steps are repeated over and over again. Just as with the JIT/TQC approach, the best way to learn how to reduce setups is through experience. Initiate a project for reducing setup times, with the objective of making this process a way of life within the company.

The first aim of this project should be to actually increase the time a given machine is available for production by reducing the time that must be devoted to setups. The second objective is to reduce the time and the cost of the setup. It's important to realize that the primary objective is not to reduce the number of setup people. Consider yourself successful if you spend the same amount of money but achieve smaller lot sizes, or, in some cases, realize more capacity on the machine. Your goal for this project should be aggressive, because spectacular results are possible, and breakthrough results will encourage additional successes. You might initially shoot for a 50 to 75 percent reduction or a single-digit changeover (SMED). A parallel objective should be to accomplish this at little or no significant cost. The idea is to achieve results not by throwing money at the problem but by improving the setup process.

The first step is to define setup time. This is the elapsed time from the completion of the last good part of the last job to the completion and verification of the first good part of the next job. Sometimes, if the actual run time of the first good part of the next job is significant, it is subtracted from the total elapsed time. What's important here is to be consistent.

The biggest obstacle to setup reduction is the same one we encounter with JIT/TQC: the failure to get started. Many of us have a hard time believing the process will really work. It does. Figure 5.2 provides some examples of the kind of success that can be achieved. As you can see, reducing setup times is not only possible, it can yield amazing results

Figure 5.2
Setup Reduction Results

COMPANY:	MACHINE:	BEFORE:	AFTER:
Toyota	Boltmaker	8 Hrs	58 Sec
Mitsubishi	6 arbor borer	24 Hrs	2.7 Min
Arakawa	500 ton press	27 Min	4.5 Min
Toyoda	Cold Forge	32 Min	7.5 Min
Hitachi	Die cast	75 Min	3 Min
HP	IC Insert	30 Min	3 Min
Omark	Press	120 Min	3 Min

SOURCES: SANDRAS
HALL
SHINGO

(see figure 5.3). Similar achievements are possible in any manufacturing environment and on any machine. The key is to closely examine the setup process in each situation.

There are two basic activities that take place during a setup: internal and external operations. Internal setups are those that take place while the machine is stopped, such as the process of unbolting and rebolting the die in the machine or of loading a program. External setup activities occur while the machine is running a different job. These include getting organized for the next job, moving the next die from a storage location to the machine, and gathering or returning tools.

Figure 5.3
Setup Reduction Results

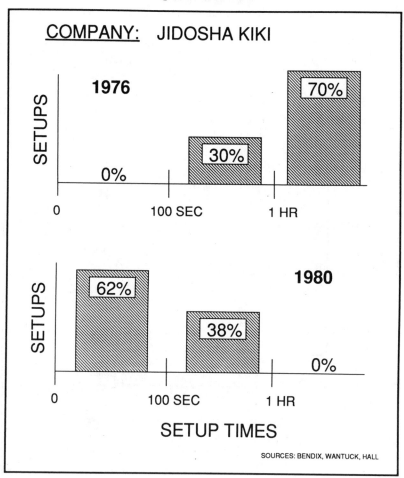

The first stage of the SMED process is to *identify the internal and external activities of a setup.* The second step is to *examine the internal events and see which of those can be converted to an external activity.* The third step is to *reduce the time it takes to perform each of those internal and external events.* The fourth step is to *repeat the process,* identifying, converting, reducing, and again repeating the process. (See Figure 5.4).

Figure 5.4
Stages of SMED

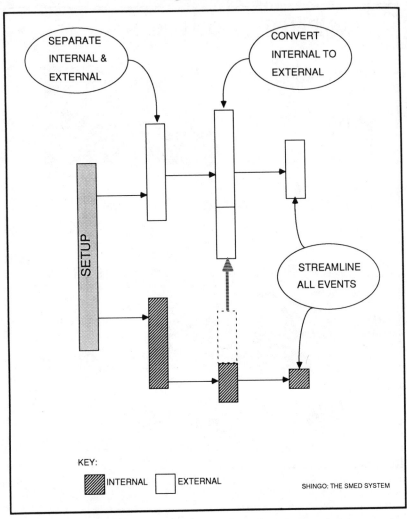

There are some very useful techniques to help us perform a scientific analysis of setup times. One of the best is to *videotape the setup*. This offers a unique opportunity to step back from the process and view each setup procedure objectively. It's best to start the taping before the last piece is completed on the previous job. Keep it running through the completion and verification process of the first part of the next job. It's also beneficial to have a camera that can display the elapsed time in the corner of the picture. The clock makes it easier to analyze the time involved in performing each setup step. Another valuable tool is a wireless microphone, which the operator can use to describe what's happening during the setup. (These devices can be rented.) If capturing the audio is not possible during real-time taping, a voice-over can be dubbed in later on. A verbal explanation offers a better understanding of the events when camera angles are difficult and allows those less experienced with the equipment to better understand what is taking place.

It's not enough, however, to tape only the internal activities. The external events should be captured as well. This may mean following the setup people around the plant as they perform their duties. By doing this you record the entire setup process.

Supervisors and managers often express their concern that, because of the presence of the camera, the operators will try and do a better job than usual, and therefore, they won't get an accurate reading on the setup time. While this is possible, it is not likely to happen if you tell the operators to perform their work as normally as they can. There's usually so much waste that even if the operator tries to do a better job, it doesn't make much of a difference. What is interesting, however, is that videos *always* turn out to be embarrassing, revealing much wasted time and movement. The embarrassment, however, is not personal in nature. In viewing the tape, the worker becomes the observer and not the doer.

Once the tape has been completed, a team should be formed to analyze it. It is critical that the operators themselves be involved in this process, along with appropriate personnel from engineering, maintenance, management, the stockroom, the tool room, and the previous and next operations. While engineering may have defined the setup process, the operators are also authorities on the equipment. They are quite capable of coming up with many ideas necessary to reduce setups. They are also able to implement many of those ideas. Given some time to use their heads and not just their hands, the operators can free up management and engineering for solving constraints that do require their level of expertise.

As the setup team goes through the tape, note each step taken and record it on a process flow chart (see figure 5.5). Better yet, use a personal computer and a spreadsheet program. Your notations should

Figure 5.5
Process Flowchart

Process Flowchart

PROCESS	PROCESS DESCRIPTION	DRAWN BY
☐ Proposed ☐ Current	_____ Start Point _____ End Point _____	Name _____ Date Approval Name _____ Date Page___ of___

SEQUENCE OF ACTIVITIES	STEP #	Description of Activity	Time	Cum Time	Run	Move	Inspect	Stock	Report	Int Setup	Ext Setup	Quantity	Distance
	TOTALS												

Column header labels under ACTIVITIES: Run, Move, Inspect, Stock, Report, Int Setup, Ext Setup include the times involved and the distances moved and should identify the internal, external, and run portions of the changeover.

Next, study the entries on the process flow chart and determine which of the items that are currently internal could be switched to an external activity. Once you identify those, make a list of action items that need to take place. It's important to remember that there is no *one* thing you can do to reduce setup time dramatically. You are probably going to eliminate page after page of constraints before you achieve a major reduction. It is essential to *identify each of those items, make an action list, and assign somebody to make those changes happen.*

Identifying which internal activities can be made external is often quite easy. The difficult part is freeing up the human resources to accomplish the external task when everyone already appears occupied. Be certain to enlist the commitment of the operators, and then let them contribute to the process and experiment with how to handle the change. (A useful way to capture these ideas regarding setup reduction is through the use of a Cause and Effect Diagram, which will be explained in the chapter 11.)

After converting the internal activities to external, the next step is to examine each item and come up with ideas to actually reduce the time it takes to perform each step. Again, make an action list for those ideas, assign someone to each task, and implement them. Now, go back to the video and repeat the process.

One objective of this project is to raise the awareness and problem-solving skills of the people doing the setup. It is important to develop the thinking worker in order to continue to reduce setup times. Another objective is to actually improve the setup design so that a higher skill set is not required. It's not uncommon for adjustments such as vertical and/or horizontal alignment of tooling to make up half of the setup time. To remove these delays, try to standardize the various elements of a setup and use visual marks so that pieces can be lined up more quickly. Quick clamps, shortened bolts, slip nuts, U-shaped washers, calibrated dials and bolts, and standard connectors are all helpful too.

Test runs also consume a significant amount of time. Whenever possible they should be shortened or eliminated. Also if a mold has to be brought up to a specific temperature, ask why and how it can be done externally. The key is to identify and challenge everything.

At McDonnell Douglas, to motivate workers by helping them visualize the ideas of setup reduction, the managers introduced the image of the Indianapolis 500 pit crew. "How long" they asked, "would it take the average person to change the tires on his car, refuel, check the oil, and get back on the road?" They then compared that figure with the 10.6 seconds taken by an expert pit crew, working in harmony and total synchronization. By applying the process outlined in this section and motivating workers through visualization techniques, McDonnell Douglas has dramatically cut its setup times.

SETUP AVOIDANCE

As mentioned earlier in this chapter, setup avoidance is also a useful strategy for achieving smaller, more economical lot sizes—as long as we build only products that we need. While continuing with setup-reduction activities in his own factory, Tim Willoughby, the manufacturing manager at NCR's facility in Waterloo, Ontario, worked with a key supplier of shafts to avoid setups. They used one of the primary aspects of group technology outlined in chapter 4, establishing a periodic fixed sequencing of similar parts through the production processes. By doing this, they replenished only the needed items, while minimizing setups as a result of the sequence in which the parts were manufactured.

NCR was purchasing twenty-two different shafts from its supplier. Each shaft required a considerable amount of setup time on various pieces of equipment. Using group-technology analysis, NCR and its supplier rearranged the production of the shafts into a sequence whereby one complete setup was required, to make the first shaft; the following twenty-one different shafts required only one-third of the original setup time, and in some cases no further adjustment was needed. This grouping, which essentially entailed one major setup and twenty-one minor adjustments, allowed for significant setup avoidance. In addition, they worked on setup reduction. They also looked at the shafts as a family and eliminated unnecessary variations in tolerances, finishes, dimensions and materials. As a result, NCR is now able to buy smaller lot quantities of each shaft with shorter lead times and obtain more frequent deliveries of each type to replace what has been consumed, all at less cost. (See figure 5.6.)

There is no secret to the process of setup reduction or avoidance.

Figure 5.6
Setup Reduction and Setup Avoidance Results

NCR WATERLOO

SHAFTS:

1.) ORIGINAL TIME   **3327 MINUTES**

2.) AFTER GROUPING   **1206 MINUTES**

3.) AFTER ENG. CHANGES   **427 MINUTES**

*   STEP (1) TO (2) = 63% REDUCTION IN SETUP TIME.

*   STEP (1) TO (3) = 87 % REDUCTION IN SETUP TIME.

Systematically attacking setups takes time and concentration. Later stages may require some expenditure, but early breakthrough results can be accomplished relatively inexpensively. By following these suggestions, setup-reduction results like those at Omark Industries in Oswego, Oregon, which pared a 120-minute setup on a punch press down to 3 minutes, or Toyota, which trimmed a press setup from 240 minutes to 3 minutes, are possible for you, too.

SUMMARY

Once companies begin to achieve the objectives of Single-Minute Exchange of Dies, does that mean they can stop lowering setups? Not if they follow the JIT/TQC process of continual, relentless improvement. The next objective becomes what is called One-Touch Exchange of Dies (OTED). This targets setup times of under sixty seconds. Some companies are even striving for No-Touch Exchange of Dies (NTED), in which either no setup is needed or the setup is accomplished in the time required to take one part out of the machine and put in another. The ultimate goal, of course, is "no setup required."

Significant setup reductions are possible and justifiable. They represent a vital step in improving most companies' competitive stance. However, like all JIT/TQC processes, reducing setup times requires more than haphazard, sporadic efforts. The process must be formalized, and should incorporate the experience of others. Finally, the most difficult part of the whole operation, as always with JIT/TQC, lies in developing the proper mindset and getting started. The goal is to achieve an environment in which the our setup process is no longer a constraint but an asset leading to significantly higher velocities.

Chapter 6
Simplifying Planning

Planning is the vision. Replanning is the response to reality.
—Walter E. Goddard

Much has been written about Manufacturing Resource Planning versus Just-in-Time, about push versus pull. Let us put one thing to rest here and now: Just-in-Time does *not* replace Manufacturing Resource Planning. *We need both* to compete effectively. All areas of the company experience change when JIT/TQC is implemented, and the planning area is not excepted. Just-in-Time and Manufacturing Resource Planning effectively compliment each others' strengths and weaknesses.

WHAT IS MANUFACTURING RESOURCE PLANNING (MRP II)?

Manufacturing Resource Planning (MRP II) is a system for managing all the resources of a manufacturing company. It is a set of computer-supported planning and scheduling tools designed to allow management to control production scheduling, cash flow, labor, capacity planning, inventory, distribution, and material purchases. It also supports marketing, engineering, and service and provides useful financial information.

Manufacturing Resource Planning evolved from Material Requirements Planning. Material Requirements Planning is primarily an order

119

ing technique to avoid shortages by determining when material is needed. Material Requirements Planning uses the master production schedule (what they plan to make), the bill of material (what it takes to make it), and the inventory record (what they have) to generate information on material requirements (what they have to get). A more powerful version, Closed-Loop Material Requirements Planning, offers the tools to establish priorities by using capacity planning, as well as a means for monitoring all these plans. Closed-Loop Material Requirements Planning also includes sales and operation planning, master scheduling, and the means for executing material plans, such as dispatch lists and supplier delivery schedules.

Manufacturing Resource Planning incorporates the elements of Closed-Loop Material Requirements Planning and considers financial figures, marketing forecasts, and engineering plans, thus allowing users to control these functions more effectively than ever before. Instead of using one set of numbers for the operating system in manufacturing and another set in finance, everyone works with the same figures. In other words, operating plans are translated into dollars. The result is better control of the company's operations and better competitive performance. (See figure 6.1.)

Figure 6.1 indicates the strength of Manufacturing Resource Planning as a planning tool. By considering the sales forecast, capacity constraints and other factors we can create a master schedule. The master schedule is then exploded by the Material Requirements Planning program to provide information regarding future requirements in terms of materials, equipment, labor, and perhaps even energy and other resources. Manufacturing Resource Planning is a powerful planning tool. But if we throw out Manufacturing Resource Planning when we implement Just-in-Time, there will be a void in the planning area. Just-in-Time is not a planning tool. It makes no attempt to plan.

From a quality perspective, Manufacturing Resource Planning is weak. If we expect to have late deliveries, we can use safety stock. If we expect to pull up the master schedule, we can use safety time. If we have a history of poor yields, we can use yield and scrap factors in our planning. In fact, Manufacturing Resource Planning makes it relatively easy to compensate for poor quality. Using Just-in-Time, however, we find ourselves lowering the inventory, increasing the velocity, and reducing the margin for error. If we haven't been successful in our quality-

Figure 6.1
Manufacturing Resource Planning

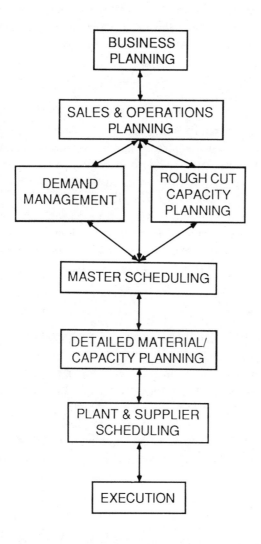

improvement efforts before, Just-in-Time will force us to seek out and eliminate the root causes of the problems it exposes.

It is on the shop floor that the real choices lie. Manufacturing Resource Planning has a very structured approach to production based around work orders. Even at lower velocities, the shop-floor control module is the weakest link of the entire Manufacturing Resource Planning package. It requires the most effort to implement, the highest number of transactions, and the most computer resources to be processed in a timely fashion. At higher velocities, work orders become an even bigger constraint. Just-in-Time also has a structured approach to controlling the shop floor. Just-in-Time's approach is based on kanban, a simple visual-control technique.

What we would like is the best of both worlds. This is possible. Manufacturing Resource Planning and Just-in-Time *are* compatible. We can use Manufacturing Resource Planning for macro planning of our resources and Just-in-Time for micro-execution on the shop floor.

A survey of sixty-six factories using Just-in-Time revealed that fifty-eight were also using Manufacturing Resource Planning systems, six were using reorder point, and two used time-phased reorder point.[1]

Nevertheless as we embark on the JIT/TQC journey, *how* we use the Manufacturing Resource Planning system and the software itself is subject to change. Let's examine why these changes occur.

CONTROLLING AND TRACKING THE FLOW

In traditional batch environments, large lot sizes of material are run through various operations, often organized by function rather than by cell. Long throughput times, as well as lengthy setups, cause larger batches. The result is more inventory and slower response time and feedback on quality problems. Also, with long throughput times, priorities are more likely to change, making it necessary to expedite some

---

[1] The survey was conducted by Professor James Dilworth of the University of Alabama, and the results were published in *Target Magazine* by the Association for Manufacturing Excellence in the Spring of 1987, pp. 17–18.

Figure 6.2
Work Orders

REASONS FOR WORK ORDERS

AUTHORIZE START OF WORK

**COMMUNICATE THE ROUTING STEPS
IN MANUFACTURING PROCESS**

AUTHORIZE/CONTROL MATERIAL ISSUES

TRACK PROGRESS OF WORK

LOT CONTROL

**BASIS FOR COST COLLECTIONS &
ANALYSIS**

CONTROL MATERIAL RECEIPTS

CAPACITY PLANNING

items and de-expedite others. Dispatch reports and anticipated-delay reports are used to communicate this information.

The traditional shop order shows the routing, an order header, an order release, and maybe change orders and split orders. We issue materials, report movements, apply labor, and have completion transactions. When we have long throughput times, a lot of inventory, and jobs

Figure 6.3
Cell Layout

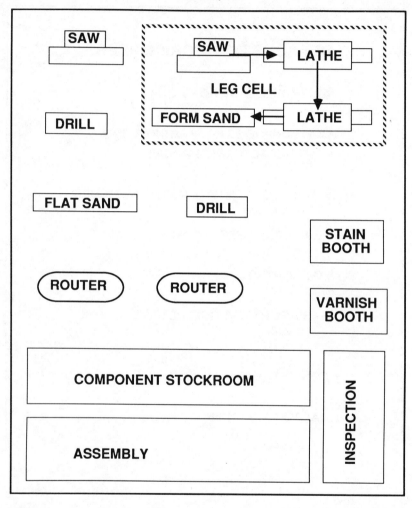

out in the shop, traditional shop-floor control-tracking systems serve us well. The work order, in fact, is used for many purposes (see figure 6.2).

Unfortunately, as lots get smaller, an increasing number of transactions will be taking place. The traditional work order and transaction-reporting procedures will become a constraint. At that point it will be necessary to address the reasons why work orders are required in order to eliminate them. It's not that the work orders in and of themselves are a bad idea. But as we move into JIT/TQC, and it becomes imperative that we lower our paper quotient, we must also reassess what information we need and how we collect it.

As we reorganize and gather operations into cells (see figure 6.3), material will move quickly from the saw to the lathe to the form sander. We can now visually track movement from machine to machine through several departments, because all types of machines are now in one compact area. As a matter of fact, someone could be sawing the fourth piece while the next lathe is working on the third piece, the next lathe is working on the second, and the sander is working on the first. The lot is actually spread throughout the entire cell. When velocities are high, it is not necessary to track material at every step. We can simply track it as it enters the cell and as it exits.

Again, the authorization to start work is based on a kanban—in this case, available "kanban spaces" within the cell. When the cell has a free kanban, it can start another job into the area. The kanban becomes the authorization, replacing the work order. Communicating the routing steps is simple, because the cell flow is obvious. Workers can be told what to build by a brand-name kanban itself or by a generic kanban authorization coupled with a customer order (or build schedule).

It is important to recognize that with this process the computer, or system, will no longer be tracking numerous slow-moving batches of material through various departments. We are changing to a visual-control system that is much more responsive to smaller lots moving at higher velocities. Unfortunately, we have become accustomed to computer controls and now balk at visual controls. There was a time not too long ago, however, when we hesitated relinquishing our visual-control capability to the computer, because so much discipline and overhead was required. Have we come full circle? With JIT/TQC, we have a better balance. We recognize that not everything needs to be done by computer. Visual controls are most effective in JIT/TQC environments because we organize to enhance visibility, and the kanban establishes the necessary controls.

We sometimes refer to an entire package of documentation as a work order. Technically, the work order is simply the authorization to start to build a specific quantity of a specific product at a certain time. Other information is often included with it for the sake of convenience. Once the work order is eliminated, however, it is important to find the means to continue providing the other necessary information. Routings are often self-evident in tightly compacted cells. If not, they may be printed on the back of brand-name kanban cards or, in very complex environments, accompany the kanban, as they did when the work order existed.

Drawings and assembly documentation typically reside in the cell in Just-in-Time environments and therefore do not move with the product. Likewise, test documentation that is captured in the cell by computer need not travel with the parts. Essentially, all the material and information necessary for the job will begin to remain within the cell.

Eliminating the work order does not mean that there will also be no top-level order. Hopefully, there will be a customer order! Turning the customer order into another document such as a work order is wasteful. However, we are less concerned about a redundant top-level work order than we are about the numerous lower-level work orders that are often generated for subassemblies or sublevel products.

Lot tracking remains possible with JIT/TQC, but batches are now recognized at the beginning and end of a cell because individual items are spread throughout.

Harris Corporation's semiconductor-assembly operations in Melbourne, Florida, provides an example of how this process works. They manufacture custom integrated circuits for commercial and military customers. In Harris's case, lot control is a legal requirement. They began with lot sizes of 500. As these decreased, lot control became more difficult. Originally, an operator would take one piece from a pile of 500 at his left hand, perform the operation, and place it in a pile on the right side, passing the entire lot on to the next person once he was finished. Today, a couple of years after Just-in-Time was implemented, people move 5 devices at a time, not 500. They still maintain lot control, but they pass five pieces at a time through the various operations in the cell. When the entire *series* of operations is completed, the material is once again collected into a lot for tracking and audit purposes. What used to take twenty days to travel through the pipeline now takes twenty minutes. It should be noted here that reducing transfer lot sizes may necessitate a changeover from batch-lot sampling procedures to continuous sampling procedures.

As we move into a higher velocity environment (see figure 6.4), with

Figure 6.4
Flow Layout

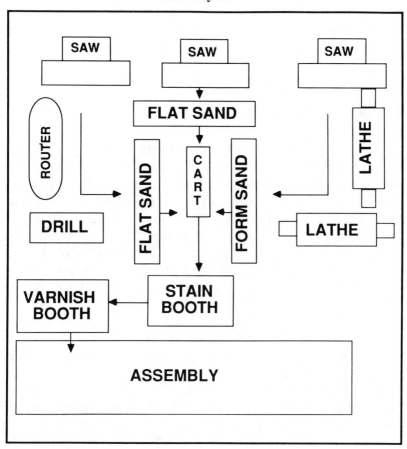

the whole factory converting to JIT/TQC, lower-level work orders are virtually eliminated. Everyone operates based on kanban authorizations, faster throughput times, smaller lot sizes, and storage of material at the point of use have obviated the need for work orders.

However, there are some cases where a company may want to continue to use work orders. If an item is only built once a year and requires unique parts, it might be preferable to leave the raw material in a locked stockroom and issue it as required on a work order, rather than store it at the point of use and have to walk around it all year. However, no matter what form of authorization is used to initiate production, whether kanban or work order, everything that flows through the manufacturing pipeline will be controlled by kanban ceilings.

PLANNING AND EXECUTION

Just-in-Time is relentless in its directive to simplify. Like all other processes in the workplace, planning and execution will have to be made more efficient. In a traditional environment (see figure 6.5), the master schedule is loaded into the Manufacturing Resource Planning system, which then drives purchases based on the schedule. Taking into account the date on which the product must be made, the material needed to build it, the lead-time offsets, the various levels of the bill of material, the purchase order lead time, and the available and ordered material, it determines when a purchase order must be placed with the supplier.

This purchase order is then placed with the supplier, given his lead time, so that the material will arrive in the stockroom shortly before the first work order is scheduled to be firmed up and the material must be used. In fact, it should arrive just when it is needed for the first work order.

Historically, the lowest-level work order is begun by pulling the material from stock, building the lot, checking it, and putting it back in the stockroom. The second-level work order is then written, using the results of the first work order, and the process continues on through the factory until the item reaches finished goods. But then the push routine changes! The *customer* indicates when he is willing to place an order for the product; the supplier does not inform him that the plan dictates a particular ship date. The customer order, in effect, pulls that item out of the factory. A company cannot satisfy its plans by *pushing* products to unsuspecting customers.

As we get into Just-in-Time, it's like bingo: Everyone starts with a free square; everyone has one piece of the pull system in place (see figure 6.6). The customer order, which pulls product from us, constitutes that first piece. Once the customer pulls an item from us, the

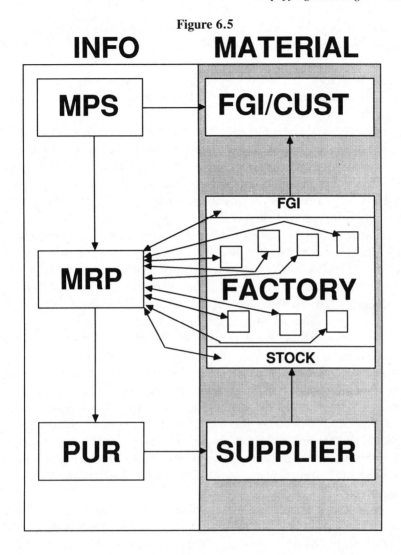

Figure 6.5

factory is authorized to begin production on the next one. If subassemblies make up the shipped product, the pull by the final-assembly area authorizes the cell to replace that subassembly by pulling material from stock. Eventually, the process travels back to the supplier and his supplier, who in turn replace the material that has been consumed.

The process by which the supplier replaces consumed material is similar to what happens in a grocery store. For example, once a certain amount of bread is purchased by consumers, the baker restocks the shelf. A factory should work in essentially the same way. (Remember, generic kanbans allow for variety and do not necessarily call for replacing what was used.)

However, when beginning the first phase of Just-in-Time, the factory is not often kanban linked to the supplier. While the factory is learning how to practice JIT/TQC internally, most, if not all, of its materials are still requisitioned with traditional purchase orders. In the second stage, the JIT/TQC operation begins to be linked to the supply base. This process is the topic of chapter 7.

If we're practicing Just-in-Time in the factory, the computer planning system is not directing our shop-floor activities via work orders. We're using available kanbans and customer orders (see figure 6.6). However, we do have to close the loop between the plan and actual incoming orders. We can't continue to plan and execute independently. There has to be a relationship. We must make sure that *the master schedule reflects the customer orders.* What we plan on the product-family side must correspond to the actual family orders that are coming in. From a planning perspective, what we use on Tuesday morning versus Tuesday afternoon typically does not matter until we have very frequent deliveries. (By then, of course, material replenishment should be on kanban and therefore be more responsive.) However, the macro planning bill should contain reasonably accurate percentage estimates of the mix of features being sold and shipped within the family. Otherwise we will be driving the resource plan—especially the material resource plans— incorrectly.

In addition, when we finish the final item, we need to relieve the master schedule (there is now one less item to build to satisfy the master plan) and the on-hand balances of the material. The latter maintains equilibrium in the planning system. One input transaction is used to relieve both the master schedule and the on-hand balance. This is called a production kanban transaction and contains post-deduct or back-flush logic. It will be discussed in greater detail in chapter 9.

When we reach the end of the planning period, what happens to the items on the master schedule that we did not finish? Do we drop them off, or do we roll them into the future? If we were supposed to make a

Figure 6.6

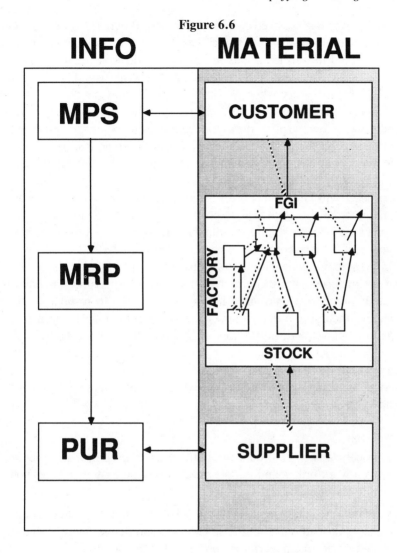

1,000 this week, but only made 900, are we supposed to make 1,100 next week? In fact, we may either roll the residual or we can forget it. This is a basic planning decision and is not unique to a JIT/TQC environment.

What happens if our production plan calls for us to build A items today, but we have received customer orders for B items? Do we build as planned, with the possibility that at least some of the production output can be stored in finished-goods inventory? Or do we capitalize on our new responsiveness and shift to building B's? Why would we want to build A's for inventory when we can build B's for payment?

Suppose then that we decide to respond to the customer rather than heedlessly follow the plan. If the plan continues to call for A's but orders continue to be for B's, we should continue building B's. We should respond to the customer demand as long as we think it is prudent, knowing full well that if the plan is not altered correctly, something in the process will fail. Whenever we start to see that the actual orders are deviating from the plan, it is important to address the situation. That doesn't mean that we shouldn't build the actual orders, but we do need to understand the consequences of each of our choices.

In many environments, the first consequence of violating the plan is that the material-supply chain breaks. Before Just-in-Time was implemented, purchasing may have had a week or two to respond to the changing incoming-order picture because manufacturing took a long time to respond, and, inventories were staged throughout the process. After Just-in-Time, however, inventories are smaller and manufacturing can respond faster.

Manufacturing's improved responsiveness results from the fact that it is no longer necessary to

- process customer orders through production control in order to open work orders and initiate production (the customer order now initiates production)

- create a stock picking list through a batch computer program, enter the work-load queue in the stockroom, and deliver the material to production (the material is now stored at the point of use)

- await completion of long runs of product before beginning a new order (smaller lot sizes now allow for more frequent access to resources)

- wait in long queues ahead of each operation which results in long lead times (lead times are relatively fixed given the kanban calculation).

At this stage of JIT/TQC, production's ability to respond to change no longer poses a problem. We are planning with the plan but executing to the customer order as kanbans become free in the manufacturing pipeline. However, purchasing's inability to respond quickly is becoming more of a constraint to further advances. The solution, therefore, is to encourage the suppliers to adopt Just-in-Time also. I will discuss how this is accomplished in greater detail in chapter 7.

MIXED-MODEL SCHEDULING

One of the initial planning changes that takes place when JIT/TQC is implemented is the substitution of rates for batches in the product build schedule. Those in higher-volume/lower-mix environments have typically planned in terms of rates. In many cases, these companies were also the first to subscribe to Just-in-Time. In lower-volume/higher-mix environments, there may not appear to be enough volume of any unique item for rate-based planning to be feasible. However, analyzing a family of products, examining it for commonly purchased materials and often-repeated processes, may make it easier to plan in terms of rates. At Harley Davidson, they refer to this mixed-model scheduling as "jelly beaning," because it enables them to handle a jelly-bean-like assortment of motorcycles on the same line.

With mixed-model scheduling and the improved responsiveness obtained with JIT/TQC, a company can begin to move in the direction of building some of every item every day that it is required. Constant progress on this front helps to level the load and allows a company to better build what was ordered rather than what it had projected would be ordered.

The traditional manufacturing batch approach shown in figure 6.7 indicates that the sample shop has a capacity of 600 pieces a week and, therefore, evenly loads the shop with product batches up to that point.

The mixed-model shown in figure 6.8 still shows a capacity of 600 a week, but now the batches are smaller, allowing the shop to produce each product more frequently.

The plan in figure 6.8 is based on the assumption that Pump R, Pump S, and Pump W are needed every day. If this is not the case, then the

Figure 6.7, 6.8, 6.9
Mixed Model Master Schedule

TRADITIONAL BATCH WEEKS

ITEMS		11	12	13	14	15	16
PUMP "R"	400/3 WKS		400			400	
PUMP "S"	600/3 WKS	200	200	200	200	200	200
PUMP "W"	800/3 WKS	400			400	400	400
TOTAL	1800/3 WKS =600/WK	600	600	600	600	600	600

MIXED MODEL PLAN
(PLANNED ORDER MIX) WEEKS

ITEMS		11	12	13	14	15	16
PUMP "R"	400/3 WKS	130	135	135	130	135	135
PUMP "S"	600/3 WKS	200	200	200	200	200	200
PUMP "W"	800/3 WKS	270	265	265	270	265	265
TOTAL	1800/3 WKS =600/WK	600	600	600	600	600	600

=120/DAY

BUILD TO ORDER
(ACTUAL ORDER MIX)   DAY OF WEEK 11

ITEMS		1	2	3	4	5	TOTALS
PUMP "R"	400/3 WKS	30	18	42	32	18	140
PUMP "S"	600/3 WKS	45	41	47	38	29	200
PUMP "W"	800/3 WKS	45	61	31	50	73	260
TOTAL	1800/3 WKS =600/WK	120	120	120	120	120	600

shop may build only those pumps for which customer orders have been received (see figure 6.9). This is more efficient than building 400 of Pump R as with the batch approach, and then bleeding down that inventory for two or three weeks before building another batch of 400. Mixed-model scheduling helps give a company the capability to economically build smaller lot sizes, due not only to faster equipment setups but also to faster changeovers of people, information, and materials.

As we reduce lot sizes even further, we may approach lot sizes of one or, at the very least, reach the point where we can run any item any day it is required. As McDonnell Douglas's Johnny Lee says, "This is the ultimate goal and should constantly be in our thinking and planning." To accomplish this, we do our planning using the forecasted rates per day of each product. While we can't know the exact mix of customer orders that will arrive, we might expect them to average out as shown in the mixed-model plan in figure 6.8, for example. When only three products are involved, master scheduling each individual product is fairly simple, particularly given the volumes shown here. However, when variety is great and volumes are low, accurately planning each specific product is very difficult. In these low-volume/high-mix environments, planning *bills* of material, in conjunction with JIT/TQC, become very useful. Let's look further at these planning bills.

PLANNING BILLS

A planning bill of material consists of a family of products combined into a common bill of material (see figure 6.10). We can use this planning bill to assist us in aggregate planning. We will plan in aggregate but initiate production as orders are received for the individual products, *not* according to plan. The planning bill is not an actual product or assembly, but a composite picture of the entire family. It will reflect the percent of the total sales each product within the family typically receives. Therefore, we master schedule at the planning bill level and use percentages to drive the detailed material requirements for each specific item in the family.

By way of example, on one production line at Hewlett-Packard, we produced only a few units each day of a product that had 6 million logical configurations. If we planned to build three units each day, the master schedule that went into the Material Requirements Planning System would show fifteen units planned for the week. Material Requirements Planning would then calculate the material requirements using the weekly plan and planning bills. (The daily rates were simply

Figure 6.10
Planning Bill of Material

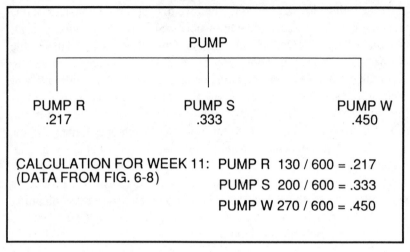

added up into weekly increments for planning purposes until we had the opportunity to modify the appropriate programs to accept data in terms of rates per day. Where kanban links to suppliers were later established, the Manufacturing Resource Planning output was used primarily for longer-range planning purposes.)

We were then able to plan the incoming-material pipeline using rates and consume materials as required by the actual order when it arrived. To provide flexibility, some unique and inexpensive purchased parts were overstocked, while all subassemblies were built as required. Is it wasteful to overstock a keycap for a keyboard, or a screw, or a wire, or a special little bracket? Certainly it is. We felt, however, that by allowing a little waste at the lowest levels, we could concentrate on substantially reducing waste in other areas. At that stage, we had greater concerns than a few extra screws or labels.

Using planning bills required us to concentrate on only four critical and expensive purchased items out of all the parts needed for the 6 million configurations. The use of planning bills, along with our ability to respond quickly in manufacturing, also allowed us to implement rate-based planning methods, even in a low-volume/high-mix environment.

It is important to realize, however, that when using planning bills, we need to compare the actual incoming-order mix with our planned percentages and adjust the latter accordingly.

At some companies where volumes are higher and more stable, planning bills are also used to initiate production. Producing to the plan smooths the flows in the incoming-material pipeline and within the factory. In these cases, however, a kanban ceiling is placed on finished goods. When the actual incoming-order rate differs from the plan to the point where the kanban ceiling is reached, production on the item halts, regardless of what was planned.

If the structure of the bill of material resembles an hourglass (see figure 6.11), planning bills might reflect items at the neck of the hourglass. The actual incoming orders are then used to specify the final configuration and initiate final production. If our bills of material appear like an inverted triangle (see figure 6.11), obtaining the correct mix of incoming materials is easier than it is when our bills resemble an upright triangle (see figures 6.12, 6.13). However, even in the latter case, planning bills and Just-in-Time provide a substantial improvement over traditional batch planning approaches.

The planning job becomes easier and the resulting schedule is easier to level as

- the number of unique purchased parts for specific items in the family decreases (the base of the triangle narrows)
- the value of unique purchased parts decreases (allowing for inexpensive overplanning in order to obtain flexibility)
- the manufacturing lead times decrease (so that raw materials need not be consumed before receipt of an order)
- Just-in-Time is linked back into the supplier base (reducing purchasing lead times and allowing planning to be done at the supplier's purchased-part level).

In situations where so many unique raw materials are required that the use of planning bills does not seem feasible, consider:

1. Beginning JIT/TQC early with a supplier of the family of unique materials. In some cases, the supplier's raw-materials bill may resemble an inverted triangle.

Figure 6.11, 6.12, 6.13
Bills of Materials

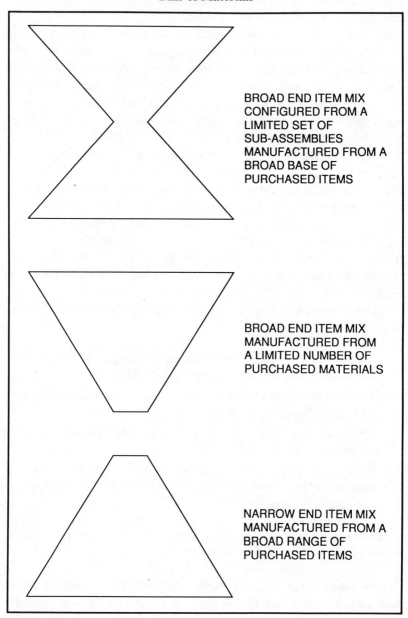

BROAD END ITEM MIX
CONFIGURED FROM A
LIMITED SET OF
SUB-ASSEMBLIES
MANUFACTURED FROM A
BROAD BASE OF
PURCHASED ITEMS

BROAD END ITEM MIX
MANUFACTURED FROM
A LIMITED NUMBER OF
PURCHASED MATERIALS

NARROW END ITEM MIX
MANUFACTURED FROM A
BROAD RANGE OF
PURCHASED ITEMS

2. Allowing overstocking of inexpensive items to gain flexibility and concentrating on structuring to plan the expensive and long-lead-time items.

3. Using planning bills for key common items even if unique items are planned individually. Aggregate forecasts tend to be more accurate than detailed ones.

4. Investigating redesign, if not for the current family, then for the next generation. (This is normally more applicable to assembly environments than to biological or process environments.)

When manufacturing lead times are longer than customer lead times, the customer order can be used only to initiate the final production steps in the process. However, as the velocity increases and lead times shorten to less than the customer lead times, the entire production process will become geared to the actual order.

Once suppliers are linked into JIT/TQC, their production may also be initiated by your customer order. A division of Metal Box, a British firm that manufactures plastic bottles, receives information from grocers by way of point-of-use cash-register-sales information. That information is sent directly to Metal Box to initiate replenishment of the appropriate bottles, which are then shipped to the bottler to be filled and delivered to the grocers' shelves.

CAPACITY PLANNING

In JIT/TQC environments, capacity considerations are typically addressed at the master-schedule level, and planning bills of material are used. Even in large companies, there tends to be only a handful of key resources that are critical. If we can plan capacity for a few key resources, the rest tends not to be much of a problem. It is important to realize, however, that as JIT/TQC exposes constraints and we eliminate them, the key resource constraints may change.

A company can actually structure its key resources into the planning bill of materials, noting the need, for example, for one part A, one part B, one part C, one hour of machine type X, two hours of skill type Y, and three kilowatts of energy type Z. When the Manufacturing Resource Planning programs are run, the resource requirements for materials as well as these key resources are calculated. Capacity is then determined from a macro level.

Another way to make a rough-cut capacity plan is to use a personal computer and spread-sheet software. The key resources are placed along one axis and the products along the other. The amount of each resource that is required is entered into each respective row and column intersection. Next, the master schedule is fed in, and the rough-cut capacity requirements are calculated. This is not unlike the approach used in pre-computer days! Again, the capacity planning needs of Just-in-Time can typically be assessed from a macro level.

Much of the need for detailed capacity planning stems from the amplification effects of larger lot sizes. The lowest-level shops in a factory traditionally tend to be either working overtime or out of work. Their load varies greatly. If we analyze why this condition exists, we discover that around 75 to 80 percent of the fluctuation is of our own doing. Customer demand doesn't typically vary to that degree (seasonality excepted), but a small change at the top is amplified by lot sizing, resulting in wild swings at the bottom. As lot sizes are reduced through setup reduction, setup avoidance, group technology, and mixed-model scheduling, small changes at the top will cause small changes at the bottom. As the load is leveled, we are able to concentrate more on the macro changes and can let kanban control the day-to-day loads. Detailed capacity planning is deemphasized, and the simpler approach of rough-cut capacity planning becomes adequate.

Some companies say they can do Just-in-Time but need, for example, a ninety-day frozen schedule. Their logic may be faulty. Just-in-Time's purpose is to improve our ability to respond. These companies are saying they can respond, but only if they are assured that they won't have to change within ninety days.

On the other hand, a company can't respond infinitely. It may find in the beginning that it is necessary to have a fixed schedule with no changes allowed within ninety days. What then stops that company from being able to respond within eighty-nine days? And eighty-eight days? Once more, we proceed "One Less at a Time," and we expose the constraints. A company can reduce kanbans to expose constraints, and/ or it can reduce the frozen schedule to expose constraints.

PLANNING AND CONTROL ON THE SHOP FLOOR

A master plan based on a rate-per-day schedule does place some minor constraints on the planning system. Most Manufacturing Resource Planning systems process in batches and are not capable of working in terms of rate per day. It's fairly easy, however, to convert a rate per day of 100 into a weekly batch of 500. With JIT/TQC, a weekly window is usually sufficient for planning purposes.

The system will then create planned orders based on this information. When the appropriate time arises, it will recommend that the order become a released order—a scheduled receipt. In a system based on shop orders, this makes perfect sense. In Just-in-Time areas, though, work orders aren't used in the traditional sense, and so the planned orders will never be released. We use the Manufacturing Resource Planning system strictly for planning purposes. We use kanban for execution. We plan with the plan, and we execute using kanban authorizations, staying as close as we can to the customer orders.

We then proceed to the shop floor. Here, kanban limits the amount of inventory in the work-in-process pipeline by controlling outbound queues. From an execution perspective, we're allowed to produce only a given amount ahead of our customer's next operation demand. That amount is defined by the kanban limits of the outbound queue.

There is a similarity here between the traditional approach of using input/output control and kanban's outbound-queue control. With input/output control, actual output is measured against the planned output to regulate the work orders released into the shop. Timely monitoring of the planned versus actual output, and disciplined release of the work orders into the shop, result in a constant level of work in the area. Kanban sets an upper limit on work in process in the manufacturing area, and only what has been consumed can be replaced. The purposes and results of the two approaches are similar, but the procedures, effort, and people required differ. Traditional input/output control uses work orders, planner/schedulers, and, ideally, on-line/real-time computer software to maintain timely control. Kanban simply uses visual controls and the operators.

As previously stated, there are some Just-in-Time environments where many operations feed a bottleneck machine or cell. This could be a large milling machine or a wave solder unit. In this situation, having an inbound-queue control in front of the bottleneck operation may be more effective than outbound-queue control. When the queue is nearly full, feeding operations slow down the rate of input into the bottleneck. When the queue is full, feeding operations stop feeding the bottleneck. Other work that does not feed the bottleneck can be performed. In each case, we need to ask why we approach or reach the kanban ceiling.

On the production floor, we also see a change in how we authorize production. Previously, the work order and the dispatch list authorized production. Under JIT/TQC, an available kanban is the authorization to produce. If the kanban is a brand-name kanban, that is all that's required. It tells us what to build and when to build it. If it's a generic kanban, then the kanban and a customer's order or a schedule makes up the full authorization. The kanban authorizes production of a variation of a family, the customer order specifies what to produce in that family.

In the initial stages of Just-in-Time development, it is not uncommon to find the build plan driving production. Later on, as we make changes in the production, marketing, and information systems, the actual customer order will be used to initiate production. We will plan with the plan but activate production with the actual customer order. To move completely to build to order, however, requires not only an improved ability to respond but also more linear customer input—a much more difficult challenge in seasonal environments, of course.

When JIT/TQC companies intend to have a finished-goods stock, they often put kanban ceilings on finished-goods levels. What is to be produced next is determined by what was consumed out of the finished-goods inventory. Often, these companies build to a planned rate, but can quickly alter the plan if kanban ceilings are reached. In some JIT/TQC factories, various combinations of customer orders, master schedules, and kanban finished goods are used. Once we have the authorization to begin and we know what to produce, there are a couple more planning questions to ask. First, is the material available? We do not want to start an item unless we are reasonably certain that we can finish it; this is a concern particularly when generic kanbans are used. An item that cannot be completed will sit idle and will occupy needed kanban authorizations in the pipeline. If there are not many part numbers involved in the cell, material availability is fairly easy to assess. The people in the area can often visually determine whether the material stored at the point of use is available or not.

In some environments, however, where there are many part numbers involved, it is much more difficult to tell visually. For example, in the process of populating circuit boards, hundreds of components may be used on one board and there may be thousands involved in the whole cell. It's not always obvious, even though we're authorized to start production, whether or not we have the material to finish. If you find yourself in this situation, a computer simulation is very useful. This piece of software, or versions of it, already exist in some Manufacturing Resource Planning systems. You notify the system that you are ready to start a given quantity of a particular product, as denoted by the kanban authorization. The system checks the on-hand balances in the cell and in the factory, and either indicates that all material is available, or specifies which items are expected to be short.

In traditional environments, a work order would allocate all of this material based on stockroom on-hand balances. In Just-inTime environments, it is still possible to allocate the material, but that level of complexity is rarely, if ever, required. It may be sufficient—and it certainly is simpler—to just use a "reserved" data field instead of maintaining all the detailed records. Suppose, for example, that the on-hand balance of a particular part is 100. We're ready to start five circuit boards. The system simply reserves five sets of parts in the separate item master data field for each part. Time phasing of allocations is lost with this approach, but if throughput times are sufficiently short, few problems are likely to arise. In most environments, because throughput times are short and lot sizes small, a simulation prior to starting, rather than reservations, is all that is required. When just beginning, it is advisable to start with the simplest approach, allowing the process to become more complex only if required.

AVAILABILITY TO PROMISE BY RATE

With these changes, JIT/TQC offers a company a new competitive order-acknowledgement opportunity—"available to promise by rate" (see figures 6.14, 6.15). Most companies develop a detailed product production plan and then match customer orders to unsold products in the plan. This process is known as "available to promise by product number." Because of the company's limited ability to respond to the

Figure 6.14
Available to Promise

BY PRODUCT NUMBER	BY RATE
PRE - JIT/TQC	POST - JIT/TQC
MANUFACTURING LEADTIME LONGER THAN CUSTOMER LEADTIME	MANUFACTURING LEADTIME SHORTER THAN CUSTOMER LEADTIME (FOR KEY PROCESS STEPS)
STOCK AT FINISHED GOODS	STOCK AT RAW MATERIALS

Figure 6.15
Available to Promise by Rate

IMPROVED CUSTOMER SATISFACTION

ENHANCES ABILITY TO BUILD TO ORDER

LOWERS FINISHED GOODS INVENTORY

MAY INCREASE RAW MATERIALS INVENTORY

LOWERS TOTAL INVENTORY

FACILITATES FORECASTING ACCURACY

ALLOWS FORECASTING BY FAMILY

REDUCES PURCHASING RESCHEDULING

REDUCES TRANSACTIONS

HELPS TO PRIORITIZE JIT/TQC EFFORTS WITH SUPPLIERS

DOES NOT CHANGE NEED FOR "WHAT IF" CAPABILITY

customer's need, the customer is forced either to fit the manufacturer's plan or to go elsewhere. Another option is for the manufacturer to disrupt the plan and attempt to squeeze in the customer order. In this environment, priorities sometimes become distorted. A company prides itself on making shipments, but then measures itself only on those shipments to customers that fit with its plan. "Available to promise by product number" makes sense when companies have long lead times. As we progress with JIT/TQC, however, the "available to promise by rate" option, which is more customer oriented, becomes more easily accessible.

With "available to promise by rate," all normal-sized orders for the family, regardless of the features specified, are routinely accepted for shipment on or before the stated lead time. A number of changes will have to have occurred in order for this new acknowledgment procedure to be possible. They are as follows:

- Manufacturing throughput times have been reduced considerably, allowing all or at least a significant portion of the production process to occur within the stated customer lead time and ensuring that material is used only on shippable products.
- Many, if not all, subassembly levels are built using generic kanbans, so that capacity is used only for shippable products.
- Rate-based planning is done to ensure adequate production capacity.
- Planning bills are accurate enough so that the correct material is almost always available when the order arrives.
- The difference between the customer and manufacturing lead time is used as a backlog to smooth the production load.
- Wasteful delays are being eliminated from the order-entry and other processes to provide manufacturing with as much lead time as possible.
- Order input has been made reasonably linear.

There are, however, certain difficulties that may arise with this process. For instance, abnormally large orders or products with very unusual features may have a different lead time than other items in the family. These atypical orders would, of course, alter the lead time, making it quite different from that for the same product with more normal features. Also, if the situation arises where the rate is sold out, then manufacturing and marketing have to make some tough decisions. Do they quickly increase capacity, refuse orders, or increase lead times? These questions come up with both "available to promise by rate" and "available to promise by product number," but the "available to promise by rate" system makes the need for such decisions more pronounced. Experience, though, has shown that when the techniques discussed here are used, many products can benefit from the "available to promise by rate" order-acknowledgment approach.

In this new environment, factories measure themselves on minimizing variation from the planned rate as well as on shipping as promised to the customer.

"Available to promise by rate" and Just-in-Time work together. Unlike other changes we have discussed, this one does not assist in making the transition to JIT/TQC; rather, it capitalizes on the competitive benefits earned by implementing JIT/TQC. We are now in a better position to respond to the customer and should not have to force the customer to adapt to us.

SUMMARY

What we have learned while progressing on our JIT/TQC journey is that the JIT/TQC production cell acts like a magnet, drawing members into the team. In many Just-in-Time environments, planning people are placed in the production area. Often, the cell management and planning become the same job. In most JIT/TQC companies, planning a family rate per day becomes a more decentralized function, rather than the task of a centralized planning department. Even in cases where the planners report directly to a central organization, it is not uncommon to see them physically located in a production area.

When we combine Manufacturing Resource Planning and Just-in-Time (see figure 6.16), we continue to do business planning as before. There is no change to the sales and operation planning. Rough-cut capacity planning becomes even more important with Just-in-Time. Master scheduling is continued, but rates per day rather than batches are emphasized. Material planning is performed in the same way but families and planning bills are often used. Detailed capacity planning is possible when planned orders are referred to, but in most Just-in-Time

Figure 6.16
Manufacturing Resource Planning/JIT

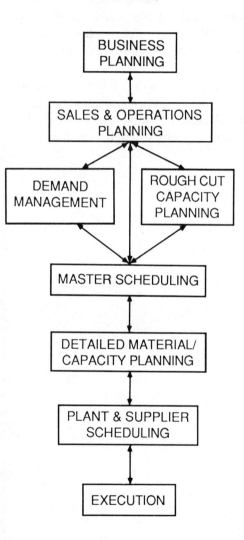

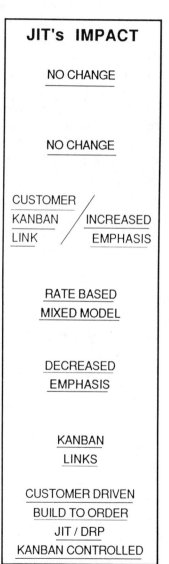

environments, rough-cut is sufficient. As for execution, on the shop floor, we move away from building to the plan by firming up shop orders, to building to order using kanban controls. The plan is simply a plan. Production is triggered by the actual customer order.

Purchase orders or supplier schedules systems remain the same until JIT/TQC is linked into the supplier base, at which time kanbans are used to initiate material replenishments, and the Manufacturing Resource Planning output is used by both the customer and supplier for longer-range planning purposes. Delivery is driven by the actual requirements rather than by the plan.

Manufacturing Resource Planning plans and controls the existing manufacturing environment. JIT/TQC controls and drives changes to the existing manufacturing environment. It is important to blend all of the power these tools have to offer to achieve High Velocity Performance.

Chapter 7

Linking to Suppliers and Customers (Purchasing, Design, Marketing, Logistics)

*In order to make Just-in-Time work, we need our suppliers'
cooperation and assistance. We solicit that. Frankly, we expect it.*
—Mike Birck

Right part, right quantity, right price, right time, right quality, right place,—*the six rights*—that's what we expect from our suppliers. It's also why we've been taught to seek out multiple sources for our parts. If one supplier has a quality problem, we can always use another to help us out. We can play one's price against another's to make sure we're getting the lowest cost possible. If one supplier delivers late, we can always use another one to bail us out. Why were we taught to have multiple sources of supply? To ensure that we would have the right part at the right time, place, quantity, quality, and price.

What's wrong with that? Why would proponents of Just-in-Time encourage single sourcing? The reason is to better ensure that we will have the six rights. In other words, Just-in-Time promotes single sourcing for the same reasons as others advocate multiple sourcing. How can both ways work? Are Just-in-Time converts speaking with a forked tongue here?

No. The objective *is* the same. The difference is in the logic. As in other areas attacked by Just-in-Time, we are required to change our way of thinking. (See figure 7.1.)

Figure 7.1
Supplier Reduction Trend

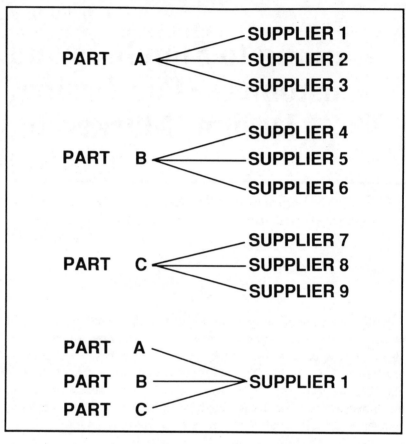

Suppose we want to practice Just-in-Time and at the same time maintain multiple suppliers. With Just-in-Time there is less inventory in the pipeline between the supplier and us, so we should expect more frequent deliveries, but the margin for error is less. As we take inventory down, we expect to expose problems.

Say, for example, Supplier 1 is having a problem meeting a specific part tolerance. Supplier 2 has a delivery problem. Supplier 3 has a planning problem. To operate effectively at lower inventory levels, we must correct these incoming material snags. Purchasing's life would be great if they could just pick up the telephone and tell Supplier 1 to improve his quality, Supplier 2 to get his delivery act together, and Supplier 3 to get a handle on his planning processes. Unfortunately, it doesn't work that way. Yes, it's each supplier's job to provide quality service and products, but it's purchasing's job to ensure dependable, cost-effective shipments. If telephone calls are ineffective, purchasing must work with these suppliers to help them correct their problems to guarantee shipment continuity.

To help eliminate the cause of the problem, purchasing will need to investigate why it is occurring. The truth is, it's hard enough to assess the incoming-material quality for Part A, much less to isolate it among three different supplier categories. But even if the data can be separated by supplier, we then must work with each supplier in order get at and correct the root cause of each difficulty. What is the root cause of supplier 1's poor product quality? What is causing supplier 2 to miss deliveries? What planning processes at Supplier 3's company are out of control? This personal attention takes time. The more suppliers we have, the less opportunity we have to spend the needed problem-solving time on each.

REDUCING THE SUPPLIER BASE

Just-in-Time contends that, if we're really serious about having the right part at the right time, place, quantity, quality, and price, we're going to have to maintain a more manageable number of suppliers. Ultimately, we should rely on the single best supplier for a part or commodity. That translates into reducing the supplier base by means of "One Less at a Time."

Suddenly, we may hear voices screaming, "No way! What about a catastrophic situation?"

What many company managers don't take the time to realize is that they already have a number of parts that are single sourced. Moreover, these parts are often the ones that make the company most vulnerable— for example, the ones with the most expensive tooling. What do we do when we are this situation? We take precautions to select only stable suppliers, and in precarious cases we develop backup strategies. The same is true with Just-in-Time.

Reducing the supplier base in this fashion usually lessens our exposure to problems, but not always. Whenever we create a potentially catastrophic situation, we must develop a strategy to protect ourselves. Certainly, continuing the practice of multiple sourcing is an easy alternative. However, if we force ourselves to think carefully about our alternatives, we may manage to reap the benefits of single sourcing while still avoiding a catastrophic situation.

For example, a multinational company with factories located in the United States might single source in North America, while its factories in Europe and Asia also single source locally. If something happened to one of the sources on one continent, the other suppliers on the other continents could serve as backups until the problem was resolved. Hallmark Cards is now experimenting with assigning lithographers to particular product lines. The company thus achieves the benefits of single sourcing, but if an emergency arises on one line, lithographers from other lines can serve as backups. Multiple sourcing, like inventory, is a traditional and easy solution, but it avoids the problem instead of solving it competitively.

Many companies fear that if they rely on a single source, the supplier will start to increase his prices above market value. Actually, it would be economically unwise for a single-sourced supplier to try to pass on an uncompetitive price. First, competitive price monitoring is still possible. Second, the purchase agreement is likely to require documentation of manufacturing cost figures and price reductions are often spelled out in the contract. This drives a supplier to continually improve his process, lower his cost, and improve his quality. And third, he'd lose *all* of his business by being so unethical. Not much motivation for being greedy.

Once the single-source agreement is set up, the supplier basically owns the business he has been allotted. All he can do from then on is lose it. And he can lose it if new management changes the business focus, or if he loses control of his processes and cannot recover in a reasonable period of time. This will be discussed in greater detail in the section on marketing later in this chapter.

It's not an easy job to reduce a supplier base. On the other hand, it's hard to imagine that a company couldn't get by with one less supplier and then another less, or that it couldn't manage logically to find one more part that can be single sourced, and then find another part and another.

In 1980, Xerox had 5,000 production suppliers. With a concerted effort, they reduced the supplier base to 300 by 1985. This resulted in reduced rejects by more than one order of magnitude, and the cost to purchase a dollar's worth of material was cut by more than two-thirds.

There is another way in which single sourcing leads to simultaneous improvements in quality, delivery, and cost. It has been observed that once the first 15 percent of a new product's design effort has been completed, 85 percent of the costs are committed and many of the future problems are predetermined. The new design teams will include key suppliers. These key suppliers will be single sourced. They will be expected to—and will want to—shorten and improve the design process by pointing out ways to improve the design, and even by assuming part of the design tasks. As always with JIT/TQC, there is not one single factor that can be credited with generating the kind of impressive results that companies like Xerox have realized. However, it is certain that those results would not have been possible without early supplier involvement.

One difference between the beginners and the more experienced JIT/TQC companies lies in how far they've progressed in reducing their supplier base. Another indication of experience is how well they have motivated their suppliers to follow JIT/TQC practices throughout their own operations. The process, however, doesn't stop with a company's immediate suppliers. Eventually the suppliers should be doing Just-in-Time with their suppliers as well.

I was once asked by some people at Toyota, "How many companies in the United States are doing Just-in-Time?" That was a difficult question. If Just-in-Time means eliminating waste, then almost everyone has attempted to get better. If JIT/TQC is the "same old way," everyone can say yes. However, JIT/TQC is not the same old way, and far fewer are formally practicing Just-in-Time's "one less at a time" when it can be evaluated. Toyota's next question was, "How many companies are doing Just-in-Time three levels deep?"

This raises an interesting point. There is often a good deal of discussion about who holds the inventory with Just-in-Time. Some say the supplier ends up holding it. But that's neither desirable nor necessarily true. During the conversion, when a Just-in-Time operation is connected to a batch operation, inventory tends to be held at the batch location. This could take place between two operations within a factory or between a factory and its external supplier. However, such an inventory situation should exist only temporarily, until the supplying operation learns how to do Just-in-Time.

When we go three levels deep in the supply chain, in most cases we find ourselves very close to the earth. For example, at Hewlett-Packard we use a plastic-molded part produced by our supplier. Traditionally, it would not be unusual for him to hold the finished assembly after he had manufactured the part. But what if the supplier is practicing JIT/TQC? Kanbans provide authorization to the molding operation, and they can quickly convert plastic pellets into finished product. The only inventory of significance is plastic pellets, not finished items, and pellets are much more economical to store, have a much higher degree of usage flexibility, and are much easier to forecast than finished goods.

Suppose our supplier is also getting the pellets on a Just-in-Time basis. Where do the pellets come from? They are made from crude oil. In other words, if we go three or four levels deep in the supply chain, we often find ourselves very close to the supplier who *should* be holding the inventory—Mother Earth.

The discussion that follows will detail how to reach the point where the earth continues to hold most of the inventory.

STRENGTHENING CUSTOMER/SUPPLIER RELATIONSHIPS

Redefining customer/supplier relations above all requires a change of attitude. For years these relationships have labored under the strain of adversarial conditions. We have purposely, in the name of checks and balances, inhibited close working alliances. This lack of trust has produced its own wasteful operations, from increased handling and inspection to increased accounting and purchasing. JIT/TQC, however, demands a stronger relationship based on mutual welfare, leading to increased confidence and well-founded trust.

Often, these bonds become at least as close as those between customer/supplier operations within a company. It is important to note that these alliances are a two-way obligation. It is this awareness that fosters change. Instead of ordering in fixed long lead times, companies work together to establish long-term contracts. The supplier feels secure because the customer has assured him of the business. The supplier can then make the capital investments and other long-term decisions that might be necessary to fulfill those commitments. These decisions, in turn, will enable the supplier continually to maintain the most competitive cost.

Once this partnerlike relationship has been established, sensitive and necessary discussions about lowering purchase price can also be initiated. In the past, material was bought on the basis of purchase price alone. Just-in-Time demands an examination of the total cost. From this perspective, the following must be determined: Is the supplier's product packaged such that it can be delivered directly to the point of use? Is inspection required? Can the very few defects simply be exchanged for good products? Will purchase orders be issued, or will kanban be used to minimize the paperwork and reduce the transaction expense? How will frequent deliveries be accomplished economically? All these elements contribute to the total cost: Price is just one factor.

Unfortunately, a key performance measure for purchasing often centers on purchase-part price variance. A certain price is projected for a part, and the variance around that price is monitored. Buyers are then measured on this variance, which, when overemphasized, may lead them in a direction contrary to that indicated by an analysis of the total cost. The variance measure is frequently counterproductive to JIT/TQC efforts, because these measures drive a company to the lowest *price,* whether it's the lowest *cost* or not. The problem is that accounting systems are not always capable of formulating an adequate total-cost picture, especially since, in many cases, the only easily determined factor is the price itself.

Some companies believe that they can reduce the waste in the purchasing process by buying sets of parts and hence ordering only one part number. This may be true, but, on the other hand, with this practice they may just be shoving wasted effort back to the supplier and paying for it under a different heading. The objective is to eliminate overall pipeline waste, not just to relocate it.

Just-in-Time also has an impact on whether a company uses a centralized or decentralized purchasing process. Though this topic is certainly open for a lot of discussion, many companies today have centralized purchasing. With Just-in-Time, we're working with suppliers to bring material directly to the person who uses it. It's difficult to imagine how a centralized purchasing organization located several thousand miles away is going to be able to establish procedures for direct deliveries to the person at the point of use, when they have never met the person or seen the work area. Just-in-Time definitely pushes a company to think about decentralized purchasing.

Even so, Xerox and others found that decentralized purchasing made it difficult to reduce the supplier base, and they centralized. As mentioned earlier, Xerox—using centralized purchasing—reduced their supplier base from 5,000 to under 300 over a six-year span.

Different strategies may be necessary at different stages of the JIT/TQC journey. As in most situations, however, the alternatives are seldom black and white. Most likely, success will result from some kind of combination of centralized and decentralized purchasing—perhaps centralized contract negotiations with decentralized kanban releases, for instance.

PURCHASING EVOLUTION

Purchasing's job responsibilities are also affected by Just-in-Time. Prior to Material Requirements Planning, a planner would break the build schedule down on a manual spread-sheet into the various components required. This was a laborious but semiprofessional job. The buyer then used this extended information to negotiate orders with suppliers for whatever material was needed.

Material Requirements Planning (MRP) essentially computerized the manual effort required by the planner to extend the build plan into requirements. Companies that implemented a Class A Material Requirements Planning process then created the position of buyer/planners. These used the Material Requirements Planning output to perform their own purchasing functions.

As Manufacturing Resource Planning (MRP II) was phased in, a professional supplier manager would negotiate the major contracts, but a supplier/scheduler, a semiprofessional person, would perform the detailed ordering and release process with the Manufacturing Resource Planning output. At this stage of evolution, information quality was typically good enough to eliminate the need for a lot of human intervention.

Now, with both Manufacturing Resource Planning and Just-in-Time, the supplier/scheduler's responsibility can be transferred to a direct labor person in the cell. The supplier manager still negotiates the major contracts and makes the arrangements for direct supplier deliveries. Replenishment material is ordered via kanban (for example, a returnable container), and execution is handled between the customer's production floor or finished-goods area and the supplier's production floor.

In this last phase, traditional purchase orders and detailed scheduled supplier deliveries have been eliminated. When we achieve daily deliveries, it will be practical to maintain the necessary level of paperwork with daily purchase orders, packing slips, invoices, and accounts-payable checks. With Just-in-Time, the output from the Manufacturing Resource Planning system is provided to the supplier for macro planning purposes. Activity on the shop floor, however, is initiated by kanban.

ELIMINATING WASTE IN PURCHASING

Once we allow kanban to pull material from the supplier, we can practice *purchasing by exception*. Now purchasing is involved only in the higher-level aspects of supplier management. The day-to-day routine is handled by kanban and the people in the cell. Now, instead of spending 75 to 85 percent of their time performing rudimentary tasks, purchasing can devote themselves to establishing more customer/supplier partnerships.

As these relationships are formed, other opportunities for eliminating waste will appear. For a positive supplier/customer relationship, the customer must reach an agreement with his supplier on pricing and payment. The intended application of the parts should be communicated, so that the supplier's expertise can help determine design specifications. Quantity, date, and delivery location also must be agreed upon. That's essentially all the information needed to make this process work.

Today's processes, however, are often loaded with waste. There are all sorts of non-value-added items such as multiple-part purchase orders, change orders, expedites, and de-expedites. There is insurance, loading, and unloading; there are packing slips, invoices, credit invoices, and checks. We pack parts in boxes we throw away. We unpackage parts and then repackage them. An enormous amount of work takes place beyond the theoretical minimum. We need to learn how to recognize these areas of waste and develop action items to make improvements.

We could, for example, create a circulating kanban container between the customer and the supplier, which would allow for the elimination of waste in the areas of packaging, trash, damage, material handling, packing slips, credit invoices, purchasing and accounting. All areas, not just production, have non-value-added activities that must be exposed and eliminated.

DEFINING A GOOD SUPPLIER

Again, improved customer/supplier relations is a two-way street. To develop them, we first must be able to recognize what a good supplier is. Like the other areas covered, this topic will be addressed according to its relationship to quality, delivery, and cost functions.

From a good supplier we should expect the following in terms of quality:

1. He ships the right quantity.
2. There is no inspection required.
3. He has good process control and lets the customer know when there are design changes.
4. He practices Total Quality Control, so that the root causes of problems can be eliminated.
5. He provides full service. This is important, because the more services a supplier provides, the better the opportunity for a customer to reduce his sources of supply.

We should seek the following in terms of deliveries:

1. The supplier delivers on time to the point of use.
2. The packaging is consistent with what is required at the point of use.
3. The supplier has short and stable lead times. He is able to execute with Just-in-Time, so there is responsiveness and flexibility within the product family.

We should look for the following from a cost point of view:

1. The supplier's prices are fair.
2. There is a long-term interest and agreement between customer and supplier.

As a supplier improves his process, the part cost should actually drop. In making any long-term price agreement, we should consider what motivation the supplier has for continuous price improvement.

Overall, with a good supplier, we should:

1. Establish a win-win attitude
2. Ensure continued use of JIT/TQC and Manufacturing Resource Planning internally
3. Determine that the supplier is financially stable, dependable, responsible, and ethical.
4. Verify that his technology is on the forefront of current advances and can provide long-term design expertise.

As customers, we don't want to go through the effort of reducing our supplier base only to find that a remaining supplier does not have the capability of keeping up with the competition. This would necessitate starting the process all over again.

WORKING WITH DISTRIBUTORS

Many companies don't deal directly or exclusively with original suppliers, but routinely obtain portions of their materials through distributors. It could be argued, of course, that with JIT/TQC the distributor should be eliminated. Theoretically, that may be true. As we will see, though, distributors can provide some valuable services and offer more than just warehousing facilities.

Distributors simplify the process of distribution. They allow original manufacturers to deal with fewer but larger customers. They also enable their customers to order in smaller quantities from a more responsive and often more local source.

There are a number of advantages to dealing with distributors. Since they buy in larger quantities, they should be able to offer price savings to offset the costs of their services. These services include breaking down their bulk order into smaller quantities for more frequent shipments to numerous customers. Also, the fluctuations in the customer's usage may be insignificant to the distributor's quantities, giving the customer some flexibility. By consolidating a number of different items, distributors can also offer customers much lower shipping costs. JIT/TQC would eventually motivate the distributor to provide improved services with less inventory.

One JIT/TQC company that used distributors wanted to eliminate waste in the purchasing area. It decided to reduce the number of distributors it was using from eight to two. Both of the distributors it wanted to employ were in the same nearby town. One had 20 percent of the business; the other had the balance. The company negotiated contracts with the two distributors for 500 different parts. It gave the distributors their best usage projection by part number, with the understanding that the actual consumption would vary depending on need. It also committed to a certain annual dollar volume of business.

The company arranged for one distributor to pick up from the other, and then drop off the material at the factory. While making the delivery at the factory, the distributor would pick up the customer's free kanban cards. The kanban cards were the authorization to deliver more material on the next delivery. In one step, the company eliminated 500 purchase orders, and the purchasing department was basically taken out of the day-to-day loop on those 500 items. Invoicing and payment were handled on a monthly basis, allowing buyers to concentrate on other areas of improvement. The production line communicated directly with the distributor. This same kanban process, of course, works with original manufacturers as well, but it usually requires more effort to incorporate so many part numbers.

As with other suppliers, there are certain attributes that define what a good distributor is.

1. He informs the customer of potential problems.
2. His parts do not require inspection.
3. He uses Total Quality Control and helps a customer establish Total Quality Control teams directly through to the original manufacturer. This is essential to establish an effective link that allows determination of the root causes of any problems that may occur.
4. The good distributor delivers on time and maintains dependable and short replenishment lead times.
5. He delivers to the point of use in logical packaging.
6. He has very knowledgeable shipping and order processing departments.
7. He delivers using kanban mechanisms, eliminating the need for purchase orders or other forms of traditional paperwork.

Overall, distributors, like suppliers, should have strong management, be financially sound, and use good information systems. They should be located relatively nearby and carry a broad product line. They should be innovative and ethical, and, of course, their cost must be consistent with the value added.

One primary disadvantage of dealing with distributors is that it may be difficult to get to the root causes of quality problems. This is why it's important that a distributor work with a customer to set up Total Quality Control links with the suppliers themselves. Another disadvantage is that lot tracking may become more difficult. And, of course, a customer has to pay for the cost of a distributor's services.

SUPPLIER-SELECTION TEAMS

When a customer wishes to select a supplier, be it an original manufacturer or a distributor, a supplier-selection team must be formed. This team is usually headed by purchasing and includes members from finance, quality, design engineering, manufacturing engineering, and transportation. If it does not have these six members, each of these six areas should at least be knowledgeably represented. The task of this team is to evaluate each supplier.

Team selection of suppliers is now more important than ever. It is ludicrous for manufacturing to be struggling to reduce the supplier base while, independently, engineering is busy establishing an equal number of new suppliers (or effectively limiting purchasing's supplier choices to one new alternative). In making its selection, the team must balance design constraints with the supplier's technical ability, delivery dependability, financial stability, quality, and total product cost.

The team works toward the common goal of selecting a supplier for the long-term commitment required by JIT/TQC. The members must carefully analyze each supplier's JIT/TQC potential. It is up to purchasing to look at delivery consistency, delivery lead times, product-line diversity, and price per part, as well as the total cost of the supply process. Finance must evaluate the financial stability of the supplier and determine his ability to minimize paperwork while maintaining adequate controls. Quality examines whether the potential supplier has a Total Quality Control system in place or is capable of installing one. Design engineering's responsibility is to assess the technology and design-support capability of the firm in question. Manufacturing engineering must evaluate the current processes and process controls used by the supplier, as well as the capacity and capability of those processes. Finally, transportation has to examine transportation alternatives and consistency with established or planned part pathways. Part pathways are formed when a customer selects suppliers with geographic consistency, allowing more frequent deliveries at less cost.

Finding the proper supplier is not just a purchasing decision anymore, nor is it a fallout of design expediency. It's a team decision, and the criteria have to be optimized. In fact, it is important to realize that when selecting a supplier, we are also choosing a member of the design team.

BEING A GOOD CUSTOMER

While we are seeking a good supplier, by the same token, the supplier is looking for a good customer. A supplier evaluating a potential customer needs to know that the customer has respect for his expertise. He needs to be assured that the customer will listen when he suggests something and will share cost savings. He would also like to know the application of the part to be purchased so that he can influence the specifications, rather than be told, to the last detail, what the part specifications must be. He would like the customer to work with him on problems. If parts are returned, the customer should be able to provide data to help him track the root cause of the problem. He would also prefer a customer with smooth order releases rather than wide fluctuations, which will tend to upend the processes in his own factory. Therefore, he would like his customer to be practicing JIT/TQC.

This was a factor Beckman Instruments encountered when it was getting started with Just-in-Time. Beckman contacted one of Hewlett-Packard's plastic suppliers who was feeding HP on a Just-in-Time basis. This supplier was also doing Just-in-Time. Beckman was interested in getting price quotes on some parts, but the supplier delayed doing business with them. The supplier actually rejected the customer. The supplier told Beckman, "You're too new to Just-in-Time at this point, and your order releases are not smooth enough. You still haven't reduced your lot sizes sufficiently, enabling your processes to run more evenly." The supplier's whole business had been converted over to Just-in-Time, and it was shipping steady quantities to Hewlett-Packard as well as to other companies. The mix of parts Hewlett-Packard needed might change, but the supplier knew that he had X amount of business capacity to supply to Hewlett-Packard every day.

Beckman, on the other hand, would order parts and then not reorder for a while. The supplier had discovered from prior experience that this lack of evenness tended to thrash his business. He told Beckman to call back in a year, once it had further developed its JIT/TQC process, and he'd be glad to sell them the parts. When evaluating a customer from a cost point of view, a supplier looks for someone who is willing to share the risks involved.

At Hewlett-Packard, we had a product that was projected to have a very fast growth rate. Prior to releasing it, we asked the supplier to build up inventory for the initial introduction. As it turned out, the product barely sold at all. We quickly tried to shut the supplier off. He told us that if we did so, he would have to absorb a significant amount of inventory, and he'd be forced to lay off fifteen people.

HP immediately took responsibility for the problem. It was our mistake, and we agreed to slow the supplier down only to the point where he would not have to lay people off. HP even agreed to buy several months of material it didn't need. We showed the supplier that we had meant it when we had agreed to share the risk with him.

This is an important point. As a customer, you've done a lot of work to consolidate your supplier base, and you're funneling a lot of business into one supplier. It is not in your best interest to put him in financial jeopardy. For one thing, if a customer puts a supplier out of business, he'll have to start the supplier selection process all over again. One of the keys to good customer/supplier relationships is establishing an overall win-win attitude.

A preferred type of customer is one who is practicing JIT/TQC and Manufacturing Resource Planning. The company is financially stable, dependable, responsible, and ethical. It is willing to transfer technology improvements to its suppliers. And it is willing to enter into a long-term commitment with its supplier.

CONTRACT CONSIDERATIONS

Now that we can recognize the characteristics of a good customer and supplier, it's time to discuss how we seal the agreement. In establishing a customer/supplier contract, we begin with the *terms of agreement*. This sets forth the effective date of the contract and how it can be canceled or renegotiated, and it also includes the usual legal information about the participants involved.

Discussions should also concern the total quantities and price of parts covered by the contract. Most Just-in-Time contracts contain the dollar volume of business that the customer intends to acquire from the supplier. Included with this figure is the best information available at the time on the part mix required. This will undoubtedly change, but there is a certain volume of business to which the customer is committed. Also, the part variations that will be allowed within the lead time and price range should be established here.

Often, the customer will specify the maximum amount of inventory he will be liable for in the supplier's process, including an agreed-upon quantity of raw materials. As the supplier advances in his own JIT/TQC journey, the liability should decrease significantly.

Customers need to *supply their key suppliers with the full Manufacturing Resource Planning horizon as well as knowledge of future products*. An increasing number of companies are using electronic data interchange to communicate this information. The more timely the information the suppliers have, the more effectively they will be able to help the customer. As a safeguard, maintenance of confidential information can be part of the contract.

Xerox found itself in a situation in which sharing information with its suppliers ultimately saved a new product line. Xerox had brought its suppliers together on a new product. They returned with their bids. Unfortunately, in the meantime, Xerox discovered that a competitor had just introduced an extremely well-designed competitive product.

It told its suppliers that the project would have to be scrapped. The various suppliers suggested that by working together on a redesign, they might be able to bring the costs down. They did, and Xerox was able to resurrect the project and successfully produce a competitive product. When we have a limited number of suppliers, they become key members of the design team. It follows, then, that early supplier involvement in the design is critical to achieving better designs in less time.

Another contractual point that must be addressed is *how quality is going to be measured*. Will Total Quality Control teams be established? What communication channels will be set up? A common communication chain—and one that often fails—is as follows: production worker to production manager to quality assurance to purchasing, and then to a sales representative to supplier factory quality assurance to supplier manufacturing manager to supplier production manager to supplier production or design. It is virtually impossible to communicate a simple message, much less a complex problem, accurately through so many people. It is important for a customer to identify direct problem-solving channels to key suppliers so that if a problem in the production area arises, the customer will know exactly whom to contact in the supplier's factory.

Other sections of the contract must deal with delivery frequency, delivery authorization, and invoicing. Will the traditional purchase orders, packing slips, invoices, and individual checks be required? Will kanbans authorize shipment, with invoicing to be done periodically, or will electronic funds transfer take place each time a kanban shipment arrives, thereby eliminating even the invoice? Whatever the case, the terms of payment can be adjusted to avoid a financial impact on either company.

CONTINUOUS DESIGN IMPROVEMENTS

Just as purchasing deals externally with suppliers, design also links JIT/TQC outside the company to suppliers and customers.

There are those who insist they can never find the time to begin implementing JIT/TQC. "This product wasn't designed to be built at all," they say, "much less with JIT/TQC." It may not be the best design, and there may be plenty of room for change, but that is no reason to postpone JIT/TQC. You start where you are and make improvements from there.

The improvements must come in the form of faster and more manu-facturable designs. To accomplish this, design teams are a necessity. Design may head up the effort, but every functional area will be involved: Purchasing will source the materials; finance will determine the product cost; quality will project reliability; manufacturing will build prototypes, identify equipment, and process needs; and marketing will research customer needs, applications for the product, and set its price. In addition, early supplier involvement in the design process will allow the team to benefit from the valuable expertise of those few remaining suppliers that have earned your business. With each idea for improvement from a nontraditional designer and with each generation of design, teamwork is strengthened.

Occasionally JIT/TQC begins in engineering design, as was the case at Tektronix's Lab Instrument Division. Their 11K oscilloscope was designed nearly from the beginning to fit with JIT/TQC. Typically, however, other areas will be learning Just-in-Time at the same time that design is incorporating the new knowledge into its designs.

In most instances, design engineering is not actively involved in the pilot (though typical, this is not necessarily desirable). However, as the manufacturing processes are simplified and ideas for improvement are fed back, designers become more involved. Typically, three to nine months into the implementation, design begins to work with manufacturing to incorporate ideas gleaned from the pilot into the next generation of design. Designers can see the improvements that have occurred. They don't want their product to drag through the factory for weeks or months, when it could be built in a fraction of that time. At this stage, JIT/TQC begins to influence and prioritize interest in design for manufacturability (the ability to be consistently and economically produced).

Another team activity that is critical to the design process, is competitive benchmarking. In a booklet entitled, *Competitive Benchmarking*, Xerox defines this as "the continuous process of measuring our product, services and practices against our toughest competitors or those companies renowned as the leaders." In other words, while Just-in-Time has us compare ourselves with a theoretical no-waste state, competitive benchmarking has us compare ourselves with today's best.

Competitive benchmarking consists of five phases. In the planning phase, we determine what products, processes, or services will be benchmarked. We then decide who is the industry leader in each area of interest. In the analysis phase, we attempt to understand our and our competitors' strengths and weaknesses. In the integration phase, we develop and communicate a strategic plan to capitalize on our strengths while minimizing our weaknesses. In the action phase, we implement the plan and adjust our course as required. We are trying to be proactive rather than reactive vis-à-vis our competitors and customers. Finally, we enter the maturity phase, where competitive benchmarking has become a way of life. We have attained and are able to maintain a leadership position in the industry.

Figure 7.2
Hewlett-Packard Roseville

	BEFORE	AFTER
INVENTORY	2-3 MONTHS	2 WEEKS
TURNS	4-6 TURNS	26 TURNS
PURCHASED $ MATERIALS		20% RECEIVED DAILY
		58% WEEKLY
		17% MONTHLY
		5% > MONTHLY
		48% FAR EAST
		44% USA
		8% EUROPE
SUPPLIER RELATIONSHIPS	ADVERSARIAL	EXTENSION OF HP
NUMBERS		REDUCED 40%
ON TIME DELIVERIES	25%	75 - 80%, TIGHTER
		CONTOLS
		0 DAYS LATE, 3 EARLY
QUALITY	INSPECTION	PROCESS CONTROLS
SYSTEMS	BATCH MODE	MRP FOR PLANNING
		JIT EXECUTION
		TQC PROBLEM SOLVING
PAPERWORK		90% REDUCTION

SOURCE: HEWLETT-PACKARD; TARGET

One of the better examples of team design and competitive benchmarking occurred at Hewlett-Packard's Roseville, California, factory (see figure 7.2). Max Davis, the manufacturing manager, first implemented JIT/TQC to simplify and streamline the traditional processes used to manufacture computer terminals. Then Roseville began to feel extreme pressure from offshore terminal manufacturers. Total Quality Control analysis showed customers liked HP's quality but not its price. Further analysis indicated that there was no inherent reason why offshore manufacturers should be able to produce terminals more inexpensively than a domestic company. HP responded by forming a design team to work on the next generation of computer terminals. Representatives from virtually all functional areas, as well as key suppliers, were included on the team. They knew the new product had to be designed quickly and be inexpensive to produce, while quality and delivery had to be maintained or improved. Each contributed in his area of expertise, but difficult tradeoff decisions were made as a team. As of the time of this writing, HP Roseville now makes the world's most inexpensive computer terminal; it is able to sell the product for a price that is 5 to 45 percent lower than the competition's.

Davis seriously doubts that HP could have accomplished this feat without first doing JIT/TQC, which enabled the company to

- reduce costs of current manufacturing and supporting processes
- better understand how to simplify the product from a cost and a process point of view
- understand the value of having fewer parts and suppliers from a cost and a process point of view
- develop teamwork
- become familiar with continuous-improvement philosophies, processes, and techniques.

Just as JIT/TQC leads toward automation and computer-integrated manufacturing, it also encourages design for manufacturability. It helps build the necessary teamwork, develop the thinking worker, prioritize areas of emphasis, and force action to eliminate design constraints that prevent economically achieving higher velocities.

MARKETING AND SALES

Once a company has accomplished breakthrough improvements in its manufacturing process and is able to respond economically and quickly, it has provided its marketing and sales force with an effective selling tool. *The ability to offer quality, delivery, and cost in a responsive manner is a powerful competitive weapon.*

In virtually every successful Just-in-Time installation, factory tours have become somewhat of an unanticipated problem. Everyone wants to see how JIT/TQC works. Moreover, as the company becomes more successful with JIT/TQC, marketing will want each potential customer to see the manufacturing processes. With Just-in-Time, manufacturing becomes a key factor in closing the sale. In fact, the customers' interest has had some drawbacks for other outsiders wanting a tour. Because these successful Just-in-Time companies are in the manufacturing business, not the tour industry, many of them have been obligated to limit their tours to potential customers only.

As a company becomes more proficient with JIT/TQC, it can begin to capitalize on its newfound gains. JIT/TQC will eventually take some supplying factories to the point of selling by exception, the corollary to purchasing by exception, which was discussed earlier. Selling is an expensive activity. There are costs involved both in obtaining the order and in processing it. A JIT/TQC supplier who is linked to a JIT/TQC manufacturer, however, can avoid a large portion of the overhead involved.

Basically, once a long-term contract is negotiated, sales and order processing are out of the day-to-day loop. At this point, sales is involved only in making certain the customer is satisfied and in determining when it is time to renegotiate the contract. Otherwise, the supplier's production department routinely fills empty kanbans received from the customer. Just as in a grocery store, it is the supplier's responsibility to keep the shelf stocked.

Another important incentive for initiating supplier/customer links was illustrated in a recent magazine article. It pointed out that a number of Japanese auto manufacturers that have opened factories in the United States, have persuaded their Japanese suppliers also to open up new factories in America. The article went on to say that many U.S. suppliers were having a difficult time trying to sell to the Japanese manufacturers, principally due to inferior quality. However, even those suppliers with excellent quality were having trouble.

Let's look at why that might be the case. Suppose you and one of your suppliers were actively performing JIT/TQC. That supplier would likely have all or most of your business. Quality would be extremely high. If a problem or an opportunity for improvement arose, both you and your supplier would be competent in Total Quality Control, and could efficiently develop a permanent solution for the trouble or capitalize on the chance to improve. Waste would be constantly driven out of the processes. Both you and your supplier would participate in the design process, which would result in very competitive costs. In addition, all deliveries would be triggered by kanban, eliminating expensive sales, order entry, purchasing, and warehousing activities. Because of kanban, deliveries would also be frequent and responsive.

Now suppose someone wanted to take all or part of that business away from your supplier. What would they have to offer? The present supplier is providing exceptional quality, delivery, and cost. If you changed suppliers, the best you could hope for is to achieve the same degree of excellence. The reality is, once a JIT/TQC arrangement is established between a customer and supplier, the supplier owns the business. He can lose it, but only if he loses his competitive edge in quality, delivery, or cost, and if another supplier can better serve you.

It is because this stable relationship offers so many benefits that some of my clients have hired me to help their better customers implement JIT/TQC. Both the supplier and customer win with a long-term arrangement.

There is still another reason for establishing JIT/TQC links with customers. With Just-in-Time, orders are placed in frequent and smooth increments, not in the batches that most non-Just-in-Time factories use. As stated before, 75 to 80 percent of the unevenness in our factories is due to our own lot sizing. Once that is smoothed out by JIT/TQC, 20 percent still remains (seasonality again excepted). To make further progress, it is important to avoid marketing incentives that promote unevenness at month's end, quarter's end and year's end. The customer's inputs must also be smoothed out in a manner that serves both the customer and supplier.

Naturally, one approach is to change sales compensation practices in a way that would emphasize smoothness without eliminating the ability to plan or the motivation to maximize sales. This, of course, is easier said than done. Another solution is to deal only with customers who already have smooth demands emanating from Just-in-Time processes. The latter is the approach adopted by the Just-in-Time supplier who refused Beckman's business. As uncommon as that may seem, it may become increasingly important for these Just-in-Time supplier companies to maintain the evenness of their process rather than subject it to the thrashing of a little added business from a nonlinear customer.

Tellabs is pursuing yet another alternative, which will provide it with smoother input and a competitive edge at the same time. Now that it is capable of quickly and economically providing smaller lots, it will tell its customers it no longer needs a purchase order from them. Instead, Tellabs requests a contract allowing it to supply the needed products up to a predetermined inventory level, a kanban ceiling. For planning purposes, Tellabs will refer to its customers' Manufacturing Resource Planning output. For execution, though, Tellabs will use electronic data interchange with the customers' computer systems and read their on-hand balance. The contract will give Tellabs a standing authorization to replace every item up to a certain level, so as a customer uses an item out of its on-hand balance, Tellabs will build what was consumed. The customer minimizes the expensive routine purchasing function, and inventories can be kept lower. Tellabs minimizes the expensive sales process, smooths inputs, and essentially provides a service that the competitors are unlikely to be able to duplicate for some time. This will prove to be good for both the customer and Tellabs. It will also effectively lock out the competition.

Where seasonality exists, smoothing the load can be accomplished only with very flexible capacity or by building inventories. Some companies, such as Briggs and Stratton, have redesigned their products to make them more seasonably flexible, which in turn allows for less inventory. Certain seasonality constraints are particularly difficult to resolve. For example, how do we smooth the input of raw materials tied directly to a crop harvest? What about Christmas sales or the year-end frenzy of governmental agencies spending their remaining budgets? The answers to these questions are not clear, and until they are, inventory and excess capacity, although wasteful, remain necessary. One thing is clear, however: As long as we understand where Just-in-Time is taking us and are careful to develop and focus the thinking worker, we will continue to be astounded at the clever ideas and solutions that will emerge.

As we convert to rates per day, acknowledging customer orders based on that rate (available to promise by rate) another change in marketing and sales takes place. Master scheduling and order entry become very closely linked and eventually merged. The resulting new position reports through the manufacturing organization. Credit checks and the like may remain in marketing, but actual order acknowledgment and planning will be done in manufacturing. The organizational merger becomes more apparent as we see the need to integrate the order entry and master scheduling information systems.

As Just-in-Time forces us to take more waste out of the system, our competitive advantage will lie in our ability to respond economically. How can marketing and sales use Just-in-Time as a competitive weapon? That depends on where we are in the process. During the initial years, the cost of our products is not greatly affected. We may reduce scrap, rework, and required space, but there is still a lot of overhead left in the factory. We improved the quality, but most customers have always seen good quality, if only because we've spent a fortune screening out the bad quality. How then do we turn Just-in-Time into a competitive weapon the first few years? One of the ways is to sell our process improvements. While the customer may not see much improvement in our external quality, the processes in use after JIT/TQC is implemented should demonstrate that the cost of obtaining that quality can be expected to decrease. The customer should be able to tell from our processes, both in the factory and in the office, that costs are going to remain competitive in the future.

Another marketable improvement is our ability to respond. Storage of material at the point of use, kanban authorizations, reduced lot sizes, and shorter throughput times all combine to shrink manufacturing lead times, frequently by 50 to 90 percent.

One reason marketing takes potential customers on tours of the manufacturing area is to demonstrate that the right processes for competitive, long-term quality and cost are in place, even if only responsiveness is noticeable today. Once the entire factory has been converted to Just-in-Time, once a substantial number of suppliers have implemented the same practices, once we have incorporated what we have learned into new product designs and when we have had time to realize the savings JIT/TQC provides, then we should see the actual cost of our product going down. This, of course, includes the cost of quality.

In *The Third Wave*, Alvin Toffler talks about three major historical waves of change. From a manufacturing perspective, the first wave took place prior to the industrial revolution. At that time, everything was custom-built. It wasn't until the second wave came along, signaled by the advent of the industrial revolution and the invention of the revolver, that manufacturing developed interchangeable parts. This is when high-volume mass production began. Most companies are still struggling with the second wave. But Toffler also describes a third wave, in which he describes the efficiencies of the second wave combine with the customizing abilities of the first wave. We will accomplish this through new processes and new technologies.

On one production line at Hewlett-Packard, we manufactured a product with 6 million logical configurations at a rate of a few per day. It is always easier to build a product with a few features than it is to build one with many. However, given a product with many features, it is always better and easier to build it using JIT/TQC than it is using traditional work orders. This is because JIT/TQC provides us with a better capability to build to customer orders and to respond quickly to changes.

This does not mean, however, that we should strive for products with many features. It is still more difficult and expensive to build a product with many features than it is to build a standard one. Whether to build standard items or products with a lot of features is decided primarily at the business level, taking into account all the marketing, design, and manufacturing considerations. However, when features provide a competitive advantage without generating disadvantages of cost, quality, and delivery responsiveness, JIT/TQC will be of great help.

The ability to respond provided by JIT/TQC affects even those products that a company is planning to phase out. Once a company has finished converting its active products to JIT/TQC, it now can turn to those products that have a planned obsolescence. At first glance it would not seem to be worth the effort, but remember, the objective is not Just-in-Time per se, it is to run the business better. Many companies feel that the responsiveness provided by JIT/TQC can benefit them in the somewhat unpredictable phaseout process. Products slated for obsolescence are not necessarily good choices for pilot projects, but they are worthy of consideration once other products have been converted.

Marketing can also make use of the improved forecasting that results from Just-in-Time. As inventories are lowered, we will need more accurate forecasts if we are to maintain dependable delivery schedules on products and features that have a variable demand. Fortunately, JIT/TQC enables us to improve the accuracy of our forecasts; Total Quality Control can be used to get at the basic causes of inaccurate forecasts. This process is discussed in detail in chapter 11. Once we clearly understand these causes, we can develop countermeasures that will lead to greater accuracy.

One countermeasure involves shortening the time span in which detailed forecasts need to be made. As we crush our manufacturing lead times and our suppliers do likewise, we find ourselves in a position to forecast our suppliers' raw-material needs rather than the finished goods required from them. For example, instead of forecasting thirty-eight different pieces of plastic parts from a supplier, we will forecast the quantity of plastic the supplier needs on hand to cover our aggregate demand. Essentially, while the planning bills in the Manufacturing Resource Planning system may contain the mix of purchased parts required from the supplier, they will be used primarily to determine the mix of raw materials and capacity to be purchased from the supplier. The supplier will then use this information to purchase the correct materials and provide adequate capacity. As he receives customer orders, he will use JIT/TQC processes to quickly convert the raw materials into the required finished products. For example, if a customer requires molded plastic parts, forecasting the aggregate pounds of plastic pellets is more accurate and simpler than forecasting individual pieces, particularly when the composite figure is based on a shorter time period than the traditional forecast for the detailed end item. As both customer and supplier progress with JIT/TQC, the improved responsiveness begins to pay off not only at the level of quality, delivery, and cost but in terms of simplicity as well.

JUST-IN-TIME'S IMPACT ON TRANSPORTATION

When applying Just-in-Time to transportation, the goal is to receive more frequent deliveries and deliver more frequently with less cost. Sound impossible? It's not. In fact, the challenge to transportation is consistent with the challenges Just-in-Time issues to other areas. The shop is required to perform more setups at less cost. Stock must provide smaller lots of material at less cost. Purchasing and shipping is also required to make more frequent deliveries at less cost. Similar challenges will be issued to all areas; transportation is no exception.

As with materials suppliers, many companies are involved with multiple carriers for both inbound and outbound freight. Again, utilizing the notion of "One Less at a Time," Just-in-Time seeks to reduce the number of these carriers, for many of the same reasons that it condenses the supplier base. Like any other Just-in-Time supplier, the carrier will be as much a part of a company's operation as anybody else.

It may be difficult to picture a trucker taking material directly to the user on the production line. Normally, the drivers don't know anything about the factory to which they deliver, and under most circumstances, they don't have any authorization to go walking through the factory. There's usually good reason for this; a company rarely knows who the delivering trucker is going to be.

As might be expected, within a Just-in-Time environment, we find a very different situation. A contract carrier may make a periodic milk run. It's the same person driving the truck day in and day out. Like the milkman, he services his customers according to a regular, prescribed route. At one factory, a contract carrier's driver was actually issued his own name badge and went to company picnics like everybody else. He just happened to be an outside source, but he was still part of the team.

One Tektronix site had progressed so far with its supplier relations that a supplier arrived with several carts of crating material every day. He brought the material right onto the shop floor, stored it where it belonged, and then entered the receiving information into Tek's computer system.

In order to permit relationships like these to exist, there will, obviously, have to be a more careful selection of carriers. Oftentimes, the customer does not select the carriers for incoming material; it is the supplier who makes this decision. The customer usually determines how outbound freight is to be transported. With Just-in-Time, it will be necessary to combine the processes for inbound and outbound freight to receive more frequent shipments and deliveries at less cost.

Just-in-Time will also affect the routing of freight. More customized routes will be developed. Instead of one supplier shipping to ten customers, we may have one customer picking up from ten suppliers.

A company that receives multiple deliveries from several suppliers may opt for another transportation alternative, having its suppliers feed a centralized hub where the freight can be consolidated. This is exactly what New United Motors (GM/Toyota) in Fremont, California, does. Every day, suppliers deliver to a rail hub in Chicago, and seventy hours later, a day's worth of material arrives in Fremont.

Once again, Total Quality Control must be involved. The carrier, instead of being an unknown third party in this process, will be part of a Total Quality Control team educated to work through transportation/distribution problems and opportunities.

It is important to realize that as a company experiences more frequent deliveries, there is less room for variability in the delivery window. Rather than specify a certain day or week in which deliveries will arrive, companies will detail the actual hour of delivery. For example, a supplier might be scheduled to deliver his parts between 10:00 and 11:00 A.M. Hewlett-Packard developed four-hour windows with some of its suppliers who provided their own delivery. A proviso in their contracts stated that if these suppliers missed their delivery windows three times within a year, their contracts with HewlettPackard could be renegotiated; in other words, they could therefore lose HP's business.

How does all of this translate into more frequent deliveries with less cost? Again, taking Hewlett-Packard as an example, the company chose a selected number of parts and determined a logical supplier for each of those part families. It then called the suppliers and asked them to rebid on all of this material. Traditionally, price quotes included shipping charges. HP asked the suppliers to formulate quotes excluding shipping, as if HP would pick up the material. HP's first surprise was to discover how much freight had been buried in the cost of materials.

The next step was to call Trans-Western Express (TWX), a Denver-based transportation company, and request the price for running a truck through a route that would begin at HP's factory, make a circuit through HP's suppliers, and then return to the factory. TWX said that, regardless of whether the truck was full or empty, it would cost X amount a mile to operate the truck and Y amount to pay the driver; based on these rates, it formulated a total trip cost. HP's second surprise was how much lower that figure was than the sum of the various suppliers' individual freight charges.

When negotiating a contract, HP stipulated that the carrier would pick up the material from the supplier at a specific time. If the supplier failed to have it ready, however, then he had to airfreight it to HP at his expense. It was fairly easy to add this provision, since no supplier was about to negotiate that he would miss shipments.

HP hired TWX, which now makes a circuit on a fixed schedule. This is how one HP site was able to get more frequent deliveries at less cost. Material is picked up from the supplier and delivered directly by the trucker to the point of use according to a dependable schedule. The success of this pilot so excited TWX that, recognizing the potential for new opportunities to provide service, they had the sides of their forty-foot trailers emblazoned with the words "Just-in-Time Carriers."

A factory in Idaho established a similar approach, except in the winter it tends to store one extra day's supply of material because of the weather. New United Motors carries a three-day supply, but it has said it plans to drop it to two days because of dependable daily deliveries.

At a JIT/TQC implementation class that I taught in England, an attendee named Mark Fernandez said that his company, BRS Midlands, didn't make anything, but rather provided transportation services. He was there so that he could help his company understand the changes that JIT/TQC was causing in the transportation industry. He also wanted to be able to provide the needed services and thereby capitalize on the opportunities the changes would offer innovative companies.

Packaging is another aspect on transportation that will be affected. Materials will no longer be packaged without regard to the customer; instead there will be more standardized, returnable, collapsible and reusable containers, as well as cartridges that plug directly into production lines at the point of customer use.

From a financial viewpoint, we will see companies making more periodic payments rather than paying for every delivery, especially as customers and suppliers approach economic daily deliveries. Just-in-Time will also have a major impact on traffic personnel. No longer will choosing a transport company consist of simply calling up a trucking line or stating "ship best way." It will be a professional-level job. The responsible employee will have to understand the transportation industry, regulations, and negotiations and be able to assist in the development of part pathways.

TRANSPORTATION TRENDS

The technology of transportation is also changing. In addition to the standard rear-load-only trucks, there will be more side-load vehicles, which are already common in England. Side loading allows a much wider variety of products to be shipped and affords much easier access to the goods; it is not necessary to unload everything in order to retrieve an item in the front of the truck. Companies are also developing the ability to trace material more efficiently by using bar codes. In addition, customers are increasingly able to change transportation modes midstream. Carrier-mode switching originally took the form of "piggybacks," in which loads were transferred from truck to train or from train to truck. Now switches can take place from truck to air, in the middle of delivery. Some innovative transportation companies, such as Skyway Freight Systems of California, can also inform customers when a shipment was, or was not, picked up, as well as state the current location of the shipment and the estimated time of delivery.

We are also going to see changes in the characteristics of Just-in-Time shipments themselves. First, there will be more shipments of higher velocity. The average weight of these shipments will be lower, and as delivery windows narrow, there will be a reduced margin for error. Companies must also be aware that unless they do something about the paperwork process, there could be increased administrative costs.

As we begin to eliminate waste from the manufacturing process, we will find that the transportation/distribution network becomes more and more of a constraint. Ensuring frequent, on-time deliveries will be of paramount importance. Not too surprisingly, this will give local suppliers an advantage, if they are competitive in the areas of quality, delivery, and product cost.

LINKING JIT/TQC INTO THE SUPPLIER BASE

As stated earlier, it is usually better if the customer understands and practices JIT/TQC in his own company before he expects it of his suppliers. By doing JIT/TQC first, he is in a better position to know what to ask for, what to expect, and how to help the supplier. He is better situated to capitalize on the advantages to be gained by linking into the supplier base. When the time comes to begin working with suppliers, however, getting started is once again the key.

One alternative, but certainly not the only one, is to host a Supplier Open House. The trouble with this approach is that you'd be hard-pressed to find a grumpier group of people than the suppliers invited. Time and again, they have been beaten over the head by customers who really don't understand Just-in-Time or Total Quality Control. The suppliers often misunderstand JIT/TQC themselves. Their customers constantly pressure them to deliver more frequently at lower cost and higher quality in the name of JIT/TQC. Customers want "Just-In-Time deliveries," but this is often just another way of demanding more frequent deliveries.

The important thing is not daily deliveries but crushing the supplier's manufacturing lead times. Which would you rather have the supplier do, ship daily using a manufacturing process with a sixty-day lead time, or reduce the process lead time to five days and deliver weekly? With JIT/ TQC we are after the five-day lead time. If the supplier can reduce his manufacturing lead times, more frequent deliveries will follow.

In reality, it is fortunate for many of these companies that the suppliers cannot economically provide daily deliveries when they demand them. One pioneering Just-in-Time company, which had not yet implemented Just-in-Time internally, gathered its suppliers together and stated a goal of daily deliveries. Luckily for the company, the suppliers didn't have the capability to deliver every day. If they had, the company would have ended up with twenty times the material handling, and paperwork, because it didn't need the goods every day to complete its still monthly batches. In its enthusiasm, it had jumped ahead of itself.

When you are ready to link JIT/TQC into the supplier base, however, a pilot approach is again useful. This time it will be used by the supplier for his own JIT/TQC efforts. It can also be used by the supplier and customer to learn which changes in policies and procedures are needed to accelerate the velocity through the supply pipeline.

To initiate the effort, and to leverage its energies, many companies hold a supplier open house. When done properly, open houses have proven to be a reasonably effective communication tool for getting things started. But who should be invited? One consideration is to select suppliers with whom you can get started quickly. Or perhaps one of the key items you purchase comes from abroad, and you'd like to bring that supplier on board. However, JIT/TQC progress with this supplier may be lengthy because of distance and language problems. You might also select suppliers that supply expensive and/or bulky parts. Cardboard and packaging suppliers are often selected for early pilot cases, because their products are not only expensive and bulky, they're usually locally manufactured. Another choice is to select suppliers who are clustered together or fit a certain part pathway.

One question that frequently arises is whether competitors should attend the same open house. It is okay. They know they compete with other companies, and they all need to know what you're looking for in the suppliers you retain. Use this forum to explain why, how, how fast, and by how much you intend to reduce the supplier base.

Mike Birck, president of Tellabs, told a group of suppliers gathered at one of its open houses, "In order to make Just-in-Time work, we need your cooperation and assistance. We solicit that. Frankly, we expect it." Open houses are for letting suppliers know what you expect. They should also know that the reason they were selected is that you consider all of them to be good suppliers, but the company can't deal with as many suppliers in the future. Everybody is given fair notice of what is being planned. It's not a threat; it's just a statement of necessary condition.

Who from a supplier's organization attends? It is critical that an influential manufacturing person familiar with the product be present. A sales representative should not be the only one from the supplier's operation in attendance. The supplier should be instructed that a key manufacturing representative must attend. A person from manufacturing quality should also be present. The people from the customer's operation who should attend are the materials manager, purchasing manager, the materials engineer, and the appropriate buyers and supplier managers.

While the open house does provide an opportunity for dialogue, the suppliers' questions will likely be restrained because of the mix of people in the audience. One way to get better, more direct inquiries is to allow for anonymous written questions. However, the best feedback of all comes from one-on-one discussions with suppliers in the days following the open house. This is when purchasing needs to be prepared for questions and ready to support the suppliers. In anticipation of that encounter, Black and Decker gave each of its suppliers a personalized packet as they left the open house. Inside the packet were documents that laid out what B&D expected from that particular company.

Once the suppliers have heard the customer's presentations (see figure 7.3) and had a chance to ask some initial questions, there should be a tour to show Just-in-Time and Total Quality Control being practiced. It should demonstrate, graphically, the results the customer is achieving. It's also a good idea to point out those areas where the suppliers will be required to deliver to the point of use.

The issue of support is important. Most companies have their hands full just doing JIT/TQC themselves. They do not have the resources to teach all their suppliers how to do Just-in-Time and Total Quality Control, nor should they have to. (Early critical suppliers may get more assistance on a pilot basis.) The suppliers should be capable of learning JIT/TQC themselves. Some assistance is going to be required, but

Figure 7.3
Supplier Open House Sample Agenda

8:00 - 8:30	Registration (Coffee, rolls)
8:30 - 8:45	Welcome (Introduction, agenda)
8:45 - 9:45	Company Vision (Top exec., company orientation, why started JIT/TQC, marketplace changes, competition, why you are here, how selected)
9:45 - 10:00	Break
10:00- 12:00	JIT/TQC (Philosophy, customer/supplier interface: use a pro here)
12:00 - 1:00	Lunch
1:00 - 3:00	Factory tour (we are doing JIT/TQC, not clubbing suppliers)
3:00 - 3:15	Break
3:15 - 4:15	Expectations (New expectations, supplier & customer; quality, delivery, & cost; certification, price reductions, teamwork,...)
4:15 - 5:00	Panel questions and answers

basically the suppliers will be responsible for getting themselves up to speed.

The host company should also make sufficient copies of its presentation material to pass out. Buyer commodity lists should be available, along with annual reports. It is also helpful to provide some information regarding how the company initiated JIT/TQC, including what education courses they took, what books they read, what consultants they used, and what tapes they saw. All of this is offered to help the suppliers help themselves.

SUMMARY

It should be obvious by now that Just-in-Time fosters teamwork—not only within the company but between supplier and customer as well. The resulting awareness can and will lead to better service levels, more efficient problem-solving, and better prices. However, the process of linking requires change, time, understanding, and education on both the customer's and the supplier's part if it is to be done safely and with improved results.

Chapter 8
Challenging Accounting

Companies are being held hostage by the inadequacies and inappropriateness of old management accounting practices.
—**National Association of Accountants**

Just as setups are a constraint to higher velocities, paperwork is too. It is for this reason that the financial community is being asked to readdress many of its practices. Accounting's responsibility is not just to supply stockholder financial information. Today, accountants must provide management information as well. Just-in-Time/Total Quality Control is challenging the financial community by intensifying the need for more and different cost-accounting information.

The potential avalanche of invoices, packing slips, checks, work variances, and labor-collection transactions that Just-in-Time stands to generate will have to be contained. As lot sizes shrink, the increase in paperwork will be overwhelming unless this issue has been carefully addressed in advance.

We also need to reconsider how we report inventory. Traditionally, if we receive 100 items into stock, store them, and later issue forty on a work order to the production floor, we're left with sixty items in raw-material stores and forty in work in process (see figure 8.1). This is the case even though it may be a week before somebody gets around to working on those forty items on the production floor. Typically, we still call that work-in-process.

Let's look at another example. Suppose 100 pieces are received into an overcrowded stockroom, requiring forty to be taken out and stored just outside the stockroom fence, perhaps on the production floor. Now, what do we call that inventory? It is still raw material; it's just not in a locked area. But what if those forty items are deliberately stored at the

183

Figure 8.1
Inventory

	STOCKROOM	PRODUCTION	FINISHED
REC'D 100	100		
ISSUE 40	60	40	
REC'D 100	100		
STK-STK 40	60	40	
REC'D 40		40	

point of use? They're still not work in process. They're raw materials stored at the point of use.

The question is, what is work in process and what are raw materials? No matter how you slice it, both are still inventory. Eventually, we're going to try to store all materials at the point of use. We can call them whatever we like, but essentially they're raw materials stored at the point of use. *The difference between raw materials and work in process is based not on whether the materials are behind a fence, but on whether they are actually in process.*

I have already pointed out the importance of eliminating work orders on the shop floor. Doing away with work orders is an emotional change, but it is not too technically difficult. The same is true for purchase orders. Purchase orders, as we know them today, will also change. We can't expect daily purchase orders and invoices to accompany our daily deliveries. However, the extensive changes in the purchase-order and accounts-payable-and-receivable areas typically begin later in the process and progress much more slowly than those associated with work orders.

If we don't have work orders, how then do we track material through the factory? Today it is technically possible to know the location of every production person or job anywhere in the world, give or take eighteen inches. If we have enough money to buy the proper equipment, we can have perfect tracking. The question is, do we need to know where everything is every second of the day? Why would we care if a part was in operation 1 at 10:00 A.M. and in operation 2 at 10:15, and in operation 3 at 10:30? Meaningless detail is also a waste.

With Just-in-Time, material moves through a fixed pipeline; kanban sets the ceiling on work in process. As velocity increases, knowing how things are going is simply a matter of watching the rate of flow coming out of the pipeline at a certain point. If the rate of flow starts to dwindle, we know there's a blockage, and it is located wherever the kanbans have reached their ceiling. Just-in-Time uses visual controls, and they are fast, simple, and effective. We simply don't need the same number of checkpoints to track material.

The key is to avoid going overboard with tracking. Start with a minimum number of critical and logical checkpoints, and as the velocity increases, begin to reduce the checkpoints by using "One Less at a Time."

Kanban is a simple but very formal and effective control system. Work orders also control, but they become a constraint with Just-in-Time. Management must discipline itself as well as production to follow the kanban rule of "no kanban-no production." We cannot use the kanban technique only when production is problem-free, say for the first three weeks of the month, and then freely interject inventory into the system at month's end. We must adhere to the kanban discipline or adhere to the work-order discipline. Failing to do so results in chaos.

Traditionally, material is picked on a work order, and as soon as the material is cashed, raw-material inventory is relieved and work-in-process inventory is increased. If a production manager's performance is partially measured on the amount of inventory he has in his area, he is being encouraged to complete work orders as quickly as possible and push them along to the next customer.

Even in situations where financial measures are not a factor, we typically have the feeling that our job is finished when we complete the work that is in our area. That is an incorrect attitude under Just-in-Time. With Just-in-Time, the producer bears the responsibility for his output until his customer buys it (longer, actually, from a quality standpoint). This true for the company and its customers, and thus should be applied throughout the company's operations. When we become inundated by our internal supplier, it encourages us to push the material out of our system and into the next internal customer's inventory as fast as possible.

By now, we should know that the word "push" is not a synonym for

Just-in-Time. Production areas should be mentally, if not financially, responsible for their produced inventory. A worker doesn't convert the inventory, build the assembly, or make the product until just before the customer wants it. In this way, production managers are responsible for their actual work in process and their output. The next work center does not pick up ownership of that part until it actually uses it.

If a supplier wants to build the part a week ahead, then it is going to stay in their inventory budget until the customer operation is ready for it. *If you own it until I consume it, then you will be motivated to wait and build it "Just in Time" for me to use it.* This shift in inventory ownership, or at least in attitude, provides a very powerful tool to motivate implementation of Just-in-Time.

KEEPING TRACK OF LABOR

Traditionally, labor is collected to the work order. A worker might report that on a specific work order he made 100 items, and it took three and a half hours. Many companies report this detail for each operation. When the work order is closed, they can compare the actual hours required to make the product to the standard hours it was expected to require. This reporting process made sense when there were large, slow-moving batches plowing through the factory. However, as progress is made with Just-in-Time and lot sizes become smaller, each time element that we have traditionally attempted to track becomes smaller too. In fact, when lot sizes become very small, the time element is just too short to bother measuring. If one job is worked on continuously for one hour, then that time can be reported reasonably accurately. Much shorter time intervals, however, will result in numerous and mostly meaningless detail.

As one company got further into Just-in-Time, it found itself spending $100,000 a month tracking $125,000 worth of labor. The company finally decided it had to find a way to break its usual work-order and labor-collection methods.

Under the traditional labor-tracking system, many companies also keep separate accounts of direct, indirect, and overhead labor. As the transition to Just-in-Time is made, it soon becomes undesirable and impossible to separate direct and indirect labor within a cell. With material at the point of use, when an operator reaches out to grasp a part, he is performing an indirect labor function. As he lowers his arm and begins production, direct labor time starts. A cost accountant with a stopwatch could stand behind each person in production and still not accurately measure these times. Direct and indirect labor activities will be intermixed throughout the day.

At this stage, Just-in-Time factories must abandon the distinction between direct and indirect labor, at least within the cell. Invariably, direct, indirect, and overhead operations will become interspersed. There will be times, for a few minutes here and there, when the entire production line may meet to discuss a quality problem. Or we may see an individual prepare data while intermittently waiting for the supplying or customer operation to be completed. Still another individual or two may be attending a class for an hour or so.

Recognizing this situation, a number of companies have begun labor collection by exception (as recommended in the pilot specifications). In other words, the employee reports that he was in a particular production cell on a given day. Accounting assumes that he was working on products coming out of that cell. The laborer will then report any exceptions of an hour or more, such as doing rework, attending a meeting, or working in a different cell. Otherwise, all the worker's time is attributed directly to the products made by the cell.

If we collect labor by exception, however, how do we know how much direct labor is required for each product? In other words, how do we set a standard? We used to calculate an average of the closed work orders to establish a standard. Now, without work orders, we need another process. One method is to do an engineering time study. Another is to build a particular product a few times and temporarily keep track of the time required. It's not necessary to track every part all the time, but whenever there's been a process change, periodically we can verify that the standard is correct.

If we have a connected-flow cell with one product, we can compute the standard simply by dividing the total units into the total labor applied. The result is the true labor per unit. If the cell produces multiple products, one series followed by another, the same approach can be applied if the start and stop time of each series is recorded.

Knowing how much direct labor is required in a connected-flow cell that practices mixed-model production may or may not be more difficult. It is more difficult when the cell builds one product (A) followed by another (B), followed by another (A, C, A, B, A, C . . .), or when the time elements are too short for most products to be logically tracked, and the labor time required for each product type varies significantly. The same holds true of a disconnected-flow cell that follows mixed-model production. Again, the time elements may still be so small that it is not logically feasible to track each product at each operation, and it is even more likely that the standard time for each product type will vary substantially.

Historically, many companies have tracked labor by product and by operation. Since larger lot sizes resulted in longer overall times, recording start and stop times was practical. We could compare the actual time the lot took with the standard and recognize a variance if one existed. We would then try to ascertain the cause. Unfortunately, the best work-order-variance analysis can do is tell us which product suffered the variance; but it is weak in pointing out the cause. Perhaps the product with the variance just happened to be the one that first used a new box of common material that contained defects.

With Just-in-Time, we use kanban to alert us to constraints as they occur, eliminating the need to wait days or weeks for work orders to close so that we can glean the necessary information. With Just-in-Time, we use Total Quality Control to explain the cause of the variance. For difficult problems, the root cause typically lies four to six levels deep in the problem-analysis tree. (How we go about uncovering the root cause will be addressed in chapter 11 on Total Quality Control.) Even the best work-order systems can't consistently reveal why a variance occurred. They also can't consistently point us in the right direction, much less track a problem down several levels. Therefore, elimination of the work order does not hinder us in explaining why a variance occurred; in fact, it forces us to use Total Quality Control.

If labor is collected by exception, however, how do we know if there is a variance? We can easily calculate the total actual time spent in the area. Everyone simply reports the total amount of time they spent in the cell on a given day, deducting exceptions. It is also quite easy to compute the total standard hours earned by the cell if we know the standard and the total quantity of each item produced. The difference between the two is the variance for the cell. But how do we allocate the variance?

Previously, we may have avoided allocation of the variance, because it was attached directly to the work order that was unlucky enough to experience the problem. At other times, variances were allocated based on direct labor hours or machine hours used per product. Under Just-in-Time, those same allocation alternatives are still open to us, but inadequacies in current procedures are forcing many companies to seriously investigate activity based costing practices, which will be discussed later in this chapter.

OVERHEAD ALLOCATION

Just-in-Time also accelerates changes in overhead allocation. Some companies allocate overhead to the product based only on the direct labor content. This practice can generate some incorrect decisions. When a heavy overhead burden is computed against a small direct labor base, it looks as if it costs a lot more to make something in-house than it does to buy it. In fact, some companies buy products offshore because it appears least expensive. Actually, if our accounting system were capable of attaching all the applicable charges (negotiations, calls, travel, inspection, rework), we'd find that offshore purchasing is much more expensive than domestic purchasing and, in some cases, even more costly than making the product ourselves.

A few years ago at Hewlett-Packard, Fort Collins, the design engineers decided to buy some small cables outside because they couldn't afford our internal prices. This seemed strange, especially since the price they cited for our own cables was ridiculously high. The cables took only a few minutes to build. The problem was that significant amounts of overhead were being allocated to those cables that we built in-house, but no overhead was allocated to those we purchased. Allocating overhead exclusively on the basis of direct labor implied that setting up external suppliers, writing purchase orders, storing the cables, and all the other activities associated with purchasing were free. In reality, however, acquisition was much more expensive than the little bit of time it took to build the cable internally from existing materials.

Recognizing this discrepancy prompted a change in the allocation method. We converted to a tribase system. Some of the overhead was allocated based on direct labor, some based on material value received, and the rest was allocated according to throughput time in the factory. We used the tribase method for a short time, until most of the factory output had been converted to Just-in-Time and all our products required a very short throughput time. When one product took three days to build and another took two months, allocating on throughput time made a difference. Once all products could be produced in three to six days, throughput time was no longer a major issue. At that point, HP/Fort Collins adopted a dual-base system that computed overhead in terms of direct labor and material purchases. Further evolution in this area is leading to activity-based costing.

ACTIVITY-BASED COSTING

A recent study by the National Association of Accountants and Computer-Aided Manufacturing International reported that "companies are being held hostage by the inadequacies and inappropriateness of old management accounting practices." Many of the deficiencies of current cost systems are being exposed by competitive pressures and the changes prompted by the adoption of Just-in-Time. Most of the current approaches value inventory and do not help management understand process and product costs. Only when manufacturing costs are accurately measured and managed at the process level can managers begin to control product costs. Overhead is most companies' largest and fastest-growing cost component. Yet many systems continue to focus exclusively on direct labor costs, which today is normally the smallest component of total product cost.

The weaknesses of current accounting systems often lead to improper decisions regarding make versus buy, pricing, resource investments, and obsolescence. Unfortunately, these systems often encourage maintenance of the status quo rather than a shift to more competitive processes such as JIT/TQC. Managers who are to make the "numbers" come out correctly and are rewarded for it are usually reluctant to change, even when they are aware of potentially better methods. For the most part, we get what we measure, even when the measurements are inadequate.

Perhaps no one accounting system can adequately address the issues of inventory valuation, operational control, and product-cost measurement. However, a growing number of companies are investigating and implementing activity-based costing methods. The activity-based costing method, or cost-driver model, allows variances to be directly associated with the processes that produce them; the product itself is linked indirectly (see figure 8.2). One premise in activity-based costing is that

Figure 8.2
Traditional Cost Accounting vs Cost Drivers

	PROCESS	JOB ORDER	COST DRIVER
Product Unit Cost	Factory Avg	Lot Avg	Sum Avg Unit Cost Of All Processes
Cost Collection Basis	Accounting Period	Completion Of Lot	Accounting Period
Product Mix	Low Mix/ High Volume	High Mix/ Low Volume	Any
Cost Visibility Direct Indirect	Product Process	Product Process	Process Product
Variance Visibility Direct Indirect	Factory Product	Product Process	Process Center Product
Indirect Cost Application	All Cost Pooled	Factory Wide Base(s) eg DL & Mat'l	Cost Drivers By Process Center

SOURCE: HEWLETT-PACKARD

every process, manufacturing and overhead alike, has a single activity on which the cost center's figures vary most directly.

For example, the cost driver in purchasing may be a line item. Purchasing's costs vary more by the number of items it acquires than by the value of the material purchased. A machine-intensive area's costs may be determined by machine cycles or machine hours rather than by direct labor. However, applied-engineering labor hours may be the correct driver for manufacturing-engineering costs. Even assembly areas in some instances may be better measured by the number of pieces produced than by direct labor hours applied. To select the cost driver, it is helpful to determine if costs vary more by product volume or by process transactions. Ascertaining the primary activity of the process, which is the cost driver, should make it possible to trace costs to the responsible organizational level and to explain the cost variances in terms of the primary measures of process activity.

It should be noted that the intent of this book is not to present an in-depth analysis of alternative costing methods, but rather to point out some of the changes taking place in the financial community. Virtually every company today struggles with changes in the financial area. The trouble is not that the finance department is reluctant to change—it is usually no more resistant than other areas—but that the changes are difficult. Adherence to the status quo usually has more to do with the mind-set of the individual in charge of the functional area than with the area itself. The changes Just-in-Time drives are difficult for everyone, and finance is no exception. However, adopting a wait-and-see attitude is no solution. Form a team to study the constraints of current financial methods and develop logical alternatives. Then try them out in the pilot.

GENERAL ACCOUNTING

Accounts payable traditionally regulates purchasing transactions by means of the purchase order. When we receive the material, we match the accompanying packing slip with our purchase order and wait for the invoice to arrive. We in turn match the invoice with the packing slip and the purchase order, and then write a check. If this process continues, as a growing percentage of suppliers ship more and more frequently, accounts payable (not to mention purchasing and receiving) will be buried in an avalanche of paperwork.

Instead of paying upon each receipt, we could collect the receipts, get a composite invoice, and pay for the total on a periodic basis. This practice is already very common in other businesses, such as grocery stores. We could also use electronic funds transfers. When we received a container, we would run a wand over a bar code printed on it, thereby initiating a receiving transaction and a transfer of funds from one account to another. Once again, however, just because we are technologically capable of processing thousands of transactions at the speed of light, it does not necessarily follow that we should spend the money to do so. Unnecessary transactions, particularly if processed by expensive dedicated computer hardware, are wasteful.

A third approach, currently being practiced by Hewlett-Packard, Vancouver, with at least one supplier, eliminates the need for both receiving and invoicing transactions. The plastic housings for the printers HP/Vancouver builds come from only one source. At the end of an agreed-upon period, HP/Vancouver simply determines how many printers it has shipped and sends a check to its supplier. The procedure is mathematically correct, and with good vendor relations, frequent deliveries, and high quality, the risk is minuscule. The point is, there are ways to eliminate transactions besides simply automating them.

SUMMARY

While Just-in-Time sometimes gets the blame, or credit, for the reevaluation of current cost-accounting practices, the financial community is beginning to examine the need for changes anyway. Just-in-Time does not necessarily initiate all of the modifications that take place in accounting systems during its early stages. They were merely integrated with the Just-in-Time implementation in order to take advantage of an opportunity to change.

Our traditional practices are not necessarily wrong, but some are becoming obsolete. We do not need to feel guilty for having used them in the past, but we should feel guilty for trying to perpetuate inadequate methods in the future. We must work to ensure that our accounting systems and accounting personnel support rather than inhibit conversion to the new and more competitive manufacturing practices. Like all other areas, accounting too must adjust. There are no easy answers here, just difficult changes; the reward, however, is better information and, ultimately, a more efficient organization.

Chapter 9
Realigning Systems and Procedures

Never confuse motion with action.
—**Ernest Hemingway**

Maintaining a healthy body is not a matter of either eating correctly or exercising. We must do both to obtain our peak performance. Similarly, in manufacturing, we cannot choose between planning and execution. We must do both to compete. As mentioned in chapter 1, we need not decide between Just-in-Time and Manufacturing Resource Planning. Nor does it matter that one is a "pull" system and the other is a "push." Techniques differ, but the philosophies are compatible. Both seek to improve a company's ability to respond to change. If we are to compete effectively, we need excellence in planning *and* execution. However, to make JIT/TQC and Manufacturing Resource Planning work effectively together, we may need to make some software changes.

MATERIAL REQUIREMENTS PLANNING SYSTEMS

As one analyst/programmer put it, the initial software changes and enhancements that are required to support Just-in-Time are not major, nor are they minor. Typically, two to three man-months of effort are required to satisfy the breakthrough pilot specifications. The 120-day implementation plan allows time for these changes. The changes, however, should begin early in the pilot development stage to avoid a setback in the planned implementation date.

In addition, it is useful to remember that not everything need be done by the computer. It is acceptable to process some information manually, particularly for the pilot. During one implementation at Hewlett-Packard, we were wrestling with a needed change in the accounting system. Suddenly, it dawned on us that doing the job manually would require only one journal entry a month. We did not plan to make manual journal entries for all products on an ongoing basis. However, for the pilot project, it was the correct decision.

Often, companies with newer Manufacturing Resource Planning software packages find that they need to make no modifications and few enhancements when embarking on the Just-in-Time journey. Most other companies, however, will end up making some changes. The detailed-capacity-planning module is still functional after Just-in-Time has been implemented, but its purpose is often better served by simpler rough-cut capacity planning. There is usually no reason to purchase a detailed capacity requirements planning module after the implementation of Just-in-Time.

In Just-in-Time areas, rough-cut capacity plans are developed for key resources, such as key pieces of equipment and critical skills. As we begin to level the work in the factory by reducing lot sizes and building more to daily rates, we reduce the wild fluctuations that cause sporadic bottlenecks. Smoothing, therefore, allows us to concentrate on the consistently crucial areas. Some companies simply build a spread-sheet in a personal computer, placing product families down the side and key resources across the top. The amount of the key resource that is required is entered at the intersection and the master-schedule quantity is multiplied by the spread-sheet matrix to obtain a rough-cut capacity.

Others structure the key resources into the planning bills of material. When Material Requirements Planning is run, the requirements for each key resource are computed automatically.

Another significant planning change instigated by JIT has to do with the frequency with which Material Requirements Planning is run. In the past seventeen years I have gone full circle on this topic. After developing Hewlett-Packard's first successful Material Requirements Planning system in 1972, we quickly realized that weekly replanning runs were not sufficient to keep up with the changes on the shop floor. We struggled to run Material Requirements Planning two and three times each week. We desperately wished that we could afford on-line, real-time hardware and software, which was particularly expensive in those days, even for a computer manufacturer.

Today the hardware is available, to run on-line, real-time shop-floor-control software. However, now with Just-in-Time, weekly replanning is again acceptable. The simple but visual concept of kanban has eliminated the need for on-line, real-time processing capability. In fact, if we stop to think about it, we realize that the visual controls provided by kanban allow us to assess the situation on-line, in real time, at the speed of light, and then process the data with the most powerful computer of all, our mind!

As we move further into the JIT/TQC process, it may eventually become necessary to modify the master-production-scheduling module to accommodate rate-based planning. Initially, most systems simply translate the planned production rates per day into the weekly quantities expected by the master-production-scheduling system. In one of my production areas, we began to do rate-based master scheduling using a spread-sheet program, and then fed that data into the Manufacturing Resource Planning master-schedule file. Because it was not a major problem, we waited until several months later to modify the existing master-scheduling system to use rates.

BILLS OF MATERIAL

Where the bills-of-material module does not support phantom structures, that capability is frequently added. A phantom structure code instructs the software to act as if the structure level did not exist, except for selected purposes. When a product is converted to the Just-in-Time process, we may actually delete from the bill of material the various subassemblies that are no longer scheduled and produced separately. This is known as flattening the bill of material. However, it is not always desirable to flatten the bill altogether. We may want to keep the structure level for service or accounting purposes. Also, restructuring is time-consuming and may not seriously affect computer processing times. Therefore, at least during the pilot stages, most people code the unused structure levels as phantoms. Not all lower-level substructures need be coded as phantoms, but if they are, the result will be a single-level bill of material—a top-level product composed of purchased parts, since the phantom assemblies are ignored for most purposes. As time permits, and conditions warrant, we can actually flatten the bill-of-material structure and remove the phantom entries. New products introduced after the implementation of JIT/TQC, of course, should have a logically flattened bill from the outset.

INVENTORY SYSTEMS

We immediately encounter another potential software change as soon as we put material at the point of use. One of the most serious software shortcomings we find is the lack of capability for multiple on-hand balances for the same part number. This is the ability to recognize each quantity of a part stored in several locations, and is necessary when the same material is stored at the point of use in one or more cells as well as in an overflow stockroom. If this software capability is missing, material at the point of use is considered "issued" and thus not available for Manufacturing Resource Planning purposes; work-order allocations keep the planning process in sync. In a Just-in-Time environment without work orders, however, if material is considered "issued" rather than stored at the point of use, Manufacturing Resource Planning will direct us to order replenishments.

A possible solution is to put only a small amount of material at the point of use to minimize the financial impact of reordering. The side effect, however, will be an increase in material handling to replenish the line frequently. If we perform Just-in-Time correctly, we should see a reduction in material handling, not an increase.

Another possibility is to place a reasonable amount of material at the point of use, leaving the rest in the overflow stockroom. Manufacturing Resource Planning would know the total but not the amount at each location. This will keep planning straight, but it will make it difficult to reconcile inventory-record inaccuracies in all but the smallest factories. Without the multiple on-hand balance capability, you are not prevented from beginning Just-in-Time, but progress is hampered.

In chapter 4, I discussed how to determine how much material to put at the point of use. To replenish this material, kanbans are typically recirculated between the overflow stockroom (or supplier) and the cell. When the material is relocated from the overflow stockroom to the cell, the on-hand balance and value in the stockroom decreases and the cell increases by the same amount. As completed products are shipped from the cell, the on-hand balance and value of the component inventory in the cell decreases as the result of a backflush transaction. (See figure 9.1).

Figure 9.1
Accounting for Material at the Point of Use

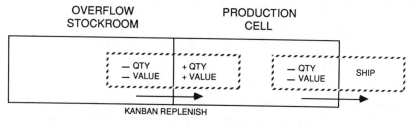

Figure 9.2
Accounting for Material at the Point of Use

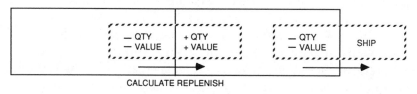

Figure 9.3
Accounting for Material at the Point of Use

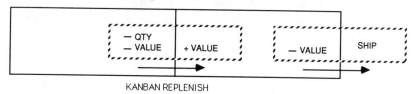

A variation of that replenishment approach was developed for a low-volume/high-mix environment by Jackie Reed and Gary Utter at NCR's COMTEN factory in Minneapolis. Their approach minimizes both handling and the preparation of kanban cards. It operates as follows: Material Requirements Planning is run weekly, using daily increments. Each day a "demand organizer program" is run that summarizes the planned requirements for each part coded to be stored at the point of use. If enough material is not on the floor to cover the next twenty-four hours of projected usage, a notice is given to the overflow stockroom to transfer material to a specific cell location (see figure 9.2). To determine how much material to transfer to the cell, the "demand organizer program" adds up past unfilled demands and adds projected requirements for, say, the next month. That projected quantity is transferred from the overflow location to the cell after package quantity and available space are factored in. Note that when the total inventory for a given item is the amount required for one month or less, it is all stored at the point of use. Once the material has been transferred from the overflow stockroom to the point of use, on-hand balances for both locations are adjusted accordingly. As products (or subassemblies) are completed, the onhand balance of the assembly or (sub-) is incremented, and the floorstock on-hand balance is postdeducted or backflushed. In this fashion, the quantity and value of material in each cell are tracked. Verification of the accuracy of the resulting records requires cycle counting.

At Northern Telecom's Research Triangle Park in North Carolina, however, Bill Boyst's team developed an approach that eliminates the need to cycle count. The environment is high volume/low mix, and throughput times are measured in hours. Point-of-use containers are physically sized not to exceed one week's supply of material. When a returnable kanban container is filled by the overflow stockroom, the stockroom value and the quantity of the material are reduced, but only the value of the material is added to the cell. Quantities are not tracked in the cell. When a product is completed by the cell, only the value is backflushed. Unless the cumulative value of material in the cell exceeds an upper or lower control limit, inventory is considered to be under control; there is no need to cycle count (see figure 9.3).

KANBAN TRANSACTIONS

One very common software change is made to the inventory-control module. This enhancement calls for one transaction after the completion of a product. It is designed to relieve the master schedule and/or increase the on-hand balance of the product, while also relieving the on-hand balances of the components used in production of the product. It is frequently called a postdeduct or backflush transaction, although it does more than just relieve the on-hand balance inventories. To convey the broader scope of the transaction, some have begun to call it a production kanban transaction.

Similarly, the purchasing module is often modified as suppliers are linked into the JIT/TQC process. When kanban is used to initiate replenishments, a single transaction figures the quantity and value purchased on the contract, adds to the on-hand balance in the storage location and initiates accounts-payable activities. This process is usually called a purchasing kanban transaction or blanket-order kanban transaction, since an individual purchase-order line item showing a release date and quantity is not expected for each receipt.

Let's take a closer look at the production kanban transaction. As previously mentioned, the method used most often to relieve inventory at the point of use, in both connected- and disconnected flow environments, is called "postdeducting" or, in common parlance, "backflushing." By way of illustration, the postdeduct transaction would take place once a product had been completed through operation 6 in the connected-flow diagram. (See figure 9.4) A single production kanban transaction is made to simultaneously deduct the completed quantity through operation 6 from the quantity left to build on the master schedule. That same transaction would extend the quantity shown on the bill of material and subtract that amount from the on-hand balance of each of the components that have been used from the cell's inventory. Hence the term "postdeduct": We've used the material, and we're telling the system after the fact (see figure 9.5).

Once material has been consumed, a postdeduct transaction should be processed at most within a few days: in most cases, you will inform the system within a few minutes or hours. There are times, however, when reporting may take longer. A delay of over a week can seriously

Figure 9.4
Production Kanban Transaction

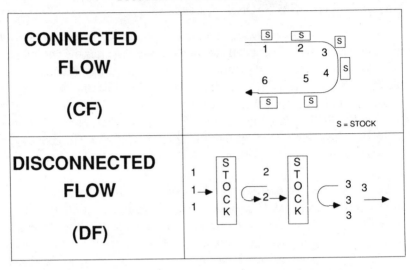

affect the Manufacturing Resource Planning system. There are exceptions, but when operations begin to exceed five days, most companies will postdeduct the material at intermediate points along the way as well as at the end, such as after steps 2, 4, and 6 in the connected-flow illustration, or after 1, 2 and 3 in the disconnected-flow diagram. (See figure 9.4). These postdeduct transactions will, therefore, occur at least every few days. As the throughput time speeds up, a company may decide to eliminate one of these intermediate reporting steps. And as velocities get even faster, the company may drop all intermediate points and simply postdeduct after the last operation.

Only the newest software packages are likely to include production-kanban-transaction capabilities. Those with older software will have to write their own program for this function. Essentially, this entails telling the computer the quantity of the product or subproduct we have just completed, including the engineering effectivity date or revision if applicable. The program should then look up the bill of material and create transactions to relieve the component inventories and reduce the master schedule total by the quantity completed. The postdeduct logic should search down through the bill-of-material structure chain, passing all phantom structures, until a "real" structure level is encountered.

Figure 9.5
Post Deduct

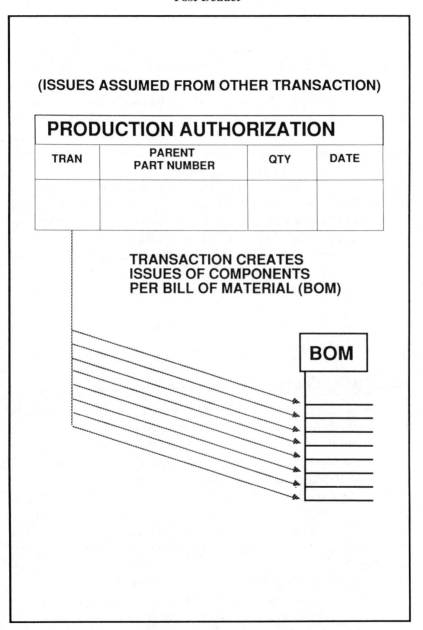

This "real" structure may be a purchased part of a lower subassembly level not coded as a phantom. If no subassembly levels are encountered, the bill of material basically appears to the postdeduct program as a single-level bill of material.

Most of the logic for the postdeduct portion of the program already exists in the work-order program that creates the stock picking list. Also, codes to search through the bill of material, recognition of engineering effectivity dates, and lookups in the on-hand balance file are already present. Therefore, it is not overly difficult or time-consuming to develop your own production-kanban-transaction program, but the job does need to be planned into the implementation schedule if it is to be completed in time for the pilot start-up.

To use the production-kanban-transaction capability, it is also necessary to be able to designate the location to relieve. By way of illustration, when a specified quantity of assembly "A" is completed, the production kanban transaction subtracts "one" from the master schedule and "one per" each component from the on-hand balance of the specified production cell. No work-order number is required.

Some companies expense low-cost items as they are moved onto the production floor in bulk quantities. These items should be on the bill of material but can be coded not to be part of the postdeduct process if that is desired.

INVENTORY RECORD ACCURACY

People sometimes believe that when you put material at the point of use it is all right to give up some inventory accuracy. That is incorrect. If you're going to use a Manufacturing Resource Planning system, you must have accurate bills of material and inventory records regardless of where inventory is stored. Remember, Just-in-Time does not replace the planning aspect of Manufacturing Resource Planning; putting material at the point of use is no excuse to lose accuracy. The transition, however, takes careful preparation. At one factory, accuracy actually rose from 75 to 99.8 percent when it moved its stock onto the line. When you initially make the changeover, it is reasonable to expect some sort of fluctuations in accuracy levels. You are, after all, changing a lot of things and involving new people. *You must identify and correct the root causes of inaccuracy problems when you put material at point of use.*

CYCLE COUNTING

Unless you adopt the Northern Telecom approach discussed earlier or your velocities are very slow, you will need to find a new way to cycle count material stored at the point of use. With even modest velocities, cycle counting on the line works only while production is stopped; otherwise, the material can be consumed and moved faster than it can be counted.

The trouble is, if the line is stopped and you use a traditional cycle counter from the stockroom, everyone but the counter must sit idle. As you probably suspected, with Just-in-Time it does not make sense to cycle count in the "same old way." Instead, the people in the production area should be held responsible for their own material. It's stored at their location; they should be the ones to control it. When you first start up, it helps to rotate someone from the stockroom to the production area. Stockroom people have certain skill sets with which people on the production line are not likely to be familiar. In a short time, however, you will not be able to tell the stockroom person from the production people. They form a team.

Now, suppose it has been decided that at 8:00 A.M. a given team is to count its inventory. Everyone in the production area gets a zone assignment. Operator 2 counts the appropriate part numbers at his position as well as what's on shelves A and B. Worker 3 counts the items at his position as well as the pre-determined items between positions 2 and 3, and those at location C. When you make these territorial assignments, every place where inventory might be stored is assigned. When the time comes to cycle counts, everyone tends to his assigned zone. The results are better than when one person must track down every location of a given part.

Each person should record the counts for each of the part numbers in his assigned areas. The computer, not the people, should sort the entries and develop the total for each part in the entire cell. However, during the pilot, this process can be handled manually until the appropriate software is developed.

Software support will be necessary in environments where a variety of high-part-count assemblies, such as circuit boards, exist in various states of completion throughout the line. We do not want to have to identify and count the installed components on each assembly that resides between operations 2 and 3. We want to report that we have one partially completed assembly between operations 2 and 3, and let the system figure out what components are in it. The system can then add that number to the total.

For this second function, the bill of material needs to reflect what components are used at each operation where a partially completed subassembly may exist. We have to know that part 123 is used in steps 1 and 6, and that part 456 is used in step 2. By applying some common sense and purging certain sections of the production pipeline, we find that the material content of the product must be ascertained only at a limited number of operations.

Total Quality Control is essential to establish and maintain inventory-record-accuracy. Our cycle count reconciliation data should include the reasons for any variances and the amount of each variance. If, for example, our records are wildly out of tolerance, that's one level of problem. If they are barely out of tolerance, that demonstrates a better level of control. We want to know the distribution of parts in or out of tolerance and how far in or out they are.

At the appointed time, everyone counts their territory and enters their numbers in the system. The system adds everything up and then compares the total counted cell quantity with the quantities the system has assigned to the cell. Rational tolerances can be allowed. If an item is within reasonable tolerance, the count will be accepted (for instance, a weight-counted item might be allowed a ± 5 percent deviation as long as the total deviation is under a certain value). If it's not, the system should produce an exception notice that tells which part is out of tolerance. For example, the system might show 110 parts and indicate that the cell counted only 100. Now, we have a quantity to look for and can try to reconcile it. Everyone need not be not involved in the reconciliation effort. Most of the team is needed to continue production, but one person can be assigned to complete the reconciliation.

RESPONSIBILITIES FOR INVENTORY-RECORD ACCURACY

Production people must take ownership for the accuracy and reconciliation of their own inventory. It is not the stockroom's responsibility to correct problems caused by production's stock areas. Ownership by production will make the crew more responsible and disciplined and discourage finger-pointing.

Each company can define which items it makes the most sense to count: and how frequently. As a general rule, it is best to minimize activity on the very minor items and concentrate on the 20 percent that represent 80 percent of the value stored at the point of use. This is not the same as traditional "ABC" analysis, which weights the material based on annual usage. Here risk is considered on the basis of the value stored at the point of use. Many variations are possible in the selection of which items to count, of course.

Storing material at the point of use necessitates a change in overflow-stockroom procedures as well. In some traditional environments, companies have maintained accuracy by counting by part number. The stockroom personnel count all locations of a given part number. If those items are in three locations in the stockroom, they count all three. Parts that have been issued to work in process are not part of the cycle-count process.

With Just-in-Time, there might be three raw-material storage locations for the same part number, one in the overflow stockroom and two in different production areas in the factory. To count by part number would be unreasonable; it would entail stopping two production lines just to count something in the overflow stockroom. Instead, the overflow stockroom is counted independently of the two production areas. Inventory is verified by part number and location rather than part number alone. That way, if the overflow stockroom wants to count a part in one of its locations, that's fine. If a production area wants to verify its inventory at a different time, that is okay also. If the counts for all locations are correct, it follows that the total is correct. If all are not correct, counts by location can be analyzed to show which areas most need to improve. Normally, if your information system is capable of maintaining on-hand balance by part number, the switch to counting by part number and location rather than part number alone is primarily procedural.

As you start looking at inventory-record accuracy with material stored at the point of use, a number of factors can emerge that contribute to errors. Not surprisingly, they are nearly the same ones that tend to be of concern with a locked stockroom, such as bill-of-material errors, count errors, and inadequate training both in counting and reconciliation. Many are procedural, having to do with the reporting of scrap, use of substitutions, and the processing of engineering changes. You've probably heard them: "Oh, I didn't count these parts. I didn't know there were any over there." "I counted them, but I didn't enter my transaction. I lost three pages." "Yeah, I counted them, but I didn't enter them into the computer until the next morning, because the computer was tied up." A major cause of record inaccuracy is not an open stockroom but a lack of adequate process controls.

In traditional environments, there are a number of inventory checkpoints. The material is received and counted, inspected, and counted again prior to being stored in the stockroom. Then it is counted again to be issued out of the stockroom, and often recounted when it is received at the production line. With higher velocities, each time this material is handled and counted, the chances for error increase.

One company, fairly well respected for it Just-in-Time program, was having difficulty maintaining inventory-record accuracy. They asked me to investigate. In the production area there were numerous Total Quality Control charts. None, however, existed outside of production, including in materials. After I was able to gather some data, I discovered that for certain items the system showed an inventory surplus which was equal to the deficit reported for other parts. The part numbers and locations varied from week to week, but the pattern was similar. Their errors stemmed from counting the material when it was received, when it was put away, when it was taken out of stock, when it was received in production, and again when it was used in production. As Just-in-Time enabled the company to increase velocities, they also experienced more chances to make an error. By storing material at the point of use rather than issuing it frequently, they were able to eliminate some of the handling and counting. In so doing, the firm also reduced the chances for error.

The way to control inaccuracies is to keep data on the kinds of things that are causing the problems. Then, the root cause of the problem can be determined and corrected. How this is done will be explained in greater detail in chapter 11.

COMPUTER-INTEGRATED MANUFACTURING

With batch production, a system's highest priority is to track labor and material, as well as to handle the scheduling and rescheduling of the shop and suppliers. In contrast, Just-in-Time's emphasis is on integrating information, solving problems, and regulating product flow; traditional tracking is much less important. That doesn't mean that with Just-in-Time we have to throw out all existing systems and start over completely.

As we begin to implement JIT/TQC, we experience an improved ability to respond. The improved responsiveness comes in part from the use of kanban authorizations. Kanbans allow for the elimination of lower-level work orders. They also relieve production control of the burden of opening and delivering work orders to the shop floor. Since material is stored at the point of use, the delay of creating a picking list from the open work order, picking the material and delivering it to the line is also avoided. Smaller lots resulting from reduced setup times allow for more frequent access to equipment and other resources. Quality improvements minimize unexpected delays in production, and the velocity through the factory is also higher due to smaller queues and shortened travel distances.

As other portions of the processes become faster, however, our traditional computer systems often emerge as a constraint to higher velocities. It is very common for companies to reduce their throughput times to the point where the process of taking a customer order and communicating it to manufacturing takes longer than the process of building the product. For example, when it takes fifty days to build a product and a week to get the order through the computer system, there may be no major concern over the order entry process. However, when production times drop to three days, it becomes obvious that taking a week to pass an order through the computer system is a waste of valuable response time. Changes have to be made.

To ease this constraint, companies have begun to integrate major blocks of computer modules. Modules for order entry, on-hand balance, master production scheduling, shipping, traffic, finance, and quality have become more integrated with the manufacturing processes.

As velocities increase, those portions of our processes that take a disproportionate amount of time will be exposed. In other words, Just-in-Time leads us to Computer Integrated Manufacturing. (As it is used here, the word "manufacturing" refers to the entire manufacturing company, not just the manufacturing function.)

By way of example, versions of the following process currently exist at a number of companies: The first person in the assembly operation queries the order-entry system and receives the unique configuration of a product to build, along with a bar-coded serial tag to place on the product. Intermediate operations wand the barcode and receive verbal and/or color graphic instructions on their terminals. As problems are noticed, data are entered into a computer to facilitate problem-solving. When the last operation wands the bar-code, the system verifies that the unique characteristics of the product match the customer order. It then prints out shipping papers, relieves the master schedule and the on-hand balances of the components, and updates the accounts-receivable file. This scenario integrates order entry, production, quality, planning, shipping, traffic, and finance and could even include the supplier and customer.

DESIGN ENGINEERING AND COMPUTER-INTEGRATED MANUFACTURING

We also find Just-in-Time leading us to Design for Manufacturability. Engineering departments today are experiencing mounting competitive pressures to design better products in shorter amounts of time. As a result, an engineer does not have the time to search for hours to locate an existing minor part, particularly when one can be designed in a matter of minutes. When the need arises near a new-product introduction date, the time constraint is especially acute. On the other hand, JIT/TQC drives purchasing to minimize the quantity of suppliers and part numbers. If design is adding new suppliers and designing new parts as fast as purchasing is reducing them, then we're getting nowhere. We must have faster and more manufacturable designs as well as fewer parts and suppliers. On top of that, we must do it all in less elapsed time. In other words, we must have our cake and eat it too.

The key to meeting all of these demands lies in the formation of design teams and the intelligent use of Computer-Integrated Manufacturing. To satisfy our needs, Computer-Integrated Manufacturing can be used to provide engineering with the tools to rapidly access approved material, parts, designs, processes, and suppliers.

Oftentimes we concentrate on the major design advantages a computer can provide to the design engineer, overlooking the smaller and simpler benefits. JIT/TQC focuses on the details. This area is no exception. We must make it easier to use an existing part than it is to design a new one. It is here that our integrated systems can help. The important thing to remember is that the information must be entered into the system with other users in mind. Various coding systems have been developed, such as Brisch Birn, Miclass/Multiclass, and Opitz. Categorizing information correctly will allow areas other than engineering to make use of it, such as purchasing and production. As stated before, JIT/TQC requires teamwork. The computer will have an increasing number of applications, which will not only simplify the design process, but integrate information for all customer/supplier relationships throughout the company. As with automation, JIT/TQC paves the path for this logical transition.

In addition, software tools are available now that help to quantify the ability to produce designs and highlight areas for improvement. General Electric has a package for electronic designs and Boothroyd and Dewhurst have one to help quantify aspects of mechanical manufacturability.

QUALITY-INFORMATION SYSTEMS

It is not surprising that often the savings gained by not tracking labor and material is spent tracking defects and process variations. This new effort, however, will help eliminate waste, because it will enable us to prevent defects and reduce variability about target values.

A quality-information system need not be computerized. I remember seeing what must have been more than a tenfold reduction in the number of defects at Mashusita's Quasar television factory in the Chicago area over an eight-year period. All Total Quality Control was done with paper and pencil. Nonetheless, computers are good at sorting and tabulating. There are also many software packages today for personal computers that offer very nice calculation and graphic capabilities. A well-designed package will provide the ability to examine data four, five, or six levels deep in the process. It is here that the root causes of most problems can be identified. In addition, it is useful to be able to examine the data across all process steps for a single product or product family, as well as to examine the data from all products for one process step. For example, an engineer may be interested in the product throughout all process steps, but the manager of an area may be primarily interested in the product that is causing the worst problems in his process. The ability to connect extraneous events to failures is also very useful. For example, if there were a power outage in the factory and we were able to record the time at which it occurred, a well-designed piece of software might be able to correlate that event to certain types of failures that could have resulted.

There is no need, however, to wait for computerized software to begin Just-in-Time or Total Quality Control efforts. Though computerized quality-information software is very helpful, it is not absolutely necessary. We will also probably find that over time, software emphasis shifts from labor and material tracking to quality tracking.

POWER TO THE CELL

In JIT/TQC, the cell acts as a magnet, drawing routine activities and support functions toward it—including the routine responsibility for planning and performance measurement. As a result, it is helpful for each JIT/TQC cell to have its own personal computer system with spread-sheet and word-processing software, in order to perform rate-based planning, rough-cut capacity planning, quality analysis and reporting, inventory control, production reporting, and report writing. The master production schedule and bills of material are often downloaded from the main computer to the cell, and the cell periodically sends production and inventory information to the host. The cell should have read-only access to all other relevant information on the main computer.

This setup departs from the traditional approach, with a central mainframe and central information-systems department, but it is the way of the future. Computers are becoming smaller, more powerful, easier to use, and less expensive, and more employees are becoming computer literate. JIT/TQC strives to delegate responsibilities and problem-solving to the lowest levels possible. It follows naturally that the cell will have local information-processing, planning, and analysis capability. It does not make sense to funnel all requests for information through the backlog of a central information-systems department when many of the demands can be satisfied within a properly equipped cell. The formal information systems department of the future will be responsible for providing the facilities and standards to process information, but the users will be responsible for its applications.

SUMMARY

In this chapter, as in others, the impact of Just-in-Time on information systems has been examined. While JIT/TQC is not a computer-dependent process, computers are effective in JIT/TQC environments, providing decision-makers with valuable information, facilitating analysis, and communicating information between the JIT/TQC process and other systems such as Manufacturing Resource Planning. The system changes necessary to help JIT/TQC continually and relentlessly hammer away at waste have been outlined, and the excellent opportunities offered by computers to establish an integral communication link between manufacturing and all other units have been explored.

Chapter 10
Developing the Thinking Worker

Nobody is going to lose their job because we get more productive.
—Ed McDevitt

Just-in-Time is people-dependent. It stimulates everyone to think about constraints to higher velocities. It demands and applies the often neglected talents of those most closely involved in the processes, the workers. Over the years, we have done a poor job of learning how to use our people's minds. We've hired a lot of hands, but we have rarely used the heads that go with them. We need to tap into the knowledge base of those who, on a daily basis, see the details of the operation. It has been said before, but it bears repeating: Intelligence is randomly distributed throughout the company. Manufacturing needs to develop and energize the *thinking worker.* Management, professionals, and workers must constantly be motivated and free to think about and implement improvements.

Grace Pastiak of Tellabs corroborates this point. "These [hourly employees] are the same people who go home at night and are deacons of their churches and presidents of their PTAs. They have tremendous problem-solving skills." JIT/TQC says, "Let these people have their say. They are the experts at what they do.

Omark Industries posts a drawing throughout their factory and on many announcements. (see figure 10.1). The message it carries is clear: Everyone has a brain, a mouth, and a heart. Beneath the drawing there is often an inscription: "Communicate! A shared decision is better than one that is handed down. Change should take place because the people make it happen. Get a team of people to work toward an objective—

Figure 10.1

shared responsibility! Find ways to let people put their ideas into practice. Recognize accomplishments." These are the ingredients that can propel Just-in-Time forward. They unleash a force that offers a company a problem-solver at every post.

This is exactly what is necessary in most environments. The difference between winning the championship and not even making the playoffs typically amounts to only a few points throughout the season. The difference between competing and slipping rests with how well we pay attention to detail. We must satisfy the basics just to survive; we must pay attention to the details to compete effectively. The reality is that the truly major, $10 million problems that face a manufacturer are fairly easy to identify. Fortunately, there aren't a lot of unnoticed $10 million problems lying around. There are, however, millions of ten dollar problems that go unnoticed and unresolved. If we leave the solution of these problems to a few engineers and managers, we're never going to make enough progress, first, because they don't see them, and, second, because they don't have the time to deal with them. Problem-solving and process improvement must be delegated to as many people as possible. Essentially, JIT is a way to develop people into problem solvers.

In fact, one of the best ways to develop and foster the thinking worker is to implement JIT/TQC. It forces people to think. Necessity breeds innovation, and JIT/TQC is at its best in making the need visible. Opportunities surface, and as we will see in chapter 11, on Total Quality Control, it doesn't always take an engineer or manager to meet the demands of these increased opportunities. Properly encouraged and motivated, the thinking worker becomes the core element for generating a successful JIT/TQC implementation.

At several Hewlett-Packard sites in Colorado, whenever a team completed a difficult Total Quality Control project, the story and their photos were displayed in a high-traffic area. This recognition was one way to thank them for their efforts. It also served to inform others of the improvements that were made, while teaching them many of the techniques of the problem-solving process. Often, there were several stories posted at once. Without the employees' active and willing participation in problem solving, JIT/TQC is just another management wellspring gone dry.

Walter Goddard, President of Oliver Wight Education Associates, tells a story about two rather different ways of handling the involvement of the thinking worker. "Everybody's in favor of having a suggestion program," he said, "and everybody recognizes the importance of it, but let me tell you how not to do it. Many years ago, in my youth, I was on the suggestion committee for a company that had about 1,600 employees. We had a quarterly program to reward the ten best suggestions. To encourage participation, we displayed the prizes in the company cafeteria. The best suggestion won a television set, and the next nine won clock radios. We barely squeezed out 100 suggestions, and that was with a lot of arm-twisting.

"Many years after that, I went to Japan, and when they made the request for suggestions, they received an astronomical number. The key to the number the Japanese acquired was in the percent of the suggestions that were accepted—close to 80 percent at some of the Japanese firms. Suddenly the light went on. I wasn't on the suggestion committee—I was on the suggestion rejection committee.

"We got 100 suggestions from our people, sifted out the ten best because that's how many prizes we had, made a big deal about awarding the prizes, and didn't realize the message that we were sending out to the other ninety people. They were all good suggestions. We were simply finding the best ones, but we were sending out rejection notices. Three months later, when we'd say, 'Send all your suggestions in,' we would barely get 100, with more arm-twisting. If we'd accepted 80 of the 100, we would have got 200 next time. We would have turned our people on rather than turned our people off."

This chapter will cover the profound impact Just-in-Time has on the factory population. In it, we will take a close look at the changes affecting performance evaluation, job categories, team building, employment stability, retraining, compensation, leadership, and employee attitude.

PROBLEM-SOLVING RESPONSIBILITY

With JIT/TQC, as the thinking worker develops, we may find ourselves wishing we had more design or manufacturing engineers to take care of all the opportunities that are presented. But hiring more engineers may be the least effective way to deal with this constraint. The right answer is to decide what takes an engineer to solve and what doesn't and let the appropriate level of worker worry about the problem. Not everything takes an engineer to solve, as this illustration from Beckman Instruments points out.

Early in its Just-in-Time introduction, whenever the line stopped for problems or because schedule was met, Beckman's line employees chose to spend their time on product improvements. In one instance, they contacted the supplier of a troublesome plastic part and proposed their ideas. They soon learned that the part could indeed be made more reliably and, at the same time, less expensively.

They also worked to reduce the number of fasteners needed to enclose the subassembly within a metal frame, bringing the figure from seven to two. After marking up the appropriate design prints with the proposed changes, they called in the design engineer to review them. Following discussions, he approved the fastener changes on the spot. Should seven fasteners have been used in the first place? Perhaps not, but should an expensive design engineer be used to reduce the number of fasteners or to design new products? If the line workers had not followed through, the problem would probably still exist today. In Beckman's case, the product design was improved, the designer learned how to better his new designs, and a design/manufacturing bond was strengthened to enhance new designs.

By employing the thinking worker, we can minimize the time actually required by the designer to effect the needed changes. It is not unusual, however, for the sheer number of changes to eventually to lead to an organizational change as well. In many companies, all engineering changes must go through central design engineering. But as we get everyone in the loop thinking about problems, a lot of opportunities for change surface. It's not uncommon to see engineering flooded with requests. Designing a new product is difficult enough to do without constantly being interrupted with an endless series of minor improvement proposals. When it comes to allocating scarce time either to minor changes on an existing product or to meeting design schedules for a new one, the designer's choice is easy: He meets schedule. However, the more requests are ignored or delayed for long periods of time, the fewer ideas to eliminate waste we are going to have in the future. We must find a way to design efficiently *and* change responsively.

Some companies cluster noncritical changes and process them on a periodic basis through an engineering change cell. The cell contains all the people and skills needed to make a swift decision. Other companies are beginning to see the wisdom in having a design group and a manufacturing- or sustaining engineering group. One works on new products, and the other sustains existing products. The manufacturing-engineering team typically reports to manufacturing and is responsible for released products. It has full authority to make product and process improvements.

Initially, Hewlett-Packard, like many companies, had a central design group. When an engineer finished a product design, he followed the design into manufacturing for six months to a year. This was one way for manufacturing to maintain engineering support. The process worked fairly well, but manufacturing was staffed with engineers whose hearts were in design and whose attitudes were only temporarily in manufacturing. In the next stage, manufacturing hired a limited number of permanent engineers, while the design engineers continued to rotate through with their products. In this situation, there was at least a core of people who were dedicated to manufacturing. In the final stage, manufacturing acquired a full contingent of engineers, whose job was to make any required changes to a product that was released into manufacturing. Design engineers still rotated into manufacturing with their products, but manufacturing engineers rotated into design as well, so there was some cross-training for both groups.

We sometimes hear that all design engineers should spend the first few years of their careers in manufacturing so that they can appreciate the problems faced by production. Though this would probably be beneficial, it does pose some difficulties. In some high-tech environments, the half-life of an engineer's knowledge is only five years. Putting him on the production floor for two or three years to gain some manufacturing experience, will reduce his useful life in design. We need to ensure that design engineers have an understanding of manufacturing, but they must be able to use their engineering knowledge while it's still valid. This is where teamwork becomes very important. For example, at a number of factories, the cells that will eventually make the product itself build early prototypes for engineering. In this way, manufacturing is able to provide direct feedback on the design, and some manufacturing experience is contributed to it.

PERFORMANCE EVALUATIONS

When it comes to performance evaluations, consideration and thought are also needed. Many companies use the closed-work-order data as a tool to evaluate direct labor performance. Actually, "tool" is probably not the right word; it is used more as a whip. In reality, the data may not be worth the paper it's written on, but it can nevertheless still be quite intimidating.

The closed-work-order data describes how well the employee is meeting performance standards and quality levels. After implementing Just-in-Time and eliminating work orders, we no longer generate this type of data. It is not a major loss. After all, almost everyone else in the company is evaluated on a subjective basis. Take, for instance, the way in which we evaluate a secretary; we certainly don't do it by counting the number of keystrokes made on a typewriter. The process is more personal. The same is true with clerks, managers, and engineers.

When a company implements Just-in-Time, it finds that there are five categories by which it can judge direct labor employee performance. It still looks at *quantity* and *quality,* but now it also has to include an evaluation of the *ideas* people offer. We want to encourage people to think. We want them to come up with answers about how to reduce the number of kanbans in the pipeline and how to improve product manu-facturability. We want to look at how they interact in teams. Teamwork is critical, because we have so many customer/supplier links throughout the process, we need people to share and rotate jobs in order to maintain balance. Therefore, another performance criterion is *flexibility.*

These five—quantity, quality, teamwork, ideas, and flexibility—are approximately equal weight in an evaluation. As with so many other areas, Just-in-Time makes us look differently at these categories. Quan-tity is still quantifiable, but it is now based more on the output of the team as opposed to the individual. Here we must also take into consid-eration that each team is controlled by its customer's needs and sup-plier's output.

Quality also can be measured in a quantitative manner. However, what we find is that many of the quality issues are not and never were under the operator's control. Rather, there was something inherently wrong with the design or the incoming material. And while it may be possible to trace a problem down to a specific person, it may not be his fault. We should attack the problem, not the person.

Actually, the word "fault" drives people to hide problems rather than expose them. When we try to get quantitative data on quality defects, we often seem to be seeking to blame someone. That's not what we're looking for with JIT/TQC. We want to understand the cause of the trouble. If a worker is honestly trying to do his job correctly but is still having difficulty, it is not his fault. *Problems have causes, not faults.* It is management's responsibility to understand the cause of the problem (training, design, etc.) and correct it.

Measuring ideas is also subjective. It may be easy to assess who proposes the greatest number of ideas, but to weigh those ideas is more subtle. Teamwork is also subjective. Evaluating how well people get along together can be ticklish.

Flexibility is one area that can be readily quantified. Omark Indus-tries, Tellabs, and others use a simple cross-matrix system to chart an employee's cross-training and flexibility. The workers' names are listed down one side of a graph and the various skill sets required are listed across the top. As the employees become certified in the different skills,

Figure 10.2
Omark Cross-Training Chart

	Heading	Zinc & Clean	E.R.H.T.	OPICS	Heat treat	Export	Degrease	Tooling	Other
Jeff	X			X	X				
Mike					X	X		X	
Ann		X	X				X		
Chris	X			X		X	X	X	
David		X						X	X
Pat	X		X	X					
Ellen					X	X			

the corresponding box is colored in (see figure 10.2). It can then be quickly ascertained how flexible a worker is.

A change may also occur in whose responsibility it is to evaluate personnel in a Just-in-Time cell. Various approaches are being used today. The most common is still for the supervisor to appraise his subordinates. In many companies, the supervisor has the primary input, but the team also has a say, particularly when it comes to evaluating teamwork.

At one Tektronix factory, the team was entirely responsible for assessing its members. The operators loved it and said they wouldn't have it any other way. This is certainly not the most common method, but with Just-in-Time many new alternatives develop, just as many procedures that were once common practice become obsolete.

JOB CATEGORIES

Prior to Just-in-Time, it was not unusual for manufacturing to be broken into dozens of job categories. This practice tended to place people in various pigeonholes, however, and when the company looked for flexibility, it was easy for the worker to say, "That's not my job," or "I'm on a different pay scale." Essentially, job categories inhibit adaptability. As a company seeks to maximize flexibility, the trend is to reduce job categories to as few as two or three. For example, TABC (formerly Toyota Auto Body) in Long Beach calls their hourly factory employees "associates." That is their job category. Another name would be simply "employees".

It is very difficult to minimize job categories, due to a number of factors. First, people's pay structures are often at stake. Many companies want to minimize job categories without causing their payroll costs to go up. If there is just one category, however, and everyone is at the top of it, then payroll costs could rise. AT&T in Oklahoma City, a unionized shop, lowered the number of its categories to three, but if a worker met certain cross-training criteria, he could move up in his category. Of course, it is not likely that everyone will move to the top of each category, and AT&T felt that the flexibility it gained was worth the payroll increases that did occur.

Unions usually do not make the process of minimizing job categories any easier. Though unions are often blamed for the plethora of job categories, nonunion shops also tend to have a lot of job categories. The main difference between unionized and nonunionized companies in this regard is that the latter don't have the luxury of blaming this problem on the unions. They have to blame themselves. It is highly unlikely that a company will officially minimize job categories company-wide prior to implementing Just-in-Time. It is not unusual, however, for the pilot implementation to serve as a learning and operating model for what is to come. A number of companies, both unionized and not, have used the pilot to help bridge this change. The Just-in-Time production cell is manned with employees who volunteer to be part of the pilot. They understand that there will be only a couple of labor grades, and within a short time they understand why that is necessary.

Both union and nonunion shops are choosing to ignore established job categories during the pilot stages and beyond. The jobs may still officially be on the books, but they are being disregarded until they can be formally minimized.

TEAM BUILDING

As a company moves into Just-in-Time, teamwork within and especially among departments needs improvement. You can never have too much teamwork. The key, as explained in chapter 2, is to understand how to build teams.

At a multidivisional, personnel-manager meeting at Tektronix, one attendee inquired if more classes on communications skills and interpersonal development would be required when JIT/TQC was started. Classes such as these can be useful, but one of the best ways to build a team is to pick a problem, put a team together, give them some problem-solving skills, and let them solve it. Few things unite a team better than solving a problem together.

We know that in sports being on a team means facing challenges together. Attacking this common adversity creates a rapport and encourages understanding of each other. We see this is true in Outward Bound schools, too, where executives go out and challenge themselves as a team. *Working on a problem together builds teamwork.* And this does not mean only horizontal teams among peers. As we will see in chapter 11 on Total Quality Control, it applies to vertical teams that cross different organizational levels as well.

EMPLOYMENT STABILITY

Teamwork to eliminate problems is one matter. Eliminating a worker's job is quite another affair. Whether it's stated or not, one of the earliest concerns people have about Just-in-Time has to do with how it will affect their job. This issue must be addressed.

If we crush throughput time by 75 percent, it does not mean that 75 percent of our workforce will be laid off. We're still working on a product, just as we used to, but we're taking the wait time out. We're eliminating the queues. People need to understand that reducing the throughput time does not correlate directly to releasing people.

However, as we improve, or especially if we do not improve, there will be an impact on the labor force. Following the Just-in-Time path means that we are dedicated to the systematic elimination of waste. We are trying to reduce the non-value-added labor. This includes indirect labor such as material handling. It also encompasses direct labor involved in rework or inspection and overhead activities.

As work orders and purchase orders are eliminated and kanban is implemented, we will also have less need for traditional production-scheduling and accounting personnel. We will, however, see a higher-level job emerge that blends order entry and planning into one function. The employees will then be able to establish production rates and promise orders against the planned rate per day. As for the impact on traditional accounting, the time saved in that area can be well used to explore and implement improved costing methods such as activity-based costing.

Although people's jobs change, there is still plenty of work to do. As we reduce waste in one area, the people displaced must be retrained to work in another area that is in need of help. The purchasing function, for instance, changes from opening a catalog and placing an order for a part to a much higher-level position requiring a person capable of negotiating long-term win-win contracts. We're moving away from a simple order placer to a more professional supplier manager. We also develop a need for professional-level traffic managers who are capable of setting up transportation contracts and standard routings. What happens to the people previously in these areas? Where do the new people come from?

As inspection operations are eliminated, the affected personnel can become heavily involved in tracking Total Quality Control data and performing some of the problem-analysis legwork for the cell. These employees are usually already trained to handle data. An inspector might also work to teach a supplier Just-in-Time techniques. Xerox was able to reduce its incoming inspection team from 225 people to 40. They then doubled their field-supplier quality-engineers staff, using former inspectors, to work with their suppliers. At Hewlett-Packard we found that after Just-in-Time, supervisors could manage more people. At Fort Collins, however, we decided to maintain the same number of people per supervisor, but have the supervisor do more problem-solving.

In most traditional environments, there are a lot of people performing non-value-added activities. As we get better at Just-in-Time, jobs are redefined and we don't need as many of the nonvalue-added operations.

Nevertheless, there is plenty of useful work that still needs to be accomplished. We must have a formal plan and process to train and retrain our people. Laying off the displaced workers and attempting to hire others who already possess the needed skills will, for the most part, be very unsuccessful. *We will not progress very far with Just-in-Time if we ask people to help make the company more productive and then lay them off every time they do.* If the company can't or won't make a reasonable attempt to retrain employees when their jobs change, then waste elimination will be limited to those functions performed by managers who are assured of not being displaced.

Tellabs' vice president of operations, Ed McDevitt, stood up in front of his people and announced, "Nobody is going to lose their job because we get more productive." He explained that the company was going to take a long-term approach. If the company decided it no longer needed someone in inspection, it would find something else for the effected personnel to do. Obviously, savings would not be realized until Tellabs was able to avoid hiring another person. But they were willing to take the long-term approach. McDevitt also added, however, that if orders took a nosedive, then all bets were off. If there weren't enough orders to support the business, he couldn't guarantee any jobs.

When implementing Just-in-Time, we have to make sure each worker understands that he is not an inspector or a scheduler or a material handler; he is an employee of the company. He just happens to be performing a particular job at the moment. In three months, he may be doing something else. But he will be doing something that is still necessary.

Another company couldn't make the kind of statement Tellabs did. It already had too many people, and it hadn't even started Just-in-Time. It had to begin the process without making such promises. Implementation was a little more difficult, but the company was eventually successful, because the workers were able to sense a sincere commitment to fairness. Also contributing to its success were a strong upper-management champion and impressive results in the early pilot.

A third company was in the middle of laying off in heavy doses and wanted to do Just-in-Time at the same time. It turned out the people working there were very motivated to do Just-in-Time, because they saw the handwriting on the wall. They would have nothing left unless they got their acts together.

The bottom line is that management has a moral and ethical obligation, if it asks its employees to become more productive, to try to take care of them.

At HP in Northern Colorado, permission to hire from the outside was not granted if there were excess people available from other departments or nearby divisions. We were required to transfer and retrain if necessary. When the economy took a downward turn, instead of laying people off, the company gave everyone an equal pay cut. There were times when employees were paid only 9 days out of 10, but everybody, including the top managers, was on the same payment schedule. Another solution might lie in job sharing. While this would be an administrative problem under normal conditions, it might be something the cell members could handle themselves. Still another solution is to use temporaries, who generally don't want to work full-time.

A factory in San Diego, California, had an intriguing program. They had a list of preferred retired people whom they would bring in for temporary work. These people were available quickly. They weren't interested in making a lot of money, but working gave them some extra income. The program was good for the community, the company, and the senior citizens.

Another way to avoid laying people off is to make selected products in-house instead of buying them, even if they are more expensive, until employment reaches the desired level through attrition, early-retirement programs, or retraining.

The point is that it's not good to let people go. Ethical reasons notwithstanding, these people know the company. They're valuable people and we need their skills. However, one thing should be clear: As JIT/TQC changes the company, jobs will change also. We have no ability to stop change. All we can do is control it ourselves and not let the competition do it for us.

RETRAINING AND CROSS-TRAINING

To return to a point made earlier, a key way to maintain employment stability is through retraining programs. One of the best retraining programs I am familiar with is at Hewlett-Packard, Fort Collins. The company begins by evaluating the skills of its employees. It then establishes the skill sets it will need in the future in light of changing technology, analyzing where skill gaps are likely to occur. HP then puts together a curriculum of courses to bridge those gaps.

If there isn't one school in the area that covers the whole spectrum of your curriculum, as in HP's case, you will need to put together a mixture of courses from the various educational sources available to you. At HP, the student attends class on company time but does homework on his own time. Instructors are brought into the factory whenever it is possible and the demand is sufficient. Otherwise the student attends an outside school.

HP believes it is the responsibility of the company to provide the necessary education to help employees keep up with the changing technology and HP's changing needs. It is the responsibility of the employee to take advantage of the opportunity.

People need to understand that we are entering an age of lifelong learning. Change is accelerating. To go to school and then stop the learning process will no longer be acceptable. We know that the company must remain competitive in its product offerings in order to survive. The same is true for the company's employees. They too must remain competitive in the skills they have to offer. The retraining process is crucial for JIT/TQC, which is precisely why the personnel function is an integral part of the implementation team.

Maintaining employment stability, then, is one objective of retraining. We want to keep loyal employees by providing them with the needed skills for the future, while also improving the company's performance and flexibility. These factors should also be taken into consideration when hiring new employees. We should continue to seek workers who are able to produce high-quantity and high-quality work, but we should also evaluate their ability to contribute ideas, willingness to learn and perform multiple jobs, and capacity to work effectively in a team. Before hiring new employees, however, it is important to verify that adequate positions are available for those already in-house who will eventually require retraining.

COMPENSATION

As we reduce job categories and people start to work as members of teams, we may have to alter our compensation practices. There are, of course, many different kinds of pay structures. One approach would be to pay everyone the same amount. Others would be to pay by seniority, use merit pay or incentive pay, or implement profit sharing.

Let's first consider incentive pay. If a worker is paid by the piece, his incentive is to make as many as he can, independent of anyone else. When practicing Just-in-Time, however, we must operate under a kanban ceiling. To exceed the ceiling and outproduce our customer is against the rules. Incentive pay encourages the employee to produce independently; Just-in-Time forces the employee to be linked to his customer and supplier. We send the employee conflicting messages when we attempt Just-in-Time while using piece-part incentive pay.

An alternative is to use group rather than individual incentives. Even here, however, the group is tied to the consumer, whether that's another operation, another group in the factory, or consumers external to the company. Knowles Electronics' factory, south of London, discontinued piece-part pay in its first pilot. When the company solicited volunteers to man the pilot, one of the conditions for selection was that incentive pay was to be abolished. Knowles was careful to explain, however, that the new pay rate would be based on each person's typical earnings under the old incentive approach. The company was not trying to cut its workers' pay; it was just trying to administer it in a manner that would stimulate teamwork and foster implementation of JIT/TQC practices.

Another type of incentive is profit sharing. Here, the whole company shares in the profit of the company. Many Just-in-Time companies have found that giving the worker part ownership in the process reassures him that he is truly receiving the benefits of his hard work. Correct implementation of profit sharing is critical, of course. Unfortunately, compensation issues never seem to be simple.

Another form of compensation is skill-based pay. The more skills the worker possesses, the more he is paid. A similar alternative is something called skills-influenced pay. Essentially, with skill-based pay, every time a worker masters a new skill, he receives a certain increase in pay. A problem with this approach arises when a skill becomes obsolete; should the pay raise then be taken away? With skills-influenced pay, the more skills the worker knows the higher he is ranked in the flexibility area on his performance evaluation. As skills and flexibility increase, the worker's merit rating and compensation go up too. When wrestling with how best to reward people for learning new skills, Diana Kreitling of Tellabs formed a management/worker task force, which devised a skills bonus plan called Inve$tment in Quality. Essentially, each worker is required to know a certain base level of skills for his particular work area. Other useful skills in that area, or those interfacing with that area, are identified as well. Then, whenever an employee is certified in a new skill, he receives a one-time bonus of $100. Each time he becomes certified in five new skills, he is given an additional one-time bonus of $500. This approach does not permanently inflate the payroll, yet it gives the employees incentive to learn new skills.

LEADERS AND MANAGERS

As I got deeper and deeper into JIT/TQC, I struggled to understand why there seemed to be so many managers who were unable to grasp the concepts behind it. How could something so simple be so hard to comprehend? I later came to realize, as I said in chapter 1, that it is not the JIT/TQC concept that is difficult—it is the fact that it requires leadership. Over the years, when we either had no competition or were oblivious to it, administering the status quo well was highly regarded. Unfortunately, today we must not only administer well but also lead change at an ever accelerating pace. The problem is that some companies have too many people in leadership positions who have weak leadership skills (see figure 10.3). While JIT/TQC is one of the safest and most beneficial ventures a company can undertake, it seems risky. It is not rational to expect everything that hinders implementation to change before we begin. We must get started despite the obstacles in our path. This requires a risk taker, a leader.

Where leaders exist in a nearly unbroken chain from the top manager on down, JIT/TQC moves very quickly. Where nonleaders dominate the organizational structure, the process of change is slow and difficult. Make certain you identify the leaders and nonleaders when you first embark on the JIT/TQC journey. Then, support the leaders while motivating the nonleaders either to help or get out of the way during the pilot efforts.

Fortunately, those nonleader managers who are not on the critical implementation path have more time to adjust to these changes than others do. In one very successful implementation, a manager in the production area was hampering the effort. The people on the line were ready to try JIT/TQC, as were the key support staff and upper manage-

Figure 10.3
Differences Between Leadership and Management

LEADERSHIP	ADMINISTRATION
DOING THE RIGHT THING	DOING THINGS RIGHT
EFFECTIVENESS	EFFICIENCY
LEADING OTHERS	MANAGING YOURSELF
EMPOWERING OTHERS	POWER
CONSENSUS	COMPLIANCE
SOCIAL ARCHITECTURE	ORGANIZATIONAL CHART
CREATING VISIONS	SETTING GOALS
KNOWING WHY	KNOWING HOW
PROBLEM FINDING	PROBLEM REACTING
PROBLEM ELIMINATION	PROBLEM REPORTING

(Based on information by Suzanne Schneider of Burroughs and Karin Kolodziejski of Tektronix)

ment. The implementation probably would have stalled if top management hadn't recognized its responsibility and reassigned the problem manager. When everyone saw that top management was committed to the pilot, the implementation blossomed.

As the entire factory begins to convert to JIT/TQC, management and personnel will have to help the weak leaders adopt the new methods. Management must create an environment conducive to change. If the penalty for making a mistake is severe, most people will maintain the status quo. If we want people to feel the freedom to take a risk, they need to sense the freedom to fail once in a while. We must reward people for thinking correctly and not only for good results.

In situations where people are afraid to change, I sometimes talk with upper managers about granting a 180-day grace period. This allows them to follow the 120-day implementation plan, correct a few bumps in the process, and still show good results in 180 days. On the other hand, if the hesitant middle manager fails to start the change process after a few months, everyone will realize that the risk is mounting because the grace period is dwindling rapidly.

We also must recognize that not all of our existing managers will be able to adapt to their new environment. JIT/TQC requires action-oriented management. Simply planning, organizing, controlling, monitoring, and reporting is inadequate. JIT/TQC expects management to recognize that it is everyone's responsibility, especially its own, to aggressively remove exposed constraints to higher velocities.

SUMMARY

People must recognize that global competition is accelerating the rate of change. We are entering an era of lifelong learning, and we need to keep current to compete. Everyone must understand and acknowledge that intelligence is evenly distributed throughout the organization, so that all areas will be able to contribute. The whole company must be dedicated to the process of change. Management has to create an environment in which ideas can blossom. It also must assure its employees that it will do all that is ethically and economically possible to keep them employed and competitive as the changes occur. *There is no way to stop change. The only choice we have is to control the change ourselves or let our competitors control it for us.*

Implementing the correct personnel policies in conjunction with JIT/TQC will help a company rise above the competition. It will create a powerful, thinking work force ready to respond to and eager to drive change.

Chapter 11

Solving Problems Using Total Quality Control

Problems have causes, not faults.
—**Bill Sandras**

Just-in-Time is one side of the competitive coin. The other side is Total Quality Control. Just-in-Time exposes problems and stimulates us to think about them. Unfortunately, no amount of wishful thinking is going to make these problems go away. We have to do something more. We must have an effective process for problem-solving. This is why Just-in-Time *forces* the use of Total Quality Control.

If you implement Just-in-Time, you will practice Total Quality Control. It makes no sense to implement Just-in-Time, deliberately expose constraints, and then not have an effective process to make those constraints disappear. As I have demonstrated throughout this book, constraints, problems, and opportunities are all the same thing.

It has been suggested that Total Quality Control can be implemented without Just-in-Time. In theory that is correct, but it is extremely rare. When Total Quality Control is attempted without Just-in-Time, usually very little happens. Sometimes, there are isolated pockets of success, usually in production. Usually, under 10 percent will successfully implement Total Quality Control company-wide without Just-in-Time. These successes stem from relentless pushing by a top-management champion. However, when top management places emphasis on both Just-in-Time and Total Quality Control, the rate of success is much higher. While management promotes Total Quality Control, Just-in-Time forces its use. Of course, both benefit from the involvement of top management, but the continuous improvement driver behind Just-in-Time makes it necessary to use TQC to eliminate visible constraints.

Just-in-Time and Total Quality Control are synergistic. They are more powerful together than apart. Just-in-Time exposes a problem and forces action. Total Quality Control is used to solve the problem. Just-in-Time exposes the next problem. Total Quality Control is used to solve it, and the process continues. There is no long-term advantage in doing one without the other.

THE PRINCIPLES OF TOTAL QUALITY CONTROL

Establish a Commitment to Continuous Improvement

The same commitment that is required for Just-in-Time is necessary for successful implementation of Total Quality Control. With Just-in-Time, we ask, "If we have 1,000 kanbans, why not 999?" Similarly, with Total Quality Control, we must ask, "If we have 1,000 defects per million, why not 999?" Both processes engender a continual and relentless dedication to improvement.

Just-in-Time has taught us that it is the responsibility of each individual never to pass on a known defect anywhere within the process, including to the customer. According to John Young, Hewlett-Packard's CEO, "Quality is not something you delegate; you must do it yourself." Thus, the quality-control department becomes a quality-audit or quality-advisory department. We move from inspecting the quality of products to building quality into them. A change in thinking occurs as each person becomes responsible for continuously improving his own quality and no longer expects the quality-control department to check for mistakes.

Gather Data

We quickly find that without the facts, we cannot get to the root cause of the problem. As we will see later on, the root cause lies deep under the surface. Emotion and casual analysis do not expose it; we must use facts.

Gathering data, however, demands a willingness to face existing problems honestly. It is very tempting, when upper management asks how things are going, to say that everything is just fine and that there are no problems. With Just-in-Time and Total Quality Control, both the question and the answer as stated are inappropriate. It would be better to ask, "What problem is currently exposed?" If the answer is none, it is time to lower the inventory to expose the next "rock."

With JIT/TQC, problems are a given. We are expected to have a problem exposed, as well as to know our next step to improve competitiveness. The quickest way to become noncompetitive is to allow large numbers of employees to remain oblivious of or apathetic to their opportunities to eliminate waste. It is only through an attention to detail involving everyone in the process that true excellence can be achieved.

Assign a Clear Responsibility for Action

Very few problems of any consequence involve just one person. The difficult problems involve multiple organizations and multiple skill sets. Nevertheless, someone has to be responsible. Someone has to know that he is going to be the one to head up the effort to find a solution on a given opportunity. Otherwise, it may never be addressed, and the opportunity may be lost in a morass of finger-pointing (see figure 11.1). Someone has to own up to the problem. It doesn't mean he is the only one who is going to solve it. He is just the one who will make sure the process is followed through to its completion. He'll form a team if necessary and work through the problem.

Feed Data Back to Involved Parties

It is each person's responsibility to improve his own quality. We must realize, however, that we do not work in a vacuum. Each person must also feed data back to his customers and suppliers.

With JIT/TQC, if you see a problem or opportunity, it is your responsibility to do something about it, whether the root cause lies in your area or not. You may be the only one who sees it, and if you do not feed the data back, it may never be resolved. Again, you may not be the only one involved in the solution, but you will likely be part of the team, because your data is necessary in establishing a clear understanding of the cause.

Figure 11.1
Whose Job Was It?

There was an important job to be done, and Everybody was certain Somebody would do it. Anybody could have done it. Nobody did it.

Somebody got angry about that because it was Everybody's job. Everybody thought Anybody could do it, but Nobody realized that Everybody wouldn't do it.

It ended up that Everybody blamed Somebody when Nobody did what Anybody could have done.

Unknown body

Follow the "Plan, Do, Check, Action" Circle

As explained in chapter 1, this problem-solving tool is sometimes called the Deming circle or the Shewhart circle. (See figure 11.2). The process begins with the plan section. Here, we must concisely describe the problem or opportunity. We also need to identify someone clearly responsible for following this opportunity through to a satisfactory conclusion. We must explain the symptoms, and we might want to categorize the opportunity if it relates to key performance measures, objectives, or projects. We then have to determine the priority of the problem; we have many opportunities, so we need to know if this problem commands attention over others currently competing for our time. We then need to quantify the magnitude of the problem in terms of key performance measures and state the intermediate and long-term goals. When the intermediate goal is reached, we will assess the need for any further concentrated effort on this problem. This too will be gauged in light of the priority of other opportunities.

Figure 11.2
TQC Process

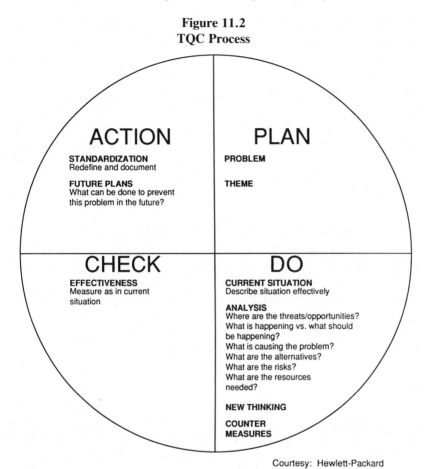

Courtesy: Hewlett-Packard

In the Do section, we need to describe the current situation in terms of its cause or causes, as opposed to the symptoms. We must ask why the problem occurred in order to expose the contributing causes to the problem at the first level. Once we have identified those first-level elements, we must uncover why each of them happened and how they contributed to the development of the problem's second-level elements. For most difficult problems, we must ask why at least four times, often more. Once we have uncovered the root cause of a problem, we can creatively develop a countermeasure. Then we must implement that proposed solution to the problem.

Once we have implemented our proposal, we must check to see if we were effective. If we have correctly identified the cause to the problem and satisfactorily implemented the correct solution, we should see the performance measures we began to track in the Plan section converge on the goal. If the performance does not change, either we have not identified the cause and effect of the problem, or we have proposed ineffective countermeasures. If we converge on the goal but do not reach it, we must go back to the Do section. Here, we will trace down another level, expose more aspects of the problem and correct them also. Once we have reached the goal we can proceed.

In the Action area, we standardize the change by asking in what other areas a similar constraint might arise. It is very difficult and often time-consuming to trace to the root cause of a problem chain. Therefore, we should leverage our efforts by implementing the countermeasures in other areas that are likely to experience the same problem.

When following the PDCA circle, we tend to move in and out of quadrants instead of following them sequentially around the circle. In addition, the precise description of what happens in each quadrant varies from person to person. The flowchart shown in figure 11.3 categorizes the steps differently from figure 11.2, but it illustrates the same PDCA process. The key is to follow the steps methodically, not to debate which step falls into which quadrant. Later in the chapter, we will walk through a Problem Solving Storyboard form that guides us sequentially through the proper stages.

If we don't follow this step-by-step PDCA process once a problem is exposed, we increase our chance of jumping straight to an incorrect conclusion. Usually, there is nothing wrong with applying our best judgment to solve a problem when it first appears. If the problem is not corrected, however, or if the solutions of today wind up being the problems of tomorrow, we will need to institute a more rigorous problem-solving procedure.

During a discussion of the PDCA process, someone once objected, "We don't have time to go through that time-consuming process. When we have a problem, we solve it right away!" If his process were so effective, it would follow that he would have no old problems. But, of course, every factory does have difficult lingering problems. Shooting from the hip does not prove to be a very effective way of dealing with difficult constraints.

Figure 11.3
TQC Process Improvement Flowchart

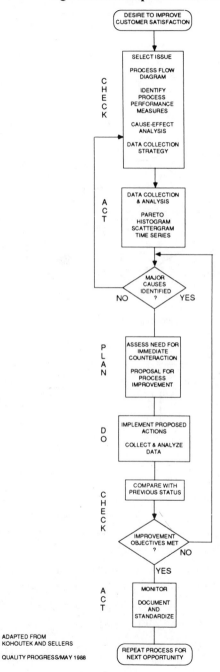

ADAPTED FROM
KOHOUTEK AND SELLERS

QUALITY PROGRESS/MAY 1988

Figure 11.4
Just-in-Time

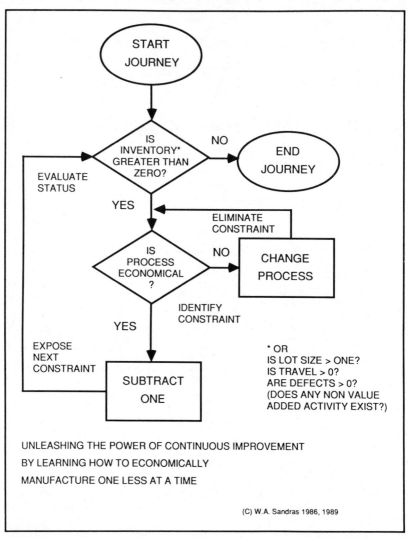

The Plan Do Check Action process requires us to analyze the problem carefully and then track the results of our countermeasures to see that our actions were correct. It also requires us to try to apply what we have learned to other areas by standardizing the change.

QUICK-START TOTAL QUALITY CONTROL TECHNIQUES

Over the years, Total Quality Control has taken on a heavily statistical flavor. However, while statistics are a very powerful tool, they are by no means the only Total Quality Control technique available. There are a number of other techniques that require no statistics. Some don't even require an ability to add, subtract, multiply or divide, or to read or write. This book does not pretend to be a treatise on all the hundreds of possible Total Quality Control techniques. I do, however, want to show some of the more powerful, immediately applicable, nonstatistical problem-solving tools contained within the framework of Total Quality Control. My aim is to get you started on the road to Total Quality Control and to help you analyze the constraints exposed by Just-in-Time, particularly during the implementation process. If you don't even routinely practice the basic techniques, it is not likely you will be successful in your application of the more difficult ones. We must learn to walk before we run.

When starting or restarting a Total Quality Control effort, it is important to assign Just-in-Time areas priority in training, education and support. Necessity is the mother of invention, and Just-in-Time makes it necessary that these areas learn effective problem-solving skills. While everyone should be made familiar with the principles of Total Quality Control and the PDCA process, it has proven much more effective to teach the actual techniques only after the need for them has become obvious to the students.

While the production department is emphasized in the discussion that follows, it should be understood that these tools apply to *all* functional areas. If you are not directly involved in production, I suggest that, as you finish reading about each technique, you stop and consider how each might apply to your particular area. Also think about how you might use each technique in your relations with other areas, such as your customers and suppliers.

FLOWCHART

The flowcharts presented in figure 11.3 and 11.4 are simply pictorial representations of process steps. Diagramming flow allows us to see the actual and ideal progressions of thoughts and patterns for any product or service in a manner that will make inconsistencies more obvious. Many symbols may be used when preparing a flowchart, but generally a diamond represents a yes/no question, rectangle or box indicates an operation, and an oval is a start or end. A small circle may represent a branch or reentry point.

One type of a flow diagram is the wall chart which depicts flows of paperwork using the actual forms. These are posted on a *large* wall and ribbon or string is used to connect documents and show flows of paper from operation to operation. The wall chart is effective, for example, in demonstrating all paper and processes involved in a traditional work-order/purchase-order process.

Another kind of flowchart makes use of a grid on a page. Across the top, we might list departments, and down the side, we might list elapsed days. Then, if we wished to diagram the order-entry process, we could show when the various departments became involved. This particular flowchart format is useful for visually exposing large segments of wasted time and/or inefficient communications.

Flowcharts can be especially helpful in nonproduction areas, where the processes are often less well defined. When beginning the Just-in-Time pilot, it is a good idea to use flowcharts to examine the existing and proposed engineering change processes, as well as the logic behind deciding which bill of material to use for backflushing highly customized products.

CAUSE-AND-EFFECT DIAGRAM

The cause-and-effect diagram is also known as an Ishikawa or fishbone diagram (see figure 11.5), and is used to help stimulate and organize the process of determining the possible causes of a specific problem or condition. It works very well in conjunction with brainstorming techniques. Briefly, the box is used to describe the effects of a problem or an opportunity. It often contains narrative and/or data in a graph form. The main branches of the diagram represent the categories on which to focus when considering the probable causes of the problem: *measurement, materials, machine, man and method,* (the five M's).

For example, if we have too many defects in product A, the logical first question is, why do we have defects on this particular product? To

Figure 11.5
Cause/Effect Diagram

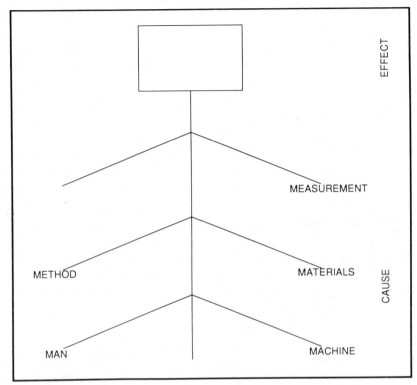

discover the cause, we might brainstorm for ten of fifteen minutes, and under each category we list the possible causes. The way we *measure* and inspect the product, or the way we *measure* and set up the equipment could be the cause of the problem. The quality of the incoming *material* could be poor, or the *machine* might not hold tolerances. Under the *man* heading, we might conjecture that the problem is due to the training of the person who operates the equipment. Finally, the problem might stem from the *method* of making the product. All of these possibilities would be laid out on the diagram.

Sometimes, instead of using the five M's, we substitute customers, suppliers, and other functional areas. The problem might be that there are too many parts shortages. The shortages could be due to record accuracy in the *stockroom,* or they might occur because the *supplier* mixes parts. There might be a problem with the way *production* reports scrap, there could be errors in the *MIS system.* Problems could also stem from *engineering changes* or bill of material errors.

For administrative problems, the four P's—*policies, procedures, people, and plant*—can be very effective. The cause-and-effect diagram can also be very useful in planning.

Basically, these categories provide a framework for examining problems in a large number of areas. However, there is no hard-and-fast rule. If other categories work better, then by all means use them, adding them off the main branch. It is not uncommon to see one of the elements of a main branch become the subject of another fishbone diagram. What we do want to avoid, however, is having twenty or thirty *main* branches.

Sometimes, cause-and-effect diagrams are placed on large walls in the work area. Under the main branches, the potential causes of the problem under consideration are listed on the left side. Immediately adjacent to the cause, on the right side, the potential solutions are documented. In some cases, these special fishbone diagrams are drawn on erasable boards. Other times, CEDAC's (cause-and-effect diagram with the addition of cards) are used, in which color-coded cards show possible causes and solutions. Truly modern companies have progressed to CEDAPN's, however: cause-and-effect diagrams with the addition of Post-It Notes! The important thing, of course, is not whether we use markers, cards or sticky paper, but rather that we keep the problem visible and make it easy for anyone to contribute ideas.

The cause-and-effect diagram doesn't actually tell us the cause of the problem or the relative importance of each element. It just lays out the potential causes for the constraint represented in the box. In order to unearth the actual cause, we're going to have to gather some data.

CHECKSHEET

One of the easiest ways to gather data is with a checksheet (see figure 11.6). Many times this is done right in the work area on a flip chart or tablet. The checksheet shown here provides a simple method for recording the number of times a given problem occurs, and is an effective tool for quantifying the causes identified on a cause-and-effect diagram.

Figure 11.6
Defect Checklist

TYPE	TALLY	FREQUENCY
WORKMANSHIP	ЖЖ ЖЖ ЖЖ ЖЖ I	21
MATERIAL	ЖЖ ЖЖ III	13
ADJUSTMENT	ЖЖ I	6
OTHER		0
TOTAL		40

When we're beginning to investigate a problem, we may not have any data. A cause-and-effect diagram gives us clues to what the potential causes are likely to be, and with a checksheet we can record how many times each of those items occurs.

One reason why this is such an effective process is that the people closest to the problem are the ones actively involved in conducting the investigation and developing a solution. This is not some amorphous computer feedback received months after the fact, confirming that a problem exists—the sort of "problem-solving data" that ends up collecting dust in a file cabinet in quality assurance.

Another type of checksheet is shown in Figure 11.7. Several work groups at Tellabs were struggling with good housekeeping, a necessity

Figure 11.7
Workplace Organization

Cell #:_____   DATE:_____   TIME: _____

		PASSED	FAILED
1)	Aisles are clear.	☐	☐
2)	Only work-necessary items are in view.	☐	☐
3)	Trash and waste are removed when trash can is full to rim.	☐	☐
4)	Floor is free of debris. Materials such as burn racks, blue bins, rivet tails have Kanban levels which are observed.	☐	☐
5)	Nothing on top of pallet boxes, parts bins, lights, etc.	☐	☐
6)	Pallets must be stored inside pallet boxes only.	☐	☐
7)	Piece parts inventory stored in designated locations only.	☐	☐
8)	Kanban levels are clearly marked at all areas.	☐	☐
9)	Graphs are posted and are neat and current: Parts Per Million; Yields; Cycle Count; Cell Volume; Scrap; Storyboards; Kanban Inventory; Downtime; Attendance; Workplace Organization.	☐	☐
10)	Are there any goodie bins? (Misc. Item)	☐	☐
11)	Scrap - clearly marked/sample boards also should be clearly marked.	☐	☐
12)	Manuals; Workmanship Standards, S.O.P.'s, within cells and available to all cell members. Also test procedures, line balances, current BOM and board schematics. All forms of documentation are neatly stored in binders or file cabinets.	☐	☐
13)	Documentation of skill certifications available.	☐	☐
14)	Safety glass and static wrist bands are being used. Proper material handling procedures are being followed.	☐	☐

OTC Signature: _____

if the visual controls of Just-in-Time are to work. They formed a team to address the problem. First, they brainstormed on the probable causes of poor housekeeping. Then, they developed a checksheet to tabulate them. They walked through the entire PDCA process to uncover the various causes of poor housekeeping. Finally, they implemented the necessary measures to ensure adequate housekeeping in the future.

Checksheets can also be applied to purchase-order changes, customer-order changes, or engineering changes. The checksheets in figures 11.6 and 11.7 capture data at only one level. We have already learned that solutions to complex problems lie four or more levels deep. Therefore, we must modify each checksheet to capture successive levels of data. These levels can be graphically displayed using multilevel Pareto charts.

PARETO CHARTS

Data can be expressed graphically in many forms. One of the most powerful is the Pareto chart. This is used to visually display the relative importance of all the elements of a problem. According to the Pareto principle, *where there are a large number of contributors to a result, the majority of the result is due to a minority of the contributors.* Dr. J. M. Juran is the person who actually popularized the Pareto principle. He called it "the law of the vital few and the trivial many." It is also called "the 80/20 rule" and a "frequency histogram."

Basically, the Pareto principle indicates that most of the dollars in inventory are contained in a minority of the part numbers, or that most of the business we receive is coming from a minority of our customers. It can be very helpful for problem-solving. If we were to take the checksheet data we've been gathering about defects and place it in a Pareto chart, the most frequently occurring reason for the problem would be represented by the first bar: the next most frequent would be shown by the second bar, and so forth (see figure 11.8).

In many factories, checksheets going back for years can be found at some inspection stations. What is amazing about this is that these often do not contain enough information for the root cause of the constraint to be ascertained. If workmanship proves to be our biggest problem, we need to break that down and understand the causes of poor workmanship. Every time we make a check mark next to "workmanship" on a

Figure 11.8
Pareto Chart

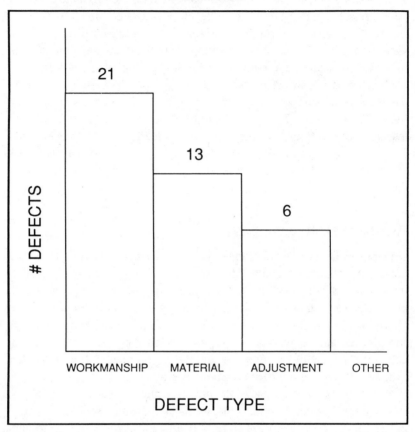

checksheet, we must narrow that category further and describe what is wrong with workmanship. Is it a missing item? Is it an incorrectly assembled item? Is it the wrong item? To further understand the probable causes of the workmanship problem, we might do another cause-and-effect diagram on workmanship. Then, to quantify this new level, we need to modify our original checksheet to capture data at the second level of the problem.

For example, figure 11.9 shows the first bar breaking up into the second graph. Once a main item emerges out of the first graph, we need to break it down. Our goal is to find a single large bar, representing the

Figure 11.9

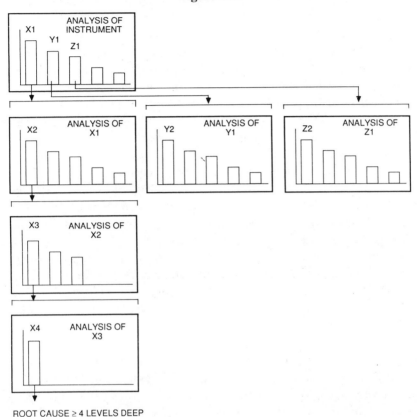

ROOT CAUSE ≥ 4 LEVELS DEEP

root cause, at the bottom of this process. Typically, that stage is four to six levels deep. We should be very suspicious if we think we have reached the root cause after two or three levels.

In the early 1980s, Hewlett-Packard's Japanese division set out to win the Deming Prize, which is one of the most prestigious quality awards in Japan. This division had a list of what they called "Rainbow Suppliers." The factory I was with happened to be the number-one supplier on that list of seven. We told them we knew we were good but had had no idea we were their best supplier. They then informed us that we misunderstood the list. This was their list of worst suppliers.

We were ready to believe we were the best, but could not accept that we were the worst. They took out their first Pareto chart. Level one showed the seven suppliers. We were the biggest bar on the Pareto chart. They showed us the second Pareto chart. Level two displayed our problems: inaccurate shipments and poor product design. We were certain we didn't have a problem with inaccurate shipments, because we had 99 percent-plus inventory record accuracy. If we made inaccurate shipments we would not have been able to maintain that record.

The Japanese division broke down the shipment problem. The third level showed that the main cause was short counts. The next-longest bar indicated we shipped the wrong material, and further down the list was overshipping. We found all this very hard to believe. There was nothing to be gained from undershipping; they were the same company. They broke that down another level. The fourth level illustrated that the product we most often shipped short was integrated circuits. We found that hard to believe too, because integrated circuits come in convenient packages of twenty-five. They broke that down, and the fifth level showed that the main problem was the integrated circuits that came in tubes of eighteen. Suddenly we understood what the problem was. People were mistakenly counting tubes of eighteen for twenty-five. For every tube that they miscounted, the shipment would instantly be short by seven. Embarrassing!

The design problems, we found, occurred mostly on one particular old product. The second level showed that the problems were mostly with the keyboard of the product. The third level demonstrated that the main problem with the keyboard was sticky keys. We knew about that; it had been that way for years. We'd done everything we could to minimize the problem, but it was an old product, and it just wasn't worth spending the extra money to redesign the keyboard. The problem wasn't bad, but the keyboard was not perfect. The Japanese division told us they were determined to win the Deming Prize and were intent on solving this problem. They needed us to help them get to the root cause. But we were not interested in putting more engineering into the problem.

Eight out of ten times, what is a priority for the customer is naturally a priority for the supplier. Even if it is not, the constraint remains, and Just-in-Time will not let us forget about it.

Finally, the Japanese division motivated us by convincing higher-level management that the problem had to be addressed. Upper management had a way of explaining the need to us that suddenly made us interested. The division sent an engineer over to help us. Initiating the fourth level of the problem-solving process, the engineer started sorting the sticky keys. We knew there was an occasional problem, but there was no particular pattern; an "A" failed just as often as a "B" or a "T." We took a sample of the defective keys and sorted them into piles. Sure enough, the "A" key pile was just as big as the "B," which was as big as the "T." They were all equally sticky. We said, "See, the problem is random."

The Pareto chart revealed nothing; bars representing each key were essentially the same height. We had beat the problem as low as it would go without an expensive redesign. But the engineer from Japan did not give up. He was determined to get to the bottom of this. As he was analyzing the keys, he looked inside one and noticed that there was a number inside the keycap. That number, it turned out, represented the cavity in which the key was molded. It was time to gather a new set of fourth-level data: The engineer sorted the keys by cavity and found that cavities 2, 4, and 6 were the main culprits. We called the supplier to see if there was a problem with those cavities. The supplier called back and said that in all those years of our complaining, he had never noticed, but there were burrs in cavities 2, 4, and 6. The Japanese engineer ordered that those cavities be plugged up, and the number-one problem died. The root cause was a burr in the supplier's mold cavities. Embarrassing!

One thing we learned, a little slowly perhaps, is that when it comes to Total Quality Control, you can strike the word "random" from your vocabulary. Problems are not random. By the way, after all the hard work, HP's Japanese division did win the Deming Prize.

We could have redesigned the keyboard, but there was still a good chance we'd have used the same mold, because it was so expensive. We did not understand the real cause of the problem. Until you get to the bottom and a big bar jumps out at you, you haven't discovered the root cause. The moral of this story: Put your detective hats on and methodically uncover the clues leading you to the culprit, the root cause of the problem. Don't jump to conclusions.

One intriguing fact about this process is that 80 percent of the time, the root cause turns out to be embarrassing. There is no real reason why that problem needs to exist. From the surface, you just can't see through several fathoms of muddy water to the root cause. You have to dive to the bottom to understand it. Probably twenty percent of the time, you may encounter a really tough problem that will take a while to resolve. Most times, though, it's simple.

People say problem-solving is hard. That is not entirely true. What's hard is problem identification. Typically, when we get to the bottom the solutions are fairly clear and obvious. But we must recognize that getting to the root cause is not necessarily easy. We watch a lot of television and movies these days, and major problems are resolved in a matter of an hour or two. It's easy to forget that real life does not work that way. The process described above took many months, partly because we eloquently denied the evidence each step of the way. Today, at HP, Total Quality Control is becoming a way of life. More problems are solved accurately and quickly because everyone has to be familiar with the process. It still takes time and effort, but most of all it takes a lot of thinking and resourcefulness. The Pareto chart is an extremely powerful tool and requires only basic math.

RUN CHART

Another effective tool is a run chart (see figure 11.10). As with checksheets, it's not uncommon to see run charts that span years and years. A run chart tells us how the process is going. It can be quite valuable, particularly when coupled with statistical analysis. By statistically analyzing a run chart, we can determine whether a process is under control or if it is varying uncontrollably. If the process is being controlled, we can statistically calculate that it is highly improbable that a data point would ever occur outside of an upper limit or a lower limit. If, on the other hand, our run chart indicates that our process frequently goes out of control, Pareto charts can point the way to improvement.

FOUR WHYS

Yet another valuable technique is known as the Four Whys, because it forces us to ask the question "Why?" four times (see figure 11.11). Let's walk through an example using part shortages. It seems that everyone implementing Just-in-Time experiences some sort of problem with part shortages. When Just-in-Time is used without work orders, back orders are eliminated, because by definition a back order is created from an attempt to pick a work order.

However, part shortages remain, and that's a much worse constraint.

Figure 11.10
Run Chart

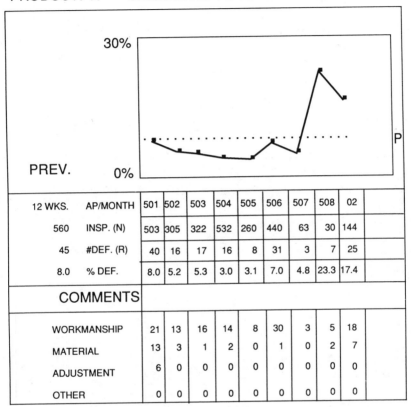

PRODUCT: X   SEQUENCE: ASSEMBLY   DATE:

12 WKS.	AP/MONTH	501	502	503	504	505	506	507	508	02	
560	INSP. (N)	503	305	322	532	260	440	63	30	144	
45	#DEF. (R)	40	16	17	16	8	31	3	7	25	
8.0	% DEF.	8.0	5.2	5.3	3.0	3.1	7.0	4.8	23.3	17.4	

COMMENTS

WORKMANSHIP	21	13	16	14	8	30	3	5	18	
MATERIAL	13	3	1	2	0	1	0	2	7	
ADJUSTMENT	6	0	0	0	0	0	0	0	0	
OTHER	0	0	0	0	0	0	0	0	0	

If a worker on the production line reaches for material and it's missing, there's a part shortage. He asks the first "why": Why isn't the part that I need available? The answer could be that the part is in the warehouse but hasn't been delivered yet, or it might be on order but not delivered by the supplier. Or the part may not even be on order. Suppose that after a little investigation, it is revealed that the part is on order but has not yet been delivered. This answer is written in the first answer box. Now we ask the second "why": Why wasn't the part delivered in time to be used? Further investigation reveals that it was ordered with a need date that the

Figure 11.11
"4 Whys"

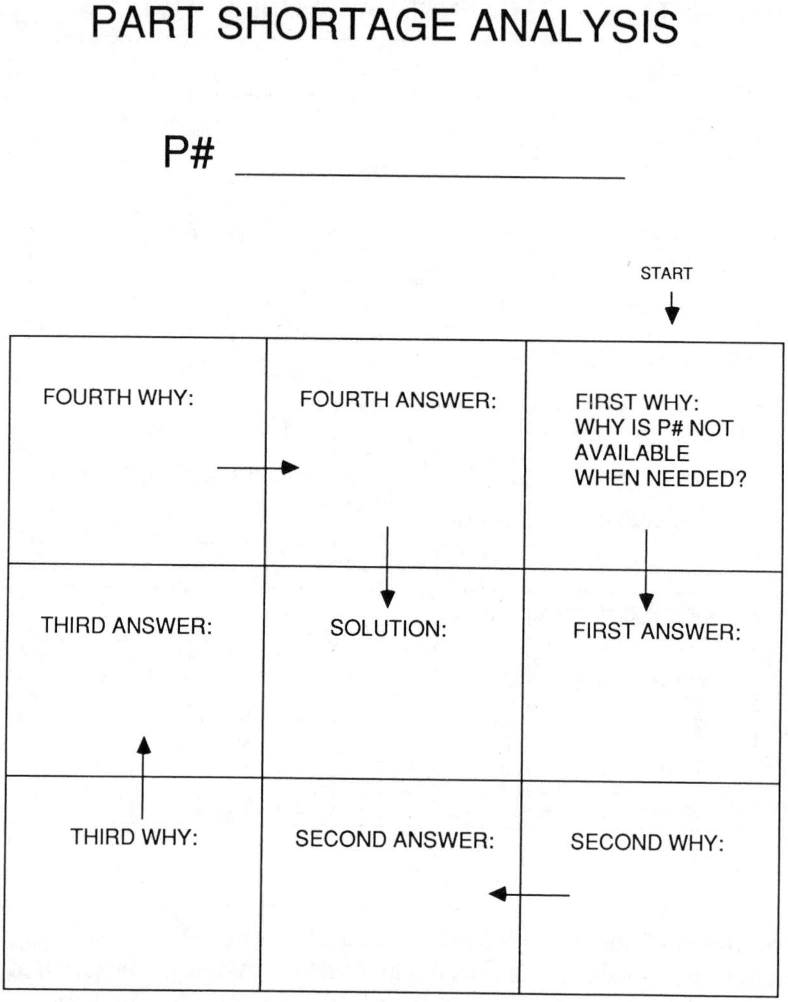

PART SHORTAGE ANALYSIS

P# _____

START

FOURTH WHY:	FOURTH ANSWER:	FIRST WHY: WHY IS P# NOT AVAILABLE WHEN NEEDED?
THIRD ANSWER:	SOLUTION:	FIRST ANSWER:
THIRD WHY:	SECOND ANSWER:	SECOND WHY:

supplier's stated lead time would not allow him to meet. That answer is written in the second answer box. Next we ask the third question: Why was the part ordered in less than lead time? A critical engineering change was made. This leads to the fourth question: Why did we schedule production of the product knowing that the part was going to be missing? Answer: Planning is not part of the critical-engineering-change-approval procedure.

When it comes to part shortages we have at best twenty-four hours to try to understand why the shortage occurred. Part-shortage data simply evaporates after a few hours. To get to the root cause, we must trace down to as many levels as possible as quickly as possible. For this reason, in some companies the production worker fills out the number of the missing part and the time it was needed, then hands the form to someone else appointed to trace the cause. Now that work orders have been eliminated, production schedulers are ideal candidates for this task. Someone needs to expedite each missing part, but we also must determine the actual cause of recurring part shortages so that we can eliminate the problem. Production schedulers have the skills necessary to accomplish the investigation. No math is likely to be required with this technique, only the ability to ask questions and write.

FORCE-FIELD ANALYSIS

Another technique, known as force-field analysis, helps us discover and explain the conflicting forces preventing change. It too works very well in conjunction with brainstorming techniques. Opposing forces are represented as they act against a center wall (see figure 11.12). For example, the problem may be an inability to break through traditional processes and move toward Just-in-Time. We must then determine what forces are motivating us to implement JIT/TQC and improve our performance. Perhaps the threat of competition and management pressure are two elements. We may also find that our performance measures are not competitive anymore as far as inventory turns, asset turnover, quality, and cost are concerned. Or we may be driving ourselves to remain a leader in the industry.

We then need to ask, Why aren't we changing? One factor that often surfaces is education: We just don't know how to do JIT/TQC. We don't know where we're headed. We understand the current, but we don't understand the different approach. Another reason may be fear of change. Performance measures may crop up once again.

Interestingly enough, performance measures can be on both sides of the wall. They may be causing us to improve in some respects, and causing us to resist change in others. For example, Hewlett-Packard had

Figure 11.12
Force-Field Analysis

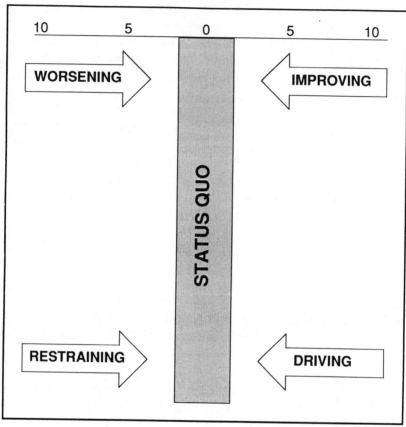

three different divisions, A, B and C. C divisions were the smallest and A the largest. In the early 1980s, when I was a materials manager, my pay was directly influenced by the size of the division I managed. Those who were managing A divisions earned more than those in the C divisions because they had more responsibility. The Vancouver factory, where I was located, was a C division at the time, but it was slated soon to become an A division, because all personal-computer-printer manufacturing was being consolidated onto that site.

A materials manager's pay was influenced by how many part numbers he controlled, how many dollars' worth of inventory he regulated, and how many people he had reporting to him. The more dollars, the more parts, and the more people, then the more pay the materials manager received.

In Vancouver we were essentially practicing JIT/TQC, although at the time, that term didn't even exist. Our objective was to minimize the part numbers and dollars in inventory and thereby minimize the number of people required to take care of it all. We would have considered ourselves blatant failures had we ever reached the materials criteria required to become an A division. Those standards were diametrically opposed to what we were trying to do. The more successful we were with JIT/TQC, the less likely it would be that we would ever meet the A division materials criteria. In some cases, then, performance measures may actually cause us to resist change. This conflicting force may also surface at higher organizational levels, such as when executive bonuses are based on something that is contrary to what we're trying to accomplish with Just-in-Time.

As will be shown in chapter 12, it is highly unlikely that performance measures will change prior to JIT/TQC. They are all too often lagging, not leading elements. That is why leadership is so critical to the JIT/TQC process. A champion must be willing and able to see the bigger picture.

Force-field analysis requires us to brainstorm and carefully examine the forces on both sides. Often, it is helpful to develop a scale and then draw a horizontal bar under each entry to indicate its relative importance. However, just coming up with the ideas doesn't make anything happen. The next step is to develop action plans. For example, if lack of understanding is one of the forces preventing change, then we're going to have to develop an educational program so that people understand what to do and get a sense of how the future is going to look. We should also show them a working pilot so that they can see the simplicity and power behind JIT/TQC.

If certain performance measures are a problem, then we must identify them and develop a strategy to eliminate or relax the forces holding progress back. In the example of the company trying to implement Just-in-Time, increasing the pressure to improve on quality, delivery, and cost is probably not the best strategy. These pressures are usually already severe. Increasing awareness of the competitive threat, however, may be in order.

Again, no math is required, just thought and action.

CHECKING

We should remember that inspection is wasteful, but it is necessary in many instances because of process and product defects and sometimes due to contractual obligations. That should not stop us, however, from attempting to achieve higher quality levels at less cost. One technique that is applicable in some environments is checking, in which each employee checks the work of the person or machine immediately proceeding his own operation. It may seem as if this extra process step will add too much time. If we use the Pareto concept, however, to check only the top failing areas, we may soon find that we can accomplish the task for free. In assembly environments, we can highlight exploded drawings to visually indicate those areas that are to be checked. The annotations are changed as each cause or error is eliminated.

MISTAKE-PROOFING

Historically, manufacturing companies had to implement inspection because they had a high level of product defects. However, inspection of 100 percent of the manufactured goods proved too expensive, and we began to sample. Statistical sampling techniques offered an economical way to understand the causes of these defects, and bring down their number. When the defect level reaches one part per million, however, a statistical sample has too great a chance of missing that one part per million. If a customer buys a television and receives the one set that's bad, then that customer is very dissatisfied with both the television and manufacturer. In some instances one part per million is too many. This is particularly true in life-or-death situations, and in this age of rapidly rising expectations for quality, it is frequently the case.

Sampling is insufficient to catch a one-in-a-million defect. We have to do 100 percent inspection. The problem is that it's too expensive, and bad parts still get through. What we need, therefore, is a flawless, 100 percent inspection for free. How are we going to do that? The way is through mistake-proofing.

The idea of mistake-proofing is not new. It has existed for years in the financial area, in the form of double entry bookkeeping and cross-footing. Cross-footing is often seen on expense-report forms. Columns are used to reflect expenses for the day. Rows are used to categorize the expenses. Columns are added down, and rows are added across. Then the sum of the columns is determined and compared with the sum of the rows. If they do not match, an internal reporting problem exists. Cross-footing is very effective, though often annoying when it turns up mistakes in expense reports.

In a manufacturing environment, there are also ways to mistake-proof. For example, one factory produced disk drives that had four feet on the bottom. It is, of course, extremely irritating to use a disk drive with three feet, because it wobbles (a fact I can personally attest to since a manufacturer recently shipped me one). The manufacturing process had been improved greatly by means of statistical sampling, but the problem still cropped up. The process had to be mistake-proofed. As the first operator finished his portion of the assembly, the product was passed to the next operator. When the second person put the product down, it rested on four sensors. If one of the feet was missing, a light went on right in front of the second operator's face. It was virtually impossible for a product missing a foot ever to get through the rest of the process. The cost of mistaking-proofing was insignificant, but the defects plummeted immediately to zero. Other techniques include weighing, templates, and go/no-go gauges which automatically shut off equipment.

We can use any number of techniques, many of which are outlined in this book, to reduce or eventually eliminate defects. However, if we are clever enough to mistake-proof, we will see defects drop to zero instantly. Mistake-proofing requires large amounts of creativity and usually costs very little. The key factor is to design the product and process so that they can't go wrong. No math, just brainpower here!

FLIP CHARTS

The most powerful technique to improve quality may be simply to put a flip chart in the work area. The objective is to capture all ideas on how to eliminate waste. As Just-in-Time stimulates people to come up with ideas, we need a convenient way for them to communicate those thoughts, which will ideally lead to action (see figure 11.13). It is very important that flip charts and pens be readily accessible in every work area. At one factory I saw, there was a flip chart, but the pen was in the

Figure 11.13
Ideas to Eliminate Waste

IDEA DATE	BY	IDEAS TO ELIMINATE WASTE	ASSIGNED TO	DUE DATE	COMPLETION DATE
		WRITE IDEA HERE IN ONE COLOR LEAVE ROOM TO WRITE FEEDBACK IN ANOTHER COLOR WRITE SECOND IDEA PROGRESS			

(HAVE A CELEBRATION WHEN ALL IDEAS ON ONE PAD
HAVE BEEN IMPLEMENTED OR RESOLVED; SAVE OLD PADS).

boss's office. If a worker wanted to write anything down he had to knock on the boss's door. It's not hard to guess how many items were listed on the chart.

These items noted on the flip chart should be discussed every day in a ten- or fifteen-minute stand-up meeting. The members of the work group and representatives from areas likely to be required to follow up should attend. At first, the meetings may take longer than fifteen minutes, because so many opportunities will be uncovered. The purpose of the stand-up meeting is not to analyze all the ideas completely; it is merely to make sure people understand each item and to assign a person to follow through by a certain prioritized date. A production-oriented work group meeting should be attended by the production people, a representative from materials, and a representative from manufacturing engineering. Over time, as different opportunities begin to emerge, other people can be invited, but in most cases production, materials, and engineering need to be represented every day. It should be noted, however, that anyone is welcome to attend these meetings at any time.

If a meeting uncovers a problem, an action item is assigned. Sometimes these action items are corrected quickly; others may take several months. Nevertheless, each item is reflected on the chart.

Each person on the McDonnell Douglas Computer Systems Company implementation team had an assignment to walk through the factory every day, and review the items on a flip chart in a specific area. The team would then meet once a week to discuss the common trends that surfaced in the various production areas. Whatever higher-level action was required was then initiated.

The filled flip chart should also be retained for historical analysis. It is extremely helpful to be able to go back to these pads, after a year or so, and pick up any patterns of problems that might be recurring. Also when you finish all the items on a flip chart, it should be the occasion for a celebration. Remember, *always recognize your achievements, especially if you want your people to continue providing new ideas!*

At one factory, that had been running its first JIT/TQC line for about forty days, a woman working on an adjacent non-JIT/TQC line noticed some very different things happening in the JIT/TQC area. She saw the flip charts, and the stand-up meetings. She noticed that whenever a significant quality problem cropped up, the line shut down. She also knew that the part she was building had too many failures. She didn't feel particularly good about the fact that what she built could be better, but she didn't know what to do to correct it. After watching the JIT/TQC line for a month or so, she finally stood up to her supervisor and declared, "I absolutely refuse to produce junk. The JIT/TQC people solve problems and if necessary shut down the line. I'm shutting down this line." Her management had a difficult and emotional time trying to explain to her that they solved problems differently on her line—they used inventory. The woman had the right attitude. Unfortunately, the necessary problem-solving tools were not in place in her area. She was, however, helping management awaken to newer methods. Later, when the manager of the JIT/TQC line needed some equipment from her line that was not being used, the two managers made a deal. If the JIT/TQC manager would list a missing part for the other line on his flip chart and get the problem resolved, then the JIT/TQC manager could have the excess equipment. JIT/TQC's ability to force problem-solving was beginning to be understood!

IDEAS TO ELIMINATE WASTE

Another tool, similar to the flip chart, is a form entitled "Ideas To Eliminate Waste" (See figure 11.14). This is an excellent device for communicating simpler problems. For instance, at Hewlett-Packard we had a box that went inside another box for double packaging. It was very difficult to push the inner box into the outer box. The operator on the line took a form and filled it out. In the *What is wrong?* section, she wrote, "It is too difficult to push the inner box into the outer box." Her *Proposed solution* was to "cut finger holes in the inner box so that I can grab it better and shove it down into the outer box."

This form then went to manufacturing engineering. At the time, we had a packaging engineer, because we were introducing a brand new-product every month. You can imagine the priority the finger-holes were assigned on his list of things to do! This improvement wasn't ever going to happen, even though this *was* a package and we *had* a packaging engineer.

On the other hand, this problem didn't require a packaging engineer. All it took was someone interested in following through. Manufacturing engineering simply reviewed the form to see if it took an engineer to solve the problem. It didn't, so the form went right back to the woman who had filled out the request. She was told that the next time she met the schedule for the day or the line shut down she should call the buyer, have him send the supplier in, and show the supplier where she wanted the finger holes. In other words she was told to take care of it. Not everything requires an engineer or a manager, and even when one is needed, often the majority of the work can be done by someone else. We have to learn how to delegate problem-solving.

PROBLEM-SOLVING STORYBOARD

Earlier in this chapter, when talking about the Plan, Do, Check, Action circle, I mentioned the Problem-Solving Storyboard (see figures

Figure 11.14
Ideas To Eliminate Waste

Ideas To Eliminate Waste

IDEA BY

PROBLEM AREA

Objective; Department; Product;...

RESPONSIBILITY

START DATE

COMPLETION DATE

WHAT IS WRONG?

Explain the symptoms of the problem.

PROPOSED SOLUTION

Suggested ideas for solution. Use the Problem Solving Storyboard form for difficult problems.

SOLUTION PROGRESS

If resources will not be allocated to this problem soon, explain why priority is low; hold for periodic review.

11.15, 11.16). The storyboard was designed to guide us through the PDCA problem-solving process and to provide a working document that continually showed the steps we were taking and the progress we were making toward resolution of a problem.

The first block of the storyboard is used to describe the *problem area*. We categorize the problem by writing the name of the department initiating the storyboard or the area or objective affected by the problem.

The *responsibility* block names the person, not the area, responsible for following this storyboard through to a satisfactory conclusion. The date the storyboard was started is entered, as well as the current date each time the form is updated. Only when the goal is met and the problem is resolved satisfactorily, is the completion date entered.

In the *problem* section, we describe the symptoms of the problem. What is the nature of the problem? Do we have too many part shortages? Are we experiencing too many engineering changes? Are customers changing their orders too frequently and at inconvenient times? General terms, feeling words, and any other device that will help convey the problem can be used here. From now on, however, it's facts and figures.

In the next block, the *history* of the problem is quantified. Here we will show graphs of the key performance measures, or characteristics, of the problem. For example, we might see the number of engineering changes that takes place each month. Included in this area are run charts, perhaps with statistically calculated upper and lower control limits. More than one characteristic of the problem may be used. For instance, a part-shortage problem might be characterized by number of shortages in a given time period as well as by the average duration of the shortages in the same period.

Also on each history graph we will indicate the intermediate *goal*—the point that, when achieved, will prompt us to reassess our efforts and perhaps move on to bigger problems. We may even tighten up the intermediate goal and continue to focus on this problem. It is a checkpoint. Also shown on the graph is the long-term goal. As we implement countermeasures, we will check the graph line of the performance measure or measures to see if we are making progress and if we have reached the goal.

It is not unusual, particularly for new problems, to be unable to graph any data. Furthermore, if we have no data to quantify the magnitude of

Figure 11.15
Problem Solving Storyboard

Problem Solving Storyboard

PROBLEM AREA

Objective; Department; Product;...

RESPONSIBILITY

Current Date _____
Start Date _____
Completion Date _____

PROBLEM

Explain the symptoms of the problem.

HISTORY ... GOAL ... CHECK

Graph historical data for the key performance measures. Indicate intermediate and long term goals on the graphs.

PRIORITY

Why should resources be allocated to this problem?

go to "Cause" section

Figure 11.16
Problem Solving Storyboard (continued)

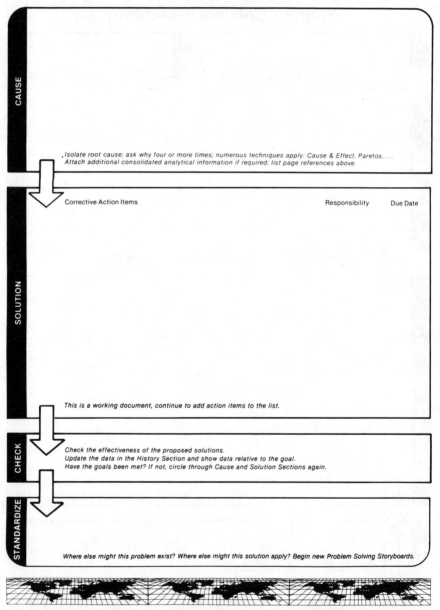

CAUSE

,Isolate root cause; ask why four or more times; numerous techniques apply: Cause & Effect, Paretos,....
Attach additional consolidated analytical information if required; list page references above.

Corrective Action Items   Responsibility   Due Date

SOLUTION

This is a working document, continue to add action items to the list.

CHECK

Check the effectiveness of the proposed solutions.
Update the data in the History Section and show data relative to the goal.
Have the goals been met? If not, circle through Cause and Solution Sections again.

STANDARDIZE

Where else might this problem exist? Where else might this solution apply? Begin new Problem Solving Storyboards.

the problem, we are often unable to specify a goal intelligently. Sometimes we know so little about the problem that we can't assess our current status or even state what it is reasonable to expect. In these instances, we must first collect data and graph it. Then, once we know enough about the problem, we can establish intermediate and long term goals.

Nevertheless, even if we cannot quantify the problem yet, we should be able to state its *priority*. Is this a key problem causing us to miss shipments? If it is, that fact should be stated in the priority section. No one ever seems to have enough time to solve problems methodically. However, if this problem is a cause of missed shipments, we can't afford to postpone finding and implementing a solution. If the priority is moderate, we may choose to begin to collect data for the history section but not spend the time just now to track down the root cause.

The *cause* section is where we trace to the root cause of the problem. It should include cause-and-effect diagrams outlining probable causes, as well as the Pareto charts resulting from data-tracking efforts. The Pareto charts should go down deep enough to clearly show the root cause of the problem, indicated by a single bar on the chart.

Considerable data can accrue in this section, so the space provided on the form is often used to refer to other supporting documents. However, most problems should require no more than four to six pages, including both sides of the storyboard form. If it takes dozens of pages to describe the problem, you probably don't really understand it clearly. The person responsible for the solution may have considerable backup data, but it should be condensed into a concise format for the storyboard. When reading the storyboard, a person unfamiliar with the situation should be able to quickly read a statement of the problem, see the steps taken, and look at the corresponding results.

In the *solution* section, we list the action items taken to explore and eventually resolve the problem. Entries will be made in this section throughout the life of the storyboard. Often, the first entry presents a plan to form a team to help resolve the problem. A second entry might indicate the development of data-collection procedures, because when the storyboard was first started, the team might have discovered it didn't have any data to graph in the history section. Each significant step en route to the root cause and each significant countermeasure is listed here, along with the person responsible for the task and the date it is to be completed.

Note that we repeatedly cycle through the history, check, goal, cause, and solution sections. We may also choose to update any other section as new information is uncovered.

As we advance toward final resolution of the problem, we need to *check* our progress against the goal stated in the history section. If our analysis and countermeasures are effective, then the data in the graph should be converging on the goal line.

When we reach the goal, we then examine how to *standardize* what we have learned. How can we apply what we have learned to other areas that might have the same problem, whether or not they are yet aware of it? For example, returning to the sticky keys on HP's computer keyboard, we would ask ourselves where else a similar problem might exist as a result of burrs in a mold. Do other products use the same mold? Are there other keycap molds? Significant leverage can be gained if we carefully consider the opportunities to avoid or accelerate problemsolving in other areas.

When the *goal* is met, it is time to decide if we will conclude this problem-solving effort or if we tighten the goal and proceed further, resolving other root-cause chains associated with this problem. If we continue, an entry in the solution section should state that the original goal was met and a new goal established. The work will continue. If we conclude, the completion date should be entered in the responsibility section. Then we should celebrate!

Problem-Solving Storyboards can be put to a wide variety of uses. My staff and I used to put all of our departmental objectives into this format to ensure that we followed a scientific process. It helped us simplify and standardize progress reviews, and it provided a concise record of the actions taken and results achieved. However, when first learning how to use the ProblemSolving Storyboard and the PDCA process, it is helpful to pick problems that can be easily quantified. This does not imply that the problems are insignificant; they are just more concrete than others. For your first several attempts, consider the projects listed in figure 11.17. For further information, refer to Appendix B, which presents a Problem Solving Storyboard preventing potential problems by storing material at the point of use.

Several times in the discussion of the Problem-Solving Storyboard process the concept of the team has arisen. Let's look now at how we organize to solve problems.

Figure 11.17
Problem Solving Storyboard

(IMPORTANT INITIAL PROJECTS)

INVENTORY RECORD ACCURACY

PART SHORTAGES

INSPECTION/TEST RESULTS

ENGINEERING CHANGES

CUSTOMER ORDER CHANGES

PURCHASE ORDER CHANGES

PRODUCTION QUALITY

SERVICE CALLS

SETUP TIME

FORECAST ERRORS

PROBLEM-SOLVING TEAMS

As stated earlier in this chapter, Just-in-Time exposes problems, and Total Quality Control offers a variety of techniques that can be used to uncover their causes. One thing should be clear: Just-in-Time makes us pay a great deal of attention to detail. There are very few problems that occur that won't eventually appear at the work-group level. What we're doing is giving the workers the ability to expose those problems, as well as the tools to communicate them to management.

An interesting point is that as a rule only 15 to 20 percent of the problems can be solved within one work group. Eighty percent either lie among several work groups or are outside of them completely. These are management's responsibility. Unfortunately, management doesn't see the bulk of the problems. They are too detailed. Part of the Just-in-Time process is to expose these problems and make them visible to management so that it can take action. This is one of the key reasons for the flip chart and the stand-up meeting. As Philip Crosby said, "Quality is management's responsibility. Without management's involvement it will never happen."

Unfortunately, some managers do not really want to hear about problems. Problems are threatening to them. Certainly they do not perceive problems as opportunities for improvement. If they express anger and hostility or even suppress others' efforts to make these problems visible, the flow of information and ideas for improvement will cease. It is difficult to get ideas to flow but very easy to stop them.

Once again, it is important to remember that problems have causes, not faults. If someone is honestly trying to do a good job and a problem continues, it is not that person's fault. Using the word "fault" in conjunction with "problem" is counterproductive. Some factories track the number of workmanship "demerits" accumulated by each production worker. The word itself will motivate people to hide rather than expose opportunities for improvement. We must understand the root cause of the problem and correct it. The most we can ask is for someone honestly to try. Under the JIT/TQC mentality, if we are living with a problem, we have an obligation to contribute to its solution, regardless of our organizational level.

A number of years ago, many companies initiated small group-improvement activities, or quality circles, though later they often disbanded them. Today, almost all Just-in-Time companies have the equivalent of quality circles, although they do not use that term. Quality has just become a natural part of the work group. In these companies, a work group and a quality circle are mutually inclusive; two names are not necessary. Typically, these people work on problems related and confined to their work area, such as housekeeping, procedures, cross-training, and perhaps even some aspects of workmanship and setup reduction.

There are times, however, when the work group cannot solve the problem by itself. If, for example, we have a chronic part-shortage problem, a number of different skills may be required to solve it. We may need someone from engineering, planning, and the production floor. We may also need someone from the supplier's organization. This second type of group is referred to by a number of different names, such as "quality circles" and "Total Quality Control team." In the work-group example, a homogeneous group of people picks the problem. In the second, Total Quality Control-team example, the problem picks the people. The "problem picks the people" category typically involves Problem-Solving Storyboards. They may focus on the causes of part shortages, engineering changes, customer-order changes, and shipment performance. The team exists for the life of a problem and then disbands. The members then move on to other problems and form appropriate teams to solve them.

Whether we call the groups quality circles, work groups, or Total Quality Control teams is not important. We must understand, however, that in one case the people pick the problem that is within their power to resolve. In the second case, the problem requires a set of greater skills and authority.

MOTIVATING QUALITY IDEAS

Another aspect of the quality issue is how we reward people for ideas. We need to be able to stimulate people to develop better ideas for improvement. As we saw in chapter 10, various payment methods can be devised. However, where significant pay is involved, there may be some side effects detrimental to the progress of JIT/TQC. Total Quality Control is designed to illuminate the root cause of problems, frequently making the solution obvious at that point. As a Total Quality Control team approaches the root cause of a problem, we do not want to tempt anyone to withhold data so that he can be the first to submit the "valuable" idea. We want to encourage cooperation and the exchange of information, not selfish competition.

Also, many pay schemes effectively encourage people to seek the big opportunities, as if they were playing the lottery. The net effect of this is that numerous small opportunities are ignored. Typically, a sincere thank you works as well as, if not better than, money when it comes to encouraging people to contribute ideas. This can be done verbally, in public, or with a letter. One factory I visited had a "wall of fame." Whenever a team finished working on a Problem-Solving Storyboard, their pictures and the storyboard were placed on a bulletin board in a high-traffic area for a month. It was just one way of calling attention to the work these people did and to thank them. This not only helped to teach the problem-solving process; it also recognized publicly those who did the work and encouraged others to contribute too.

Other modest thank-yous, such as pizza or a luncheon, are also appropriate. Payment levels that lead to temptation are dangerous. Some companies that pay significant amounts for ideas like the policy; many do not. If you have a "pay for ideas" policy, carefully evaluate its merit. If you want to terminate it, the Just-in-Time pilot again provides an excellent opportunity to make the change.

In addition to thank-yous, action is required in order to keep the ideas flowing. Again, Walt Goddard's example of the "suggestion-rejection committee" should be remembered. If we effectively limit problem solving to engineers and managers, we won't make fast enough progress. Whenever possible, we need to learn to delegate problem-solving to the person who comes up with the idea. Necessity is the mother of invention, and the person who conceives the idea often has the motivation to pursue a solution. We talk a lot about stress in the work environment these days. One of the most stressful situations is to have a better idea that no one will listen to or let you try out. People love JIT/TQC because it allows, and in fact expects them to solve problems that effect them.

TOTAL PRODUCTIVE MAINTENANCE

To some, the term "preventive maintenance" is as mentally restrictive as the term "quality control." Its historical associations prohibit us from thinking more broadly. Therefore, just as "Total Quality Control" has come to replace the humble "quality control," a new preventive-maintenance term is also emerging—"Total Productive Maintenance." Once again, however, it is not so much the fancy new name that matters, but the concept behind it.

Japan's Institute for Plant Maintenance defines Total Productive Maintenance as "productive maintenance carried out by all employees through small group improvement activities." By now it should be obvious that Just-in-Time exposes unpredictability as a constraint. It also uncovers the sources of this variability so that they can be eliminated by means of Total Quality Control. Equipment failure is one such constraint to higher velocities. Our approach with Total Productive

Maintenance is no different from the approach we will use to eliminate waste in any other area. We will use Just-in-Time to prioritize our Total Productive Maintenance efforts, and we will use Total Quality Control to determine the root cause of each maintenance opportunity.

Figure 11.18 presents the results of an analysis showing that most equipment failures occur with current equipment; failures on new equipment are the most common. Perhaps surprisingly, in this example older equipment is the least significant source of failure. Level 2 of the Pareto chart reveals that the main reason for failures on current equipment is routine maintenance lapses. Level 3 shows that this is primarily due to lubrication. Level 4 isolates XYZ equipment as the sole source of lubrication problems. Now, we know where to focus our maintenance efforts to yield the greatest benefit.

Today, in many JIT/TQC environments, routine maintenance is handled by operators in the cell, as are general janitorial duties. Operator-controlled maintenance doesn't mean that the cell members are out there waxing the floors. They are simply performing the day-to-day maintenance around their areas. The sign at one factory was quite clear on that point: "Your mother doesn't work here. If you throw it on the floor, pick it up!"

An operator is likewise responsible for the routine maintenance of his machinery. Roger Brooks, executive vice president of Oliver Wight Education Associates, devised a system while he was at the Hyster company by which he ensured that operators properly serviced their machines. He attached wooden signs in the shape of a drop of oil to each machine. On one side of the drop was a red circle with a red line through it, like an international driving sign, which meant that the equipment was not oiled. At the end of the shift, the worker would turn over the oil drop display to the "not oiled" side. This simple device reminded the next operator to check the oil before using the machine.

The area and equipment of the work cell essentially belong to the operator. They must be the ones to take care of it. Housekeeping, preventive maintenance, minor adjustments, and lubrication are now generally performed by the production people. Repairs and rebuilds are still handled by the maintenance organization.

Total Productive Maintenance is an excellent area in which to learn Total Quality Control, because the information is tangible and often readily available to the operator.

Figure 11.18

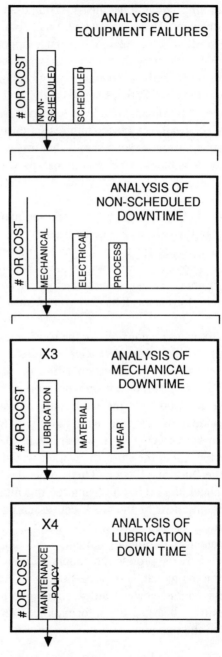

ROOT CAUSE ≥ 4 LEVELS DEEP

SUMMARY

Total Quality Control applies to every function in a company, from production quality and record accuracy in materials to engineering and customer-order changes, to office management and service calls. *Total Quality Control is a generic problem solving process.* It creates an environment in which people have both ownership and responsibility for the quality of their products and processes. Together with Just-in-Time, Total Quality Control provides the processes that enable our people to become an active, competitive weapon against the onslaught of global competition.

Chapter 12

Measuring Performance

When you can measure what you are speaking about, and express it in numbers, you know something about it.

—Lord Kelvin

Now that we have begun to use JIT/TQC to realign the manufacturing process, we should also consider how we need to change the ways in which we measure performance. There are two types of performance measures. One demonstrates the change between the way things were prior to JIT/TQC and the way they are today. It tells us how things are progressing by monitoring our current performance. The other type of measure points the way to improvement.

Around the turn of the century, the renowned mathematician and physicist Lord Kelvin said, "when you can measure what you are speaking about, and express it in numbers, you know something about it; but when you cannot express it in numbers, your knowledge is of a meager and unsatisfactory kind." Quantifying progress and change is essential whether a company is producing in batches or with JIT/TQC. As should be expected, a number of the performance measures that we use with JIT/TQC challenge traditional means.

It is important to note, however, that it is unlikely that performance measures will change prior to the implementation of JIT/TQC. This is unfortunate, because performance measures can be used to drive desired behavior. Even so, performance measures often lag behind in the process of significant change. You will most likely have to begin JIT/TQC in spite of performance measures that may hamper progress. Some of these were mentioned in the explanation of force-field analysis in chapter 11, and we have seen how Just-in-Time can be hindered when materials managers are rewarded for having more parts, more people, and more dollars' worth of inventory.

Since one of the areas we track is whether or not a company is making progress, we should describe what we mean by progress. *Progress is measured in terms of the positive impact of change on quality, delivery, and cost to the customer.* If we're really advancing, we should see improvements in these three competitive areas.

As we begin to implement JIT/TQC, one of the first things that we need to examine is the measure for implementation progress. JIT/TQC is a *process.* However, installing this process in our factory involves a *project,* the implementation of the initial pilot, and we need to be able to measure how well we're doing on the pilot implementation project. A sample form is provided that can be used by top management to review the project implementation team and evaluate the progress of the pilot (see figure 12.1).

First, we must demonstrate that the implementation team has been established. This can be accomplished by simply supplying a list of names of the recommended people for the implementation team, as described in chapter 2. (See Figure 2.1)

The next task is to assess the team's education. As noted earlier, the team has to understand what changes will be required and why. It will also need to know how to implement the initial changes. The easiest way to document each member's education is with a copy of a class certificate from a *detailed* JIT/TQC implementation course.

We then need to determine if the pilot has been selected. Proof of performance here will be a layout drawing specifying the kanban locations and quantities.

Next, we need to show if the pilot has been implemented. If it has been, top management should be able to take a tour to see how it works. Remember, it is important to talk to people in non-Just-in-Time areas on this tour in order to keep jealousy in check.

It must then be determined what progress has been made in educating the entire facility about the changes entailed by JIT/TQC. If a large number of employees have received at least minimal training in JIT/ TQC concepts, this standard has been met. How much education is required overall per person is difficult to gauge. With a project that has a definite conclusion, it is easier to state. To get started, however, the implementation team requires at least forty hours of Just-in-Time and

Figure 12.1
JIT/TQC Project Measures

MEASURE	PROOF OF PERFORMANCE	REVIEW BY	DATE COMPLETE
IMPLEMENTATION TEAM ESTABLISHED	TEAM LIST & CLASS RECOMMENDATION	PLANT STAFF	
IMPLEMENTATION TEAM EDUCATED	CLASS CERTIFICATE	PLANT STAFF	
PILOT SELECTED	LAYOUT AND KANBAN LOCATIONS	PLANT STAFF	
PILOT IMPLEMENTED	TOUR OF PILOT TO DEMO BREAKTHRU SPECS.	PLANT STAFF (ALL)	
JIT/TQC EDUCATION	EVIDENCE 95% RECEIVED 2 HRS.	PLANT STAFF	
JIT PRACTICED	3 MONTH HISTORY OF NO KANBAN VIOLATIONS; EVIDENCE OF KANBANS REMOVED	PLANT STAFF	
TQC PRACTICED	EVIDENCE OF IDEAS TO ELIMINATE WASTE * PSSB IN ACTIVE USE SUBMIT 5 EXAMPLES EA.	PLANT STAFF	
SETUPS REDUCED	3 MO GRAPH; CHANGE LIST	PLANT STAFF	
VISION STATEMENT	COPY OF VISION NARRATIVE	PLANT STAFF	

*PROBLEM SOLVING STORYBOARD

Total Quality Control education. Highly successful companies tend to devote a minimum of thirty to forty hours per person to instruction during the first eighteen months.

Since JIT/TQC drives continuous change, we must realize that we are entering a new era of lifelong learning. Education will never completely stop. We need to be especially careful to ensure that the education level does not deteriorate after two or three years. "Education, training, reeducation and retraining should be greatly emphasized," says McDonnell Douglas Computer System Division's Johnny Lee. "If this is not done, all our good work will sink into the ooze of status quo." Manufacturing Resource Planning users sometimes begin to have problems two to three years after a highly successful implementation. The reason may be that, due to job changes, the system is being used by new people who did not receive the proper education at the beginning of the project. The same sorts of problems can arise with JIT/TQC. For continued success, it is therefore essential to maintain at least the initial level of education.

Once the education process has been properly checked, we must assess whether JIT/TQC is being practiced. This can be confirmed by means of an occasional tour and sample checks for kanban violations. If you have laid out your facility correctly, maintained good housekeeping, and maximized visibility, it should require only a few seconds to verify adherence to a kanban ceiling. The results should be continuously reported, graphically, for all to see. Kanbans should never be violated, and silver bullets, as discussed in chapter 4, should be used no more than six times per year. In addition, we should also see evidence of kanban reductions, increased output with the same number of original kanbans, or both.

We also need to make sure that Total Quality Control is being performed. A number of rigorous Problem-Solving Storyboards that show progress being made on tough issues would provide ample proof of performance in this area. These storyboards should come from several functional areas and not just from production.

Progress with setup reductions must also be assessed. At a given work center, a graph should be maintained that exhibits the actual and the average setup times on a particular piece of equipment; it should show that setups are being reduced. An explanation should accompany any significant changes and may appear as the graph itself.

Finally, a copy of the vision statement, which will be described in chapter 13, should be presented as evidence that the process of change will continue as the company strives to satisfy its vision of the future.

While these proofs of performance are simple, top management can use them very effectively to verify that progress is being made on the implementation project. These performance measures will allow the company to concentrate on the project rather than the progress reports.

Up to this point, I have discussed procedures primarily aimed at measuring the JIT/TQC implementation project. Since JIT/TQC is designed to help us with quality, delivery, and cost, we will require measures that reflect, on an ongoing basis, how well we're doing in these areas, too.

MEASURING QUALITY

Most JIT/TQC companies measure quality in terms of defects per million parts. *Parts per million* provides a much greater granularity than percentages. If we have a 98 percent first-pass yield on a product, or 98 percent inventory record accuracy, that sounds very high. On the other hand, it indicates 2 failures out of 100; 20 out of 1,000; and 20,000 out of a million. If there are 20,000 defects per million parts, we should be able to discern a pattern that can be analyzed in order to correct the problem. Some companies have improved their processes to the point where they are now measuring defects in parts per billion.

Parts-per-million (PPM) quality measures apply in the cell, the work center, on product lines, and in office areas throughout the factory. They apply to incoming-materials product defects as well as to order-entry and shipping efforts. Each functional area's key positions should be measured for improvement and control. The criteria for each particular function can be developed by a team consisting of people from the area and someone from quality assurance who is familiar with this type of analysis.

One PPM measure reports defects per product. A problem arises, however, when a company is comparing the quality of a complex product with that of a simpler one. The comparison is not exactly fair, because we are likely to have more difficulty manufacturing the complex product.

Suppose a company makes computers, miscellaneous computer accessories, and software. If it measures defects per product, it will probably discover more defects per computer, because of the complexity of the product, than in a simple printer-stand accessory or a floppy disk onto which data was recorded.

If a company wants to do some sort of comparison, it could use defects per number of items on the bill of materials rather than per product. Suppose a computer had 2,000 items on a bill of material, the computer stand 20, and the floppy disk 3. Suppose further that during a given period, 1,000 of each unit was made and each had one failure. The computer would show 0.5 failures per million, the stand 50, and the floppy disk 500. The rate would be determined as follows:

$$\frac{1 \text{ failure}}{2{,}000 \text{ parts x } 1{,}000 \text{ computers}} \times 1{,}000{,}000 = .5$$

While this measure makes comparisons easier, it is essential to remember that to the customer who purchased the one defective unit, the failure rate is 100 percent.

PPM measures can also be computed by using inspection points. Again, all defects should be counted, not just those at the inspection points. Remember, we are not trying to establish fault, just determine the root cause. The main problem with this calculation is that the number of inspection points, particularly in areas that are not likely to have a problem, can be increased to make the results look better.

The PPM measure is a very early indicator of whether JIT/TQC is leading us to improve quality. But as we just saw, we can improve the answer while actually increasing the waste. A more accurate measure of overall performance is *Cost of Quality*. This is the number that must ultimately improve. Unfortunately, it is slow to change and takes some effort to measure completely.

Cost of Quality shows the expense required to obtain the levels of quality both our customers and we are experiencing. Our customers may see high quality, but we may be paying an enormous price to achieve it. At one company known for high quality, after a Cost of Quality audit of the company's operations, executives were surprised to find that 20 percent of revenues, 25 percent of assets, 25 percent of the people, 40 percent of the space and 70 percent of inventory could be attributed to poor quality. These numbers are staggering but very normal prior to intensive efforts in JIT/TQC.

Cost of Quality figures are usually subdivided into appraisal, failure, and preventive categories. Appraisal costs include inspection and testing. Failure costs, both internal and external, include scrap, rework, repair, engineering changes, and problem service calls. Preventive costs include education, mistake-proofing, and audits.

It is very difficult to capture all of the information needed to measure Cost of Quality for a couple of reasons. First, accounting systems today do not usually pull out the data for the Cost of Quality. Second, *everyone* is involved in the Cost of Quality. This includes top management, especially when it must rework a decision affecting a significant number of people. Since quantifying every aspect of the Cost of Quality is very difficult, some companies follow a simplified approach, that picks up only the easy-to-isolate costs. Typically, these items are already reported ·by traditional financial systems, such as inspection, test equipment, scrap and rework, portions of manufacturing, engineering, and the quality department. Excluded from this analysis are some of the Cost of Quality items stemming from management. The most important thing is for the company to get started quickly and observe whether its trends are going in the right direction. Later, it can develop methods to quantify costs in more ambiguous areas. How we ultimately track Cost of Quality information is a strategic decision. This measure should be reported monthly.

MEASURING DELIVERY

When we accept an order from a customer, we make a promise to ship our product by a certain date. One necessary delivery-performance measure should be a graph showing whether our products are being shipped early, late, or on time. A curve skewed to the right would indicate a late delivery problem. A tight curve centered above the promised date would indicate we have our processes under control. What we are determining here is our performance to our original promised ship date, providing, of course, that the customer hasn't asked for it to be changed. This measure is important because customer satisfaction is critical to our success. We must understand how well we're complying with our promises. This measure applies to a product line as well as to the entire factory. It may also apply to a cell, if the cell is producing the whole product or the final portion of it. In any case, we're measuring the actual ship date against the original acknowledged date for each order.

We might also consider how well we were able to satisfy the customer's initial request for a shipment date. This is important, but it may require considerable effort to validate the data. Sometimes when a customer makes such a request, he is actually negotiating with us. We need to understand the validity of the request in order to measure this accurately.

How often we ship the entire order as promised is also a valid measure. This must be determined not only from our factory's perspective but also from the customer's, especially if multiple factories are involved in the shipment of the complete order.

Notice that we have made a rather significant change. We are now measuring ourselves primarily against our promises to the customer rather than against the plan. It is still valid to compare performance with the plan. If a choice must be made, however, it is usually wiser to satisfy the customer rather than the plan. This is a rather tricky area in some companies, however. Many make-to-order companies promise shipments to customers according to when they plan to build the product, not according to when the customer wants it. If the product is not planned to be produced when the customer wants it, the customer is forced to accept the plan or go elsewhere. We then measure ourselves on how well we met the plan. This results in a sort of self-fulfilling prophecy. It is more appropriate to measure the plans according to how well they satisfied the customers, and measure shipments based on how well they met the customers' needs. The primary focus should be on the customer, not the plan. When the focus is on the plan, we see managers making "planned shipments" that result in finished goods inventory, while actual shipments that could have resulted in revenue are missed because they did not fit with the plan. Developing the ability to promise by rate rather than by product, as discussed in chapter 6, aids in this difficult transition.

Another delivery measurement is shipment linearity, which is a measure of how evenly we ship every day of the month. The more level the factory load, the more efficient we're going to be. If, on the other hand, a factory barely ships anything the first week of the month and ships 45 percent the last week of the month, it is not using its resources very effectively. This measure applies from the cell on up, and each area should determine its own output. Linearity can be assessed in terms of units per day if the effort required for each unit is relatively consistent; if not, it can be measured in standard hours shipped.

From a financial perspective, we want to know this figure in terms of dollars per day. Production, however, builds units, not dollars, and the customer orders units, not dollars. Efficiently meeting the promised customer ship date with a minimum of waste is the first objective. Dollars are a result.

If a company's rate per day is 100, and it ships 80 today but catches up and ships 120 tomorrow, then it is back on track. However, neither day was linear. The company needs to ascertain why.

People will tend to complain that it isn't their "fault" that they weren't linear, and they are correct. Shipment linearity is a complex issue. We are just trying to understand the causes of unevenness. Often 75 percent of the causes for nonlinear shipments are within the control of the company and do not actually emanate from fluctuations in customer demand. As we learn to correct those factors within our immediate control, the next step is to begin to control the input from our customers. This was discussed in chapter 7 in the section on purchasing and selling by exception. And, of course, we can smooth the hockey-stick effort at month's end with intelligent production planning, being careful to minimize the total waste between inventory and nonlinearity.

The measures we're discussing here serve to tell us how we're doing. They don't point the way to improvement. We'll talk about those shortly.

MEASURING INVENTORY COST

Inventory is only one of a company's many assets, but it's a key one. One way to measure it is by *inventory turnovers*. The actual calculation of this should be determined by a combination of finance and materials. It can be computed by dividing the value of current inventory into the annualized costs of goods sold. Materials departments typically like to use projected shipment figures, while finance usually prefers to use history. Both measures are useful, and in the long run averages of each should be equal. Most companies are struggling to maintain three to eight inventory turns. With MRP II, JIT and TQC, companies are now pushing ten times that number.

As companies adopt JIT/TQC and begin to shorten their manufacturing lead times, thereby increasing their inventory turns, many find it more useful to count days of inventory on hand. This measure provides more precision and is easier to mentally comprehend as velocities increase throughout the manufacturing pipeline. The calculation for inventory on hand is the reciprocal of inventory turns. Days of inventory on hand equals current inventory divided by the annualized cost of goods sold times the number of days per year.

At one Hewlett-Packard division manufacturing a low-volume, high-mix product, the number of days on hand for work-in-process and finished-goods inventory decreased from forty-eight to six days on hand in just nine months. Another HP factory making computer terminals now has ten days on hand for all inventory. NCR has a "target ten" plan for all divisions.

In 1980 TABC (formerly Toyota Auto Body in Long Beach) had seventy-five days on hand. Today, they have about two. You may not be able to see yet how you can move your inventory that rapidly, given all of the problems and perhaps excess inventory on the shelves today. But you should be able to segregate your bread-and-butter product lines and develop a strategy to increase their velocity by a factor of five to ten within the next five years if you want to remain competitive. The processes exist today to make this a reality in most, if not all, industries. It is not easy, but then competing usually isn't. Inventory measures, when viewed in balance with delivery and cost, are usually excellent early indicators of how much a company is improving.

As we implement JIT/TQC according to the process outlined in this book, the first inventory change we will likely see is in work in process. I have already mentioned some of the reductions companies have achieved in this area, with work in process decreasing by 50 to 90 percent. The next change some companies experience is a reduction in finished goods. Because of the improved ability to respond, we can now provide the same customer-service level with lower finished-goods and distribution inventory levels. In fact, a number of make-to-stock items may change to make-to-order as our ability to respond improves. The third stage of inventory affected by JIT/TQC is raw materials. Because a company will have to work with a number of suppliers in this area, the process is longer. Of course, this sequence of observable improvements can vary depending on the implementation process, preexisting inventory profiles, and overlapping projects.

Finally, don't ignore service-part inventory levels. Tektronix estimates that due to its improved ability to respond quickly and economically with small lots, it will be able to reduce service-part inventories by at least 50 percent on items manufactured in JIT/TQC areas.

MEASURING ASSET PRODUCTIVITY

There are other assets besides inventory that we must use productively and be able to measure. We need an assessment that tells us how well we are using our *total* resources as opposed to just our inventory resources. This is asset productivity.

Not so long ago, remember, that we thought inventory was desirable, and it was unthinkable to shut a line down or allow direct labor people and/or equipment to sit idle. Then when Just-in-Time/Total Quality Control first appeared, we started hearing that inventory was evil and that it was acceptable to shut down the line or let a worker sit idle. We even read that it was okay to have excess machinery and equipment.

It's time to step back and reconsider this. In chapter 3, I used the analogy of a multiline telephone to describe the way we sometimes think: when one push button is pressed, another pops up. Thus, inventory used to be desirable; now it isn't. Having idle labor and equipment was evil, but now it's acceptable. These statements are indicative of push-button performance measures. In fact, inventory is wasteful, but so is allowing a person or machinery to sit idle. We shouldn't waste any of our assets.

It's important that top management realize, however, that as we go through "One Less at a Time" and inventory is lowered, we're going to expose constraints. A constraint may be reached that shuts the line down periodically or forces a person or machine temporarily to stop producing, because a consuming operation doesn't need the output. Each resource will experience strain from time to time during the JIT/TQC journey. There are going to be different pressure points between labor, material, machinery, equipment, and facilities. Top management must measure performance based on the total asset productivity and not emphasize one asset over another. Our managers must be allowed the leeway to trade off on these various assets to minimize the total waste.

It's not incorrect to use inventory turns as a measure of productivity, because inventory is a large part of our asset base. However, it needs to be kept in balance with the overall asset productivity. The asset productivity measure should be determined by finance and manufacturing, and could be calculated by dividing the annualized shipments at cost by the monthly manufacturing expenses. Where I have used this measure previously, I looked at hard assets (physical equipment, inventory) and soft assets (people's payroll, taxes, and benefits) separately as well as together.

MEASURING PRODUCTIVITY

One measure of productivity that has proven valuable in JIT/TQC environments is the time the cell is inoperative or working overtime. If we must work a great deal of overtime to meet the planned schedule, or if we frequently have to shut down the line, we should be asking why. There are undoubtedly good reasons, but these reasons can provide a clue to areas where performance may be improved to eliminate waste.

One of my production lines at Hewlett-Packard was shut down a larger percentage of the time at the outset of JIT/TQC than it was a year later. At first, as we corrected the causes of the line shutting down, the percentage of downtime dropped. Then, we noticed a that it was beginning to climb again. Analysis showed that the planned output was being consistently completed fifteen minutes before the shift ended, then thirty minutes earlier, then one hour earlier. At first, the measure had pointed the way to needed improvements. Later, this same measure revealed an opportunity to shift people into areas where more help was needed.

MEASURING KANBANS

Another effective measure, particularly at the cell level, is simply to assess the number of kanbans. By visually displaying removed kanbans, we can provide excellent progress feedback to everyone, especially at the direct and indirect labor levels. As mentioned in chapter 3, McDonnell Douglas's Computer Systems Division used what they called a money line. Each time they lowered the kanban ceiling, they wrote the value of the inventory reduction on a small disk and hung it on a line stretched across a wall. NCR in Cambridge displayed the removed kanban card itself on a wall. Both visual displays showed reductions in the hundreds of thousands of dollars, providing performance feedback and a stimulus for continuous improvement.

Given a reasonably flat or moderately rising levels of business, a company should be able to make shipments with fewer kanbans in the production pipeline. If kanbans are going down while orders are flat or going up, then we are making progress toward achieving higher velocities. In some cases where orders are increasing rapidly, we may decide to hold the kanban level. This has the same net effect as reducing them during a period of flat orders, although it may feel less gratifying than having "One Less" kanban. One way to display the progress of velocity improvement is to graph the ratio of

$$\frac{\text{units produced per period}}{\text{number of kanbans in pipeline segment}}$$

This kanban measure should be charted and displayed on a monthly basis, along with the number of kanban violations observed and the number of "silver bullets" fired.

MEASURING TRANSACTIONS

Another key measure, the number of transactions, is a good indicator of what professors Miller and Vollman called "the hidden factory." This consists of the unseen overhead efforts taking place in all functions of the company. Tracking this data is not easy, but one way to begin is to put counters in key information systems. As we implement JIT/TQC, it's likely that the number of transactions will increase. We have to be careful, however, to watch the cost of these transactions.

Both work orders and purchase orders require a lot of human activity to open, schedule, reschedule, and close. To illustrate this point, suppose we give this kind of transaction a cost weight of 10,000. Another type of transaction we might see is a bar code. A person still has to be involved, but the only work required is to wave a wand across the bar code. Let's say that has a weight of 1,000. Still another kind of transaction is a computer only (CPU) transaction, taking place inside a computer. This has a weight of 1.

Thus, according to our system, the intense human effort of a purchase or work order is 10,000 times more expensive than the computer-only transaction. If we take the 10,000 point transaction and say each weight is worth one cent, then it costs us around $100 to process a purchase or work order, $10 dollars for a bar-code transaction, and one cent for a computer-only transaction. Though these figures are not precise, they are certainly in the right ballpark.

As we get into JIT/TQC, we find that expensive human transactions such as purchase and work orders are driven down substantially. However, we may see that the actual number of CPU transactions increases. The reason for this is that traditionally we have issued material to a work order for a week's worth of production. The work order involves a lot of human intervention, but the computer is activated for the issuing only once for that week. With JIT/TQC, while we probably will not have the work order and human intervention, we will likely back-flush every day. Consequently, we will have more computer-only transactions but fewer expensive human-interaction transactions.

As we start looking at the figures and the number of transactions, it is important to cost weigh them. This should be done monthly, and the Pareto principle should be applied to capture the bulk of the transactions that cost the least to obtain.

MEASURING SET-UP REDUCTION

Setup times are a key restriction to our ability to reduce lot sizes and therefore increase velocities. To track their progress, we can create a graph with setup time on the vertical axis and each sequential setup on the horizontal axis. As each setup is made, the time it took should be recorded on the graph with a dot. At the end of the month, a line will be traced through the dots. If we are making progress, we should see a reduction in the average time required to set up a given piece of equipment. We are not trying to establish an elaborate tracking mechanism here, just a way to provide feedback to the operator and interested parties. Ideally, the graph is placed at the machine, and the operator plots his own data points.

Another, related measure tracks the quantity of setups. As we progress, we should find ourselves making more setups in less total time. This measure can also be applied to mental setup in other areas, such as the "get-ready" time in nonmanufacturing departments.

MEASURING MANUFACTURING VELOCITY

We have seen the importance moving material through the factory at higher velocities by exposing and removing the constraints that hold it back. To assess the speed of this process, we can use a measure called manufacturing velocity, which is the sum of the process times, divided by the actual elapsed time. (Value-added times.)

To calculate this measure, some decisions need to be made. We must determine whether the sum of the process times should be based on today's actuals or the theoretical minimums. Either is permissible, but we should be consistent when calculating the velocities of other products. Unlike accounting standards which are revised periodically, the numerator of the manufacturing-velocity formula does not change. We have a fixed reference point over time. When parallel operations exist today, we should include only the longest path in the sum of today's process times.

Another decision is whether or not we want to include setup times that are already in the standards. Setups are wasteful, non-value-added activity, but they are part of today's standard. If we include the time and number of setups, then the manufacturing velocity number will go up considerably, because actual times will go down. As a matter of fact, it's conceivable that the figure could eventually be greater than one. If we use the theoretical minimum times, the best we can expect to achieve is one. Either approach is acceptable as long as we are consistent. The important part of the measure is the trend.

There are many other performance measures a company may choose see figure 12.2). Some assess overall performance, while others measure highly specified functions.

NOTICEABLE-IMPROVEMENT TIME FRAMES

What rate of progress should we look for? It is reasonable to expect that once the implementation team is educated, a pilot incorporating the breakthrough specifications will be up and running in 120 days. It is also reasonable to expect that the entire factory will be converted to JIT/TQC within twelve to twenty-four months. This does not mean that all suppliers will be using JIT/TQC or that there is no further progress to be made. JIT/TQC is continuous; it does not end until there is no waste left. Full conversion in one to two years is aggressive, but if you are not achieving that rate of change, you should seriously question why. More than likely, something is wrong.

If progress is being made with JIT/TQC, we should be able to see a considerable reduction in the number of kanbans within a cell during the

Figure 12.2
Other Performance Measures

SHIPMENTS AT COST/SQ. FT. OF MFG. SPACE
% OF INCOMING MATERIAL VALUE RECEIVED
VIA KANBAN PULL
% SHIPMENTS VIA KANBAN PULL (IF APPLICABLE)
NUMBER OF PART NUMBERS
NUMBER OF SUPPLIERS
INVENTORY RECORD ACCURACY
BILL OF MATERIAL RECORD ACCURACY
% OF VALUE OF MAT'L. STORED WITHIN 15' OF
POINT OF USE
DAYS WITHOUT A SPECIFIC PROCESS GOING
OUT OF CONTROL
CROSS TRAINING MATRIX
% OF PEOPLE WITH 2 OR MORE HRS. JIT/TQC EDUCATION
INCOMING MAT'L. LINEARITY (BY VOLUME, $, ...)
LINEAR FEET OF MOVEMENT
SUGGESTIONS (PER EMPLOYEE)
ENGINEERING CHANGES (BY PRODUCT)
PURCHASE ORDER CHANGES
CUSTOMER ORDER CHANGES

first few months. Finished goods for a given product line should also be reduced within the first year to an extent that is easily noticeable. Factory-wide, however, significant work-in-process and finished-goods improvements will take one to three years. Setup reduction should be considerably improved within the first year. And a major reduction of raw materials should occur within a one-to-three-year time frame. Since most factories have such a large number of assets, asset productivity will take three-to-seven years to significantly improve. Of course, the greater the percentage of inventory in the total asset base, the faster the number will change.

We should see dramatic progress on the cost of quality in three to seven years. In 1980, John Young, the president of Hewlett-Packard, said that he wanted a tenfold improvement in quality during the 80's. In 1989, the corporation achieved that goal. In eight years, Tennant Company dropped the cost of quality from 17 percent to approximately 2.5 percent. Changes will occur as soon as JIT/TQC is implemented, but it usually takes a few years to be able to begin to see that substantial progress has actually taken place.

Shipment dependability should improve relatively quickly. However, shipment linearity is affected by a number of internal and external factors and it may be several years before that improves significantly. The cost and number of transactions should begin to decrease within the first three years, as systems are rewritten and integrated to support JIT/TQC.

MEASURE NOT TO BE OVEREMPHASIZED

While there are many useful performance measures, there are also a number that can deter JIT/TQC. It's not that these measures are particularly bad; it's just that some tend to be overemphasized, and others are difficult to gauge after we implement JIT/TQC. Labor efficiency is one of these measures.

Labor efficiency is calculated as standard hours earned divided by the actual direct labor hours applied, excluding rework. The problem is that labor efficiency has received so much emphasis in the past, in some companies it is the primary performance measure. In these environments, the production line is never shut down and under no conditions does a worker ever sit idle. While the intent of the measure is admirable, its applications and measurement are inconsistent with JIT/TQC. The underlying assumption is that the only constructive thing a direct labor person can do is build inventory. With JIT/TQC, when a worker's kanbans are full, the last thing we want is more inventory. We want that person to contribute wherever else he can, such as by helping a customer or supplier operation that is falling behind, working on another line, performing housekeeping chores, updating Total Quality Control charts, or cross-training. Any of a number of choices are better than building excess inventory, even sitting idle, though that is one of the least desirable.

Another problem with labor efficiency lies in the collection of direct labor time. With JIT/TQC, we collect labor by exception, subtracting from the total time any meetings and rework that take longer than an hour. What remains are the direct expenses charged to the item produced by the cell including material-handling and Total Quality Control time as well as what was previously considered direct labor. Because it is impractical to track very small elements of time, the direct labor time prior to JIT/TQC is not consistent with the direct charge after implementation.

Once material is put at the point of use, in addition to building products, the people in the area are performing material-handling duties and doing Total Quality Control. Throughout the day, they constantly intermix these direct labor, indirect labor, and overhead functions. It's virtually impossible to separate the three. As a result, labor-efficiency measures are incompatible. If you nevertheless wish to maintain labor-efficiency measures, a baseline consistent with the new JIT/TQC figures can be established during the first six to twelve months. Attempts to adjust the old standards to include the new activities prior to implementing the JIT/TQC processes have proved to be time consuming and inaccurate.

One factory had the following results just five months after JIT/TQC had been implemented in a major production area: Work in process was down 91 percent. Prior to JIT/TQC, there had been about 9,600 pieces in inventory, counting the factory's finished-goods inventory and its primary customer's raw-material stock. After JIT/TQC started, six boxes of 400 pieces each circulated between customer and supplier and satisfied their needs. That's a 75 percent reduction in finished-goods/raw-material inventory. Overall, throughput time was reduced 60 percent, and in one portion of the process, it was reduced from eight days to two hours, eliminating the need for one inspection position. Rejects dropped 66 percent. Labor reporting was simplified, saving eight hours a day. There was an inventory savings of over $250,000. No people were added to the area, 100 percent of the material was stored at the point of use, and no shipments were missed.

Was this area doing a good job? If quality, delivery and cost are important measures then it certainly was. However, the manager was in trouble with his boss because labor efficiency looked worse. From a macro perspective, the cell was achieving breakthrough results. It was making shipments and performing more tasks, while improving quality, delivery, and cost. But it looked worse from a traditional performance-measure perspective. Why?

The cell practiced labor collection by exception, because it was impractical to separate traditional direct labor activities from the newly added tasks of material handling and problem-solving. Therefore, the total direct labor time was inflated. In addition, during the first few months, while finished-goods inventory was being reduced rapidly, the same level of output was not required. Lower outputs from the cell made efficiency temporarily look even worse.The fact is, the labor-efficiency measure was not reporting the situation accurately.

The measure also indicated that the area was overstaffed, but that fact was obvious during the first couple of months anyway. The manager could not move the people elsewhere, however, because other areas were already adequately staffed. There was no other place to productively use the people, and the company did not lay off for short periods of time.

At this point the area manager was faced with a tough choice. Should he give the company long-term progress in terms of quality, delivery responsiveness, and lower costs, or should he make labor efficiency look good? It would have been easy to start building again and look "efficient." The hard task is to continue to make shipments while achieving the breakthroughs he was.

Near the end of the five-month window, the same number of people were producing as much output as they had prior to JIT/TQC, in addition to performing material-handling tasks and problem-solving. Perhaps there was excess labor in the stockroom now, but this production area was not inefficient. Labor-efficiency numbers still looked worse when compared with pre-JIT/TQC efficiency numbers, because material handling and Total Quality Control time could not be separated from direct activities. If we look at the results from a broader perspective, the cell was more efficient and utilized its time well. The baseline for traditional measures had simply changed. Efficiency was not lost, but gained.

Overemphasis of labor efficiency can inhibit JIT/TQC, especially if it is stressed to the point where people are reluctant to stop production when kanban levels are full or if a problem arises.

In the same vein as labor efficiency is a measure for machine utilization (standard hours earned over actual hours available). Like labor efficiency, the machine-utilization measure encourages constant output. However, if a machine produces more than its customers need, then simply keeping it busy is going to result in inventory. This particular measure disregards customer needs, encourages kanban violations, and inhibits the redeployment of people to help in other areas.

Another measure to watch out for is the manufacturing overhead rate (MOH). Recognizing the impracticality of tracking minute elements of direct labor time, a number of companies begin to treat all labor as overhead, particularly as they begin to adopt activity-based costing methods. As the direct labor base shrinks, either due to changes in how information is collected or because of effective automation, the manufacturing overhead rate goes up. Overemphasis of this measure will tempt us to inflate direct labor times and/or resist needed accounting changes and automation. In the labor efficiency example just discussed, the manufacturing overhead rate would have looked better, because direct labor times seemed greater. Unfortunately, the manufacturing overhead rate was not the measure that management chose to stress.

A purchasing measure that is counterproductive to JIT/TQC is the purchase-part price variance, which measures when actual prices are varying from the standard prices we expected to pay. Unfortunately, the standard does not include the cost of purchasing, handling, inspecting, rejecting, accounting, and a wide variety of other wastes associated with incoming materials. One supplier's price may be slightly higher than another's, but the total cost may be substantially lower if the material is delivered directly to the production line, with no inspection or purchase orders required. The problem with this measure is that it motivates people to pursue only one aspect of the total cost and can sabotage our effort to reduce the supplier base. Unfortunately, our accounting systems are usually not capable of adequately determining the true total cost.

Another measure to avoid is defects per person. This assumes that a worker, rather than the system or management, is responsible for quality defects. It will discourage people from reporting problems. If a worker is conscientiously and honestly trying to do his job, that is the most we can ask. No one should feel at fault for defects. Either the worker—or the manager, for that matter—was not trained correctly, or there is something wrong with the process. We must encourage people to point out problems and waste if we hope to correct them.

HIGHER VELOCITY

Frustrated with inadequate measures and incomplete data, one manager finally instructed his staff to direct all their future decisions toward the goal of higher velocity. If what they were about to do would achieve higher velocities, they should do it. If it did not, they would stop. People argued that he couldn't make a simple statement like that. For example, what if someone wanted to purchase a very expensive piece of equipment that resulted in only marginal improvements in velocity? The manager said that he and his staff would use common sense to weed out the obviously incorrect decisions. If they made a mistake, it would only be on close calls, and he wanted to err on the side of higher velocity.

IMPROVEMENT MEASURES

The measures outlined so far reflect the changes and the progress made with JIT/TQC. Another kind of measure points the way to improvement. We examined a number of these in the chapter on Total Quality Control. Fishbone diagrams begin to point the way to improvement. Pareto charts are useful when we go down four to six levels. Employee suggestions and Problem-Solving Storyboards also help to point the way to improvement.

Measures that tell us how we are doing are important, but by themselves they are not of much use. Measures that point the way to improvement, taken alone, are sometimes frustrating—as soon as we kill one bar on the Pareto chart, another takes its place. We cannot recognize progress. But together, they show progress and highlight our next steps.

It would be very instructive to construct a display like that shown in figure 12.3 on a large wall in any work area. Initially, the wall would contain only oversize sheets of blank paper. Then, in the run-chart box, we would place a graph showing how we are doing in a selected performance-measure category. Next to the run chart, we would display a Pareto chart pointing the way to improvement. As we gathered more data, we would show the second-level Pareto charts also. When we were ready to begin to capture third-level data, we would show the checksheet being used to capture that information. When sufficient data was captured, the checksheet would be replaced with the third-level Pareto

Figure 12.3

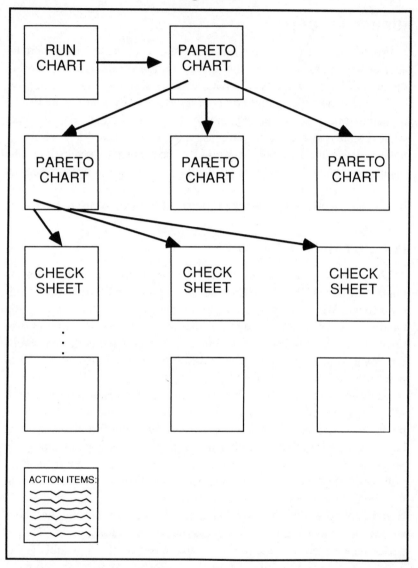

chart. Action-item responsibility could be placed underneath the display.

This display format enables us to keep the problem/opportunity visible. With it, we demonstrate that problems are multilevel. We show how we are performing and point the way to improvement. We are teaching problem-solving while solving a problem.

It is also important that each similar work area establish a standardized set of performance measures. We have standards for how we build our products, and we should also have standards for how we measure our work areas. This is not to say a work area cannot use some additional measures of its own, but each should at least track and visibly display a standard set based on the ones discussed in this chapter.

SUMMARY

If we are serious in our desire to implement JIT/TQC, then we need to understand how it is helping us in the fundamental performance areas of quality, delivery, and cost. We need measures that are consistent with and capable of monitoring the new, higher-velocity JIT/TQC environment. We must readdress those standards that motivate people to perform in the "same old way." JIT/TQC changes the traditional definition of waste, and we require measures that reflect that change. Like all other areas affected by JIT/TQC, performance measures must change. It would be naive, however, to expect them to be consistent with the new vision from the outset. We should try to deemphasize and/or modify those that are a hindrance, but we must also be leaders and help to clarify and bring about the changes needed to progress on the JIT/TQC journey.

Chapter 13
Painting the Vision

It's not enough to work hard. We must also know what to do.
—**W. Edwards Deming**

To successfully implement Just-in-Time, it is essential that management prepare and communicate a vision of where it believes the company is headed. This will provide a framework for decision-making. The vision should be developed specifically from a manufacturing point of view (although the company should of course also have an overall vision).

It is important to draft a statement of this vision to provide an overview; however, a highly detailed mapping of every move the company plans to make is not necessary. For example, if we were planning to drive from Los Angeles to New York, we would not need to know about every bump and turn along the way. What we want to describe here is where we're headed, why we're headed there, the amount of time we want to take to get there, and the kinds of things that we expect to encounter along the way. Thus, for the journey form L.A. to New York we might envision deserts, mountains, and occasional rest stops. For the factory, we will encourage new tools and organization changes and discuss the ever present pressure from the competition. This picture is not intended to be a strategic plan or a list of all the actions that are supposed to take place. Rather, it will furnish an infrastructure so that people can plan actions that will contribute to progress.

All the necessary detailed analysis and planning for our JIT/TQC journey will occur as we proceed. Our vision becomes clearly focused during the pilot. Breakthrough pilot specifications have been established, and all eyes are on the success of the pilot. After about 50 to 75 percent of the factory has been converted to JIT/TQC, however, the focus becomes less clear, and the rate of change often slows. What is next? This is certainly the time to prepare a more comprehensive vision statement. Now that we have some experience with JIT/TQC, we are in a much better position to picture the changes that will be forthcoming.

The length of the vision statement can vary. It is not unusual for it run to twenty-five pages or more, with one page for each functional area and topic.

TOWARD A COMPETITIVE ADVANTAGE

Over the years, manufacturing has taken on a number of different roles. As mentioned in chapter 1, Hayes and Wheelwright believe manufacturing has four specific stages.

During the first stage we try to minimize manufacturing's negative potential. The hope here is that it won't ruin or miss a good product or market opportunity. In stage one, manufacturing is considered "internally neutral."

During the second stage, we achieve parity with competitors; that is, we see ourselves as no worse than most others. Industry practice is followed. Status quo is the mainstay. In stage two, we are "externally neutral."

In the third stage, manufacturing provides creditable support to the business strategy. Changes in strategy are made with input from manufacturing. Manufacturing is beginning to carry its own weight. In stage three, manufacturing is "internally supportive." This marks the beginning of active manufacturing.

With the fourth stage, we begin to pursue manufacturing's competitive advantages. Manufacturing has become "externally supportive." This is where we are headed with JIT/TQC. We want to use JIT/TQC to help manufacturing become a competitive weapon. And we can do that if manufacturing makes significant breakthroughs in the competitive areas of quality, cost, and delivery responsiveness.

If a company is presently in stage one, it still must be able to envision itself as it will be in stage four. It is true that everyone seems to be interested in JIT/TQC as long as they don't have to change. But a company must accept the fact that in order to achieve the breakthroughs possible, all areas of the company will have to change. The constraints to higher velocities are not just in manufacturing.

As we compose our vision statement, we must carefully explain what we expect to happen in each functional area of the company as a result of JIT/TQC. In addition, we should outline anticipated changes to company policies, economics, technology, resources, facilities, competition, and organization.

In the policy area, we might have previously said that we would be no more than 25 percent of a supplier's business base. If we bought too much from a specific supplier, purchasing would automatically source to a second supplier. As we implement JIT/TQC, we find that there is a rational reason to move toward single sourcing. The vision statement must include this information. Other policy changes may involve the number of job classifications needed, layoff policies, training, and retraining. These areas all need to be addressed. We are painting a picture of what we expect the future to look like. Once that vision is established, those in charge of these policy areas can make decisions within that purview.

The statement should also point out the inevitable increase in factory re-layouts and frequency of deliveries and shipments that will affect the facilities area. The competitive environment should be described with explanations of factors such as the growing global competition and changes in government policies. The statement must convey the potential impact these changes will have on the business.

For example, changes in U.S. government payment policies quickly forced Beckman to switch from producing high-tech/high-price goods to making high-tech/low-cost products. When U.S. governmental regulations forced the divestiture of AT&T, Tellabs quickly moved from a safe niche to competing with international giants. Harris, too, experienced significant change when the U.S. government began to adapt more competitive policies and limited progress payments for defense contracts.

In our vision statement, we must also address whether customers and the competition will require more features and therefore more flexibility. What effect will these demands have on lead times?

We also should note that at the organizational level, the company will tend to become less hierarchical, with broader responsibilities delegated to teams. We must also consider such things as the changing role of quality, a merger of order entry and master scheduling, a merger of purchasing and production control, and a decentralization of engineering into new-design and sustaining manufacturing functions.

Technological changes will also affect how JIT/TQC is implemented. New technologies and tools such as Computer Integrated Manufacturing and automation may require us to change current processes in our factories.

It is also important to include a description of the vertical integration we're planning to achieve within the company, both directly or by linking closely with suppliers and customers.

When preparing a vision statement, we should make it easy for someone to pull out the portion of the statement appropriate to them. Since these statements tend to address the same topic in a number of different ways, you might want to make it possible for a specific area, such as finance, to condense its section into a couple of pages to be put on the wall. The various topics in the statement should also be cross-referenced and cross-indexed, so that, for instance, the finance changes that affect information systems can be noted by all departments.

The vision statement does not take a tremendous amount of time to develop. It does, however, require independent thinking. A large committee should not decide the direction of the company; involving too many people will lead to a refined status-quo approach at best. It is best to pick six to ten people who can get away for a day and brainstorm to envision the breakthroughs the company must achieve. They will not determine how the changes will occur; they will simply evaluate what will take place if JIT/TQC becomes a way of life.

These people need not come from the same level, but they should be *visionaries*. They should be aggressive and receptive to change. Their task is to free themselves from any reasonable constraints from the past and paint a picture of the next five years. At least one representative from each major functional area should be included on this team, perhaps along with an outsider with broad JIT/TQC experience.

The vision statement should begin by announcing that manufacturing is adopting the Just-in-Time and Total Quality Control processes. It should then outline the changes that are envisioned for the next five years, followed by descriptions of the changes that will be needed for each functional area.

As the vision team brainstorms and considers changes to various areas, it may make use of a tool known as the mindmap see (figure 13.1), which resembles a fishbone diagram. Each main spur of the mind map represents a major functional, policy, and/or organizational area.

Figure 13.1
Mindmap

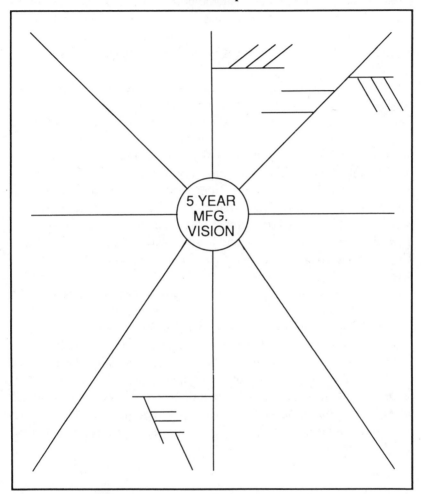

Branches are then connected to the appropriate spurs. At the end of its brainstorming session, the team should have recorded most of the key changes onto the mind map. The next task is to translate the map into words to create the vision statement. Once this document has been written, it should be circulated to the various levels of the organization that will have an interest in the projected changes.

This statement will almost certainly stir up a great deal of emotion and discussion. It's important to listen to the feedback and decide which is constructive to the process. Any helpful information can be incorporated into the statement. A vision statement does not immediately create a group consensus. It may never be officially blessed. Yet, unless another clearly defined statement is created to replace it, this one will probably take root.

Change takes a while, particularly when it is traumatic. People may need several months before they can begin to adopt this new vision. We can't expect people to love it instantly. For instance, if someone's pet project was the development of an automatic stacker retriever system, that person will be disappointed to discover that material will be stored at the point of use. Initially, he may only reluctantly participate in the process of change. Someone in information systems may have been working on a new work-order system, or someone in finance may have been devising a new but traditional cost-accounting system. Suddenly, there are no more work orders, and labor is being collected by exception. These are personal impacts that a company should do its best to anticipate.

The vision statement serves to prioritize a company's efforts with JIT/TQC and define a framework within which to make decisions. It is also important to realize, however, that, like the company itself, the vision statement is constantly evolving. Many companies find themselves reexamining these statements and adjusting them annually. There is, of course, no fixed rule about how often a statement should be revised; often, though, after nine to fifteen months a company better understands where it is actually headed and decides to fine-tune its focus. If the momentum of progress with JIT/TQC begins to slow, it is probably time to develop or update the vision statement.

Chapter 14
Taking the Next Step

What we have to learn to do, we learn by doing.
—Aristotle

The next step is yours. You have read how Just-in-Time/Total Quality Control can comprehensively change the way you do business. The opportunities are there before you. Can you continue to ignore them? If you want to remain competitive, your answer has to be an unequivocal no.

Johnny Lee of McDonnell Douglas's Computer Systems Division has said that "competition in business is like running a marathon. But in business, there is no end. There are only leaders, who are in front; losers, who drop out, and learners trying to change their pace to either catch up or stay ahead." By employing what you have learned in this book, you can effectively change your company from an also-ran into a world-class competitor.

JIT/TQC is not a process for those interested in improving their competitive stance only a little bit. It's for those looking to make powerful breakthroughs that will propel their company forward. These are breakthroughs that will lead to higher velocities with less cost, better quality, and a more rapid response to customer demand.

Learning to do JIT/TQC is like learning to ride a bicycle. You can read all the books that have ever been written about how to ride a bike, but at some point, you're going to have to climb onto the seat and start pedaling. The same is true with JIT/TQC and its pilot project. The Just-in-Time pilot project isn't designed to launch you immediately into the heights of international competition. But then you would never expect to enter the Tour de France cycling competition immediately after learning to ride a bike.

307

When you first climb onto a bike, your perspective changes. You begin to get a feel for what riding a bicycle is all about. Of course, you don't keep one foot on the curb and one foot on the pedal—you must commit to riding. It is the same with a JIT/TQC pilot. You don't "sort of" do it. You commit to doing JIT/TQC the way it's supposed to be done, with no compromises and no turning back. The pilot allows you to adjust your process while you learn. It is also small enough to allow for controlled experiments with different approaches. With a pilot, you're not going to destroy yourself or your business. You may scrape a knee or an elbow, but you won't get seriously hurt. JIT/TQC is indeed the fast track to continuous improvement, but it is relatively risk free if you follow the recommendations.

Once you learn how to ride a bike without training wheels, you never want to go back. Similarly, at companies where JIT/TQC has been implemented, the people involved never want to return to the old ways. There have even been those who have threatened to quit their jobs when asked to transfer to a non-JIT/TQC area. They wanted no part of those operations that hadn't cut over to JIT/TQC.

JIT/TQC not only changes the process of manufacturing, it changes the people who perform the operations. Donald Hogan, a data-cell electronics associate at Tellabs, attests to this. "I would never go back to batch," he says. "I like the idea of working on smaller numbers of circuit boards instead of working on lots of 125. You got bored and tired before you got through, and quality would drop off toward the end. If you were doing 125 boards, by the last 25 you were tired."

But more than maintaining people's focus, Just-in-Time alters the way people perceive the work they do. As Hogan's colleague Ken Goad explained, "The barriers of communication were broken in the cell. There was no longer a final assembler versus a hand inserter. Now, we're all doing the same things. Cross-training really helped. We all appreciate our jobs and each other's jobs. I don't understand how companies ever made it without JIT/TQC."

The way to start JIT/TQC is to put together a team of people, educate them, and try it. Once you've got the pilot up and running, you can decide whether you want to go further. With a pilot you've got tangible evidence, not just somebody's opinion.

With the pilot, you can experience JIT/TQC. As the number of kanbans in the process is dropped to accelerate our manufacturing velocities, we will expose and prioritize problems. Previously, everything was done to avoid problems. We'd dodge around them or cover them with inventory. JIT/TQC, however, forces us to eliminate the constraints. JIT/TQC lights a fire under people to turn problems into opportunities.

In the past, when problems surfaced, our first reaction was usually to find someone to blame. With JIT/TQC, problems don't have faults—they have causes. And if we can get people to communicate with each other about those problems, we have a better chance of making a profound breakthrough. Intelligence is randomly distributed throughout the organization. As JIT/TQC is implemented and people are encouraged to respond, an amazing number of creative and practical ideas are generated.

Moreover, people are not being coerced into action; they are participating because they know it will, invariably, improve the quality of life. JIT/TQC reduces the stress of manufacturing. Stress levels rise when people know they could improve something, but no one pays attention to their suggestions. Just-in-Time gives everyone the right and the duty to voice his ideas. That makes people feel good, both about themselves and about the job they are performing. They recognize that they are no longer merely hired hands—they have been hired for their minds as well.

Of course this does not mean that JIT/TQC eliminates all stress. A stress-free, noncompetitive manufacturing environment does not exist on this planet. Awareness of the realities of intense global competition fosters a healthy degree of respect and, as a result, some stress. Ignorance of the competitive nature of manufacturing may be blissful, but it is also fatal. At least, however, JIT/TQC helps to relieve some of the internally caused stress.

JIT/TQC also changes the way we deal with problems. No longer do we simply add inventory which, like a narcotic, may relieve the pain but is certainly not healthy or advisable to use regularly. Putting together a multifunctional team to begin the JIT/TQC process, as described in chapter 2, is the first step to competitive health. It is the responsibility of this team to see to it that the breakthrough pilot specifications are followed. Along with the project champion, the team makes sure the pilot is implemented quickly. These recommendations are not arbitrary; they are based on a great deal of experience. It is important that people within the company understand that JIT/TQC is not just a new production process. It is going to change the way the whole company operates. This is why it is so essential to involve a cross section of people in the initial implementation process.

The reason we begin a pilot is to create a model for the future and to experience in a controlled environment the difficult constraints we will encounter. And there will be some difficult changes. The pilot specifications have been designed to allow a company to learn how to overcome the most common constraints to continuous improvement. By mastering these problems in a pilot, we maximize our chances for success, while keeping our cost down. Then, when it is time to begin converting the whole factory to JIT/TQC, we will have models and patterns to work from which in turn, will speed that process.

Getting the pilot going in approximately 120 days is also crucial. Once we receive the green light to proceed, we must step on the accelerator, because the light will eventually change. Given that all projects expand to take up the time allotted to them, the more time we have in a pilot, the longer we have to misdirect our focus. If we don't act within that limited time frame, we may miss the green light because we find ourselves too busy or improperly organized. A lot of hard work can be accomplished in 120 days. Experience shows that a pilot usually does not require more. The key to action is starting and focusing on a clear objective.

With a few exceptions, in any reasonably well-run factory, a JIT/TQC pilot can be implemented. We don't have to be perfect to do Just-in-Time. If we fixed everything before we started Just-in-Time, then we wouldn't need it. JIT/TQC is not a list of ten or twelve things to do, but a way of prioritizing a never-ending series of constraints that we will encounter between today and perfection.

We may reach a point, however, of diminishing returns. The rate of change may slow down in certain areas, and the number of kanbans may have been reduced to a small number. That is not the time, though, to break our arms patting ourselves on the back. It is the time to focus even more clearly, and ask, "How can we be better?" JIT/TQC does not end at a point of diminishing returns.

Once our production areas have become more simplified and are running at higher velocities, we need to check if significant amounts of inventory exist between us and our external supplier. If they do, we must begin linking JIT/TQC externally. We may find that excess inventory is stacking up between us and our outside customer. That's the time to begin doing JIT/TQC with our external customers. JIT/TQC exists throughout the entire manufacturing pipeline—from the earth itself, through each successive manufacturing level, to the end customer. Some companies are even beginning to use JIT/TQC for refurbishing used equipment.

It all begins, however, with the first step. Bringing JIT/TQC on-line quickly and successfully requires a time-priority decision. Something will have to be deemphasized so that JIT/TQC can be fit in. Nobody ever has enough time to do JIT/TQC. But then, nobody really has enough time not to do it.

This book has provided you with the basic tools for JIT/TQC. It has demonstrated how to reduce setups and eliminate paperwork. It has detailed the impacts on purchasing and transportation. It has depicted the challenges to your accounting procedures. It has outlined the influence JIT/TQC has on systems, engineering, facilities, and marketing. It has shown the effect it will have on performance measures, and it has illustrated how to paint a vision for a company's future. These tools are worthless unless they are used. If they are used, however, JIT/TQC will make your operations worth far more than you ever could have projected under your present system.

You can make the comparison yourself. In chapter 1 I stated that based on conservative estimates, companies should obtain the following results:

- 50-90 percent reduction in throughput times
- 50-90 percent reduction in work in progress
- 60-80 percent reduction in scrap and rework
- 50-90 percent reduction in setup times
- 30-60 percent reduction in manufacturing space required
- 10 to 1,000 times improvement in selected quality areas
- 5 to 10 times improvement in overall quality
- 4 to 10 times improvement in inventory turns

Go out into your facility and find out where you stand in these areas today. What is your present throughput time? How long are your setups? How many days of inventory do you have on hand? How great is your required manufacturing space? How good is your quality?

If these levels were to drop by the percentages listed above, what would they be? How competitive would that make your company? The out-of-pocket costs for starting JIT/TQC are insignificant. The savings are enormous. Now, how can you afford not to start JIT/TQC? The answer is, of course, you can't.

JIT/TQC is not magic. There is no secret, no hidden tricks to making JIT/TQC work. There *is* plenty of hard work. Just-in-Time and Total Quality Control may be simple in concept, but they are difficult to accomplish. But then, no one ever said it would be easy. The payoff, however, is competitiveness.

The truth is, JIT/TQC is not the only thing you will need to compete, but it now appears unlikely that you will remain competitive for long without it. With your business at stake, can you afford to stick to the same old ways?

The other riders are beginning to wake up. Their horses are stirring. The choice is simple: You either make dust or eat it! The choice is yours.

Kanban Cards and Calculations

A sample kanban card format is shown here that will serve a variety of purposes (see figure A.1). This kanban card was designed after I observed several implementation teams allocating too much of their 120-day implementation schedule to kanban-card layout. The design and color scheme suggested here are just one of many workable formats. In fact, many people now design their card so that it can be printed by a personal computer, thereby simplifying the clerical effort involved in preparing the document. It is important not to have too many different styles, however, as it will just inhibit flexibility in moving from one production area to another. The best time to settle on a design is before there are too many. If people need to express their creativity, let them express it in problem-solving, not in coming up with a new kanban format.

PRIMARY KANBANS

The *Production Authorization* kanban (green) is used to limit the inventory of items in production. One kanban in this instance may represent one part, one container with a specified number of parts, or one job. The card stays on the completed product until "purchased" by the "customer." Only then is the card removed, thereby allowing the kanban to recirculate back to the beginning of the production process. Only when a Production Authorization kanban is available may production start.

The *Restock Authorization* (or move) kanban (yellow) is used to

Figure A.1

KANBAN CARDS

Production Authorization (Green: Recirculates)	Restock Authorization (Yellow: Recirculates)
Rework Authorization (Orange: Recirculates)	Startup Excess (Pink: Use once)
Emergency Authorization (Silver: Use once)	Other Authorization (Blue: Follow Instructions)

PART NUMBER

DESCRIPTION

OPERATION

Production Authorization
(Green: Recirculates)

FROM:

TO:

TRANSFER
QTY / CONTAINER
LOT SIZE
QTY / KANBANS
MAXIMUM | REORDER
QUANTITY | POINT
REPLENISH
MAXIMUM QTY

1987 by W.A. Sandras, Jr. of PCI, Johnstown, CO 80534 U.S.A.

Production Authorization
(Green: Recirculates)

Card#_____ of_____

Permission to reprint granted with inclusion of copyright

(Front)   (Back)

replenish materials typically stored at the point of use. When the inventory level has reached the order point, the kanban card is removed and given to the supplier to authorize replenishment. The supplier may be external or internal.

SPECIAL-SITUATION KANBANS

The *Rework Authorization* kanban (orange) is used to limit the inventory of products in rework and to show that a returned product is not in violation of the kanban control process (no item can exist without a kanban authorization). When an item is returned to the production area for rework after the Production Authorization kanban has been removed, the Rework Authorization kanban may be used. The Rework Authorization kanban helps limit the amount of rework and provides a visual feedback on the amount of rework in process. If a large mass of orange color is visible on a wall in the rework area, we know that not much is in rework. If the wall is empty, we know that rework has reached its peak. In most instances the Rework Authorization kanban is not used; items requiring rework that have not yet been "shipped" out of the production area simply retain their Production Authorization kanban, and items being returned from outside of the production area are simply matched to a free Production Authorization kanban. Normally, it is only when this simpler method does not work that a Rework Authorization kanban is used.

The *Startup Excess* kanban (pink) is helpful when first converting over to kanban control. Production Authorization kanbans are used to authorize items in production up to the limit calculated. In many instances, however, when a company is beginning Just-in-Time, inventory in production exceeds the kanban ceiling. When this is the case, the excess in inventory needs to be identified until it can be used up. Failure to authorize each item in inventory at the start will make it difficult to see which items without a kanban exist due to prior conditions and which have been created in violation of the kanban control process. It is easier and more consistent if everything has a kanban authorization from day 1. When a product with a Startup Excess kanban is "purchased" by the customer, the kanban is not recirculated, because we do not want to replace excess inventory. Many people choose to display the card with the inventory value written on it, to show the progress that has been made with "One Less at a Time." As Production Authorizations are later removed, they are displayed along with the Startup Excess kanbans.

The *Other Authorization* kanban (blue) is used for very special instances. On one of my production lines, we assembled engineering-workstation computers. One of the options was an internal printer. If the customer order did not require a printer, the process still required us to build and test the unit with one to make certain the computer would function properly if a printer was added on later. When a computer passed the test, if the printer was not ordered, it was detached and put back on the kanban shelf with an available Production Authorization kanban. If one was not available, a special Other Authorization kanban was used to show that the excess printer that resided on the shelf was a result of this special situation. The blue kanban was later replaced with the next free Production Authorization kanban.

The *Emergency Authorization* kanban (silver) is used to allow inventory temporarily to exceed calculated limits. Normally it takes at least two higher-level managers to approve emergency kanbans and they are used no more than six times in a twelve-month period. This is the "silver bullet" kanban. When a product with an Emergency Authorization kanban is "purchased" by the customer, the kanban is not recirculated, because we do not want to replace excess inventory.

KANBAN DATA ENTRY

A description of the data that goes into each field follows. Most people fill in only a minimum amount of data, thereby avoiding data-entry effort and visual distractions where the information is obvious.

Part Number:
If this is a brand-name kanban, enter the part number authorized by this kanban. If it is a generic kanban, enter the family number of products authorized.

Description:
Give the description of the part number entered above, that is, the name of the part number or part family authorized by the kanban.

Operation:
Enter the operation or series of operations authorized by this kanban to occur. That is, enter the operations within which this kanban card circulates.

From:
For Production, Rework, Emergency, and Startup Excess authorizations, enter the supplier's location of the part to be "purchased" with this kanban. For the Restock Authorization, enter the supplier's name and/or location for the replenishment part number. The name and location may be for an external supplier, an internal supplier operation/

location, or a stockroom location. When deliveries begin directly to the point of use, simply change the entry from stockroom to the supplier name. For all cards, if the "from" location is obvious or not relevant, leave it blank.

To:

For Production, Rework, Emergency, and Startup Excess authorizations, enter the outbound-kanban storage location where this work-in-process part number will be placed when this segment of the production process is completed. The location may be a work position or another point-of-use storage location. For the Stock Authorization, enter the destination of the replenishment part number. This location may be a work position or another point-of-use storage location. For all cards, if the "to" location is obvious or not relevant, leave it blank.

Transfer Quantity:

Indicate the maximum number of kanbans allowed at one work position before movement to the output-kanban location or next work position is required. The work position is only for active work, not for storage. This field defines the maximum amount of temporary storage that is allowed at the position if it is inconvenient to move each item individually. (Usually not required for Restock Authorization.)

Transfer Container:

Specify the container in which to move the material if a particular container or conveyance type is required.

Lot-size quantity:

Specify the lot size for this part. When the lot size is accumulated, the kanban (s) must be put in the priority queue to initiate new production. (Usually not required for Restock Authorization.)

Lot-size kanbans:

Specify the number of kanban cards equivalent to the lot size. For example, if the lot size is 100, and each kanban card authorizes production of 20 units, 5 kanbans represents the lot size. (Usually not required for Restock Authorization.)

Maximum Quantity:

Required only for Restock Authorizations using the order point replenishment method (i.e. a min./max. or dipstick approach). No item is allowed to exist without a kanban ceiling; therefore, specify the maximum allowable inventory for this part at this location.

Reorder Point:
Required only for Restock Authorizations using the order-point replenishment method (i.e. a min./max. or dipstick approach). Specify the minimum inventory point at which the Restock Authorization must be submitted to ensure replenishment in the required turnaround time.

Replenish Maximum Quantity:
Required only for Restock Authorizations using the order-point replenishment method (i.e. a min./max. or dipstick approach). Enter the difference between the Maximum Quantity and the Reorder Point. This quantity represents the maximum amount of inventory that can safely be replenished without exceeding the allowable level. It is permissible to restock less than this quantity, but not more. If the full amount is not restocked, the result will be that the Restock Authorization will be turned in sooner next time. Ideally, the quantity is a multiple of the supplier-package quantity.

Blank space on back:
Most often used to affix a bar code to simplify transaction processing and facilitate quality data collection. Sometimes used to show complex routings.

Card #— of—:
Used to identify the sequence number of each kanban card for a given part number or product family. Numbering each card will make it easier to know how many exist in the series and will permit detection of an additional or missing card.

Note that the card design is the same for all types; only the name of the card changes. It is possible to use only one type of card, with the heading "Do it!" authorizing production, movement, etc. Sometimes, however, color coding can help to simplify the process. Just remember to keep it simple. For that reason also, many data fields are left blank if they do not apply or if the information is obvious.

GENERAL GUIDELINES FOR KANBAN CALCULATIONS

1. Establish a reasonable number of kanbans. When establishing the maximum number of kanbans you'll need on the shop floor, pick a unit

of measure that will allow for a reasonable number. Suppose, for instance, there are four containers between a supply operation and a customer operation. Each container holds 100 parts. When a container is returned, you are authorized to build 100 more parts. If a container is considered to be a kanban, one less container would result in a 25 percent inventory reduction in one step. If, however, you change the unit of measure from container to pieces, you could then take one or more pieces out of each container and reduce the inventory much more gradually. It's easier to reduce kanbans one at a time if you're working with a "reasonable" number.

2. Consider transfer-lot multiples. Suppose your lot size is 200, but you utilize containers of 100 for handling convenience. You may not need to complete work on all 200 before you can move any material to the customer operation. Hopefully, you can determine a practical way to move the first 100 or fewer to the customer while the supplier is working on the second 100 of the lot.

The reverse also applies. If a kanban is one, it doesn't mean you have to move only one. Ideally, you should, but distances may make it economically not feasible. It is, therefore, necessary to establish a maximum number of kanbans, which, when reached, must be transferred to the next operation. In lower-volume production environments, forcing all completed material to move at least every hour helps to keep product moving and to level the flow.

3. Avoid daily or weekly multiples. When you have ten kanbans and are making ten products a day, there is a tendency to think that if your rate per day goes to eleven, then you will need eleven kanbans. This is not true. You can still use ten kanbans with an output of eleven products per day; your ten kanbans will simply turn over faster. A mental problem can arise for people when the number of kanbans is exactly equal to the number of products produced per day or week. To avoid this mental trap, it is best not to make the number of kanbans equal to the rate per day, particularly in the beginning of a Just-in-Time implementation. While there is nothing technically wrong with this, it could become confusing for some people.

4. Consider downstream unevenness. If, for example, there is a lot size of twenty-five for most of the items run through one machine, it is possible that one of those items could require an abnormally large amount of a subsequent resource because of its unique processing

requirements. When this uneven load requirement is the exception rather than the rule, it's best to break the problem lot size down to avoid an abnormally large and abrupt capacity requirement in the downstream operation. You are trying to keep the factory at a level load, and the unique processing requirements for this particular product will result in added inventory for all products because of the time it will occupy in the subsequent operation.

5. Kanban calculations should include rework. Rework should not escape kanban controls. Rework does not offer an infinite black hole into which faulty product can be dumped in order to free up kanbans to authorize replacement production during repair. If a product fails prior to shipment, it will typically retain its kanban authorization. This will prevent the kanban from recirculating to initiate production of another replacement product. If you are inattentive enough to allow all kanbans to divert into rework, the entire production process will shut down until at least one of the failures is repaired. The total number of kanbans, however, should allow for a "normal" rework level for that product. Extra kanbans due to rework are especially wasteful, but they may be necessary given the rework conditions that exist at the start of JIT/TQC.

If a failed product is returned by a following operation (internal customer) after the kanban has been recirculated, it must obtain another kanban authorization in order to exist legally in the supply operation. Some companies simply intercept a recirculating kanban and put it with the failed product, along with rework instructions. Others control the number of products they will allow in rework by using rework kanbans. When products are failing at a rate that rework cannot keep up with, all rework kanbans will eventually become attached to products in the rework queue. When this happens, no more production is allowed until at least one product is repaired and the associated rework kanban is freed again. Hopefully, if rework begins to fall behind, management will shift resources in to the repair area and investigate the problem.

Rework kanbans often reside on a wall until needed. If rework kanbans are orange, a mass of orange on the wall indicates that not much is in rework; a scarcity of orange indicates trouble.

Returns from outside customers often go to separate repair areas and typically are not part of this control mechanism, but they certainly could be.

6. Look for natural kanbans. In many environments, the potential for

kanban control exists naturally, and the kanbans just haven't been formalized. This is often the case in areas where containers or pallets are used to transport material through a series of manufacturing operations. The number of containers you have in process during normal times may very well be the number you begin with under Just-in-Time.

KANBAN CALCULATIONS FOR PRODUCTION ITEMS

Now, let's take a look at how to actually calculate the number of kanbans necessary for your pilot. We will focus in this section on the major production items.

As previously stated, the number of kanbans may represent the maximum number of pieces allowed in the manufacturing pipeline. The calculations for the maximum allowable kanbans are based on the rate per day times the total replenishment time. Under normal conditions, this is the elapsed time from the moment you use a piece, to complete production of a replacement, that is, the total elapsed time required to replace what was used.

Of course, the calculation thus far allows no room for rework, machine downtime, part shortages, or errors of any kind. Therefore, when you're just getting started, you may have to give yourself some room for error. Adding safety will increase the number of kanbans and thereby decrease the velocity of the system. Adding slack is wasteful, but it may be necessary given today's conditions.

The manufacturing lead time used by the Manufacturing Resource Planning system includes the elapsed time through the manufacturing pipeline segment. It also often includes planned safety time but typically does not include the planning time required from consumption of an item by the customer until reentry of a replacement into the manufacturing pipeline. For the kanban calculation, the entire replenishment loop is taken into account.

Often, however, only through-put time is emphasized—the time from entry into the queue, authorizing the start of production, until the moment the product is again available for consumption by the customer. This is because the time required to recirculate a free kanban is negligible. Traditionally, with work orders, the process may require a week, an entire planning department, and a long computer run. With JIT/TQC, the kanban simply returns to the beginning of the process loop. The bulk of the time is now in the manufacturing pipeline itself.

If you're producing in lot sizes rather than making one at a time, you have to allow for the accumulation of the lot size as well. For example, if a lot size equals fifteen, fifteen kanbans have to be accumulated before an operator is required to begin production. The kanban calculation in this case is as follows:

	replenishment days	3 days replenish
+	safety days	+ 2 days safety
	total days	= 5 days total
×	rate/day	× 2 per day
=	# of pieces	= 10 pieces
+	lot size	+ 15 lot size
	total pieces = # of kanbans =	25 kanbans or pieces

(or, where the kanbans are containers with more than one piece, total # pieces / # pieces per container = # of returnable kanban containers)

The addition of the lot-size quantity to the total number of kanbans allowed applies primarily to lower-volume operations. If your rate per day is two, and the sum of the throughput and safety days is five, you would require ten kanbans. If your lot size is fifteen, however, you will never collect enough kanbans to initiate production if you don't also include the lot size. In higher-volume production environments, particularly where setups are minimal, the addition of the lot size is often insignificant.

It is important to realize that the replenishment time may change dramatically as Just-in-Time starts up. Initiating the replenishment takes less time, and the product travels through the manufacturing pipeline itself more quickly. At Hewlett-Packard, throughput times decreased from thirteen days to two days at the Vancouver division and from forty days to three days at the Fort Collins division. Almost overnight, Tellabs' throughput time went from twenty-two days to two days, and at Beckman it was lowered from sixty days to three.

Due to the possibility of dramatically higher velocities, it's important to compare the number of pieces authorized by the kanban calculations with the number of pieces in inventory prior to JIT/TQC. If the number of calculated kanban pieces represents a substantial cut, it's critical to understand why. If you cannot explain why the kanban result is lower, you should rethink your kanban calculation. You should be able to

Figure A.2

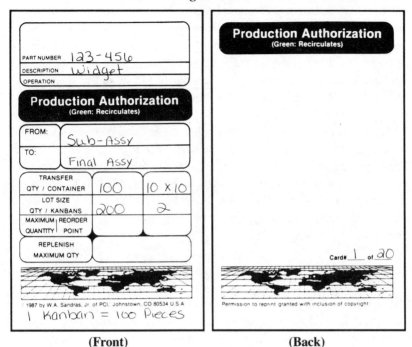

(Front)   (Back)

The *replenishment time* required for the part—that is, the time required to replace the part once it has been "purchased" by the customer operation if no problems occur—equals two days. The *safety time* allows one day extra for problem—wasteful but necessary in this environment. Therefore, the *total replenishment lead time* we will use is equal to three days. We have a planned production rate of 600 per day. A lead time of three days, multiplied by a planned requirement of 600 per day, results in a need for 1,800 kanbans. If the lot size is 200, we must also add that quantity to the 1,800, resulting in 2,000 kanban cards. To simplify the mechanics of the process, we may decide to move the product in containers of 100 each, thereby requiring us to have only 20 kanbans (2,000 divided by 100). Now, a kanban might actually be in the form of a returnable container rather than a card, or we may choose to use 20 cards (as shown) and affix them to any available container when the card is returned to the beginning of the production process.

adequately justify why the calculation has resulted in a lower inventory level. It may be due to a changed layout, shorter queues between certain areas, or reduced setup times. However, just renaming the current process Just-in-Time is not sufficient in itself to cause lower inventory levels; something must actually change. When in doubt, begin with kanbans equal to the steady-state number of pieces in the system. Just-in-Time, of course, won't cause you to have more pieces than are required today. But be careful; you don't want too many kanbans, because you'll have trouble with longer queues and be more susceptible to scrap and rework problems. On the other hand, you don't want too few kanbans, because you'll expose too many problems all at once. You must establish a reasonable number with which to begin JIT/TQC. Then, for the first thirty days or so, you will learn how the kanban system works. After that, each customer/supplier pair will gently lower the inventory levels to expose the problems.

KANBAN CALCULATIONS FOR REPLENISHMENT ITEMS

It isn't necessary to have a kanban card for each nut, bolt, or screw. However, it is important to be consistent: everything has a kanban ceiling. With parts like these, you can use a simple dipstick approach. This is similar to the device we use to determine when our car needs more oil. The dipstick approach tells us when it's time to add a standard quantity (this should be consistent with the supplier's package size).

You can also control minor items by using multiple small returnable containers that hold a fixed quantity of parts, such as a two-bin system, or by drawing a line at a particular level on a container to denote the maximum quantity of parts allowed. When the point-of-use inventory drops below a certain point, the operator will signal the supplier, or possibly the stockroom, to reload the bin to the kanban maximum. The signal may be in the form of a kanban card, a light, positioning of the stock bin, or a phone call. Or it may simply be the supplier's responsibility to keep this bin filled. No other action is required by the customer.

The number of minor items stored at the point of use should be sensible. You don't want to spend too much effort counting them, but you don't want to buy too many either. Handling is waste. Inventory is waste. Both must be minimized. During the initial stages of implementation, you should have to replenish these materials only infrequently, so

Figure A.3

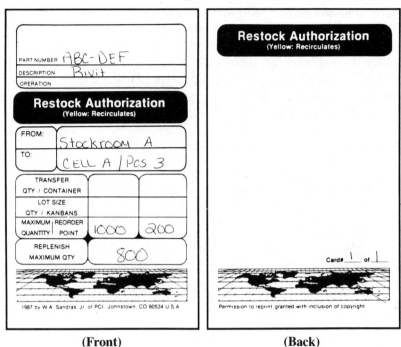

(Front)	**(Back)**

In this example, material is being withdrawn *from* Stockroom A and transferred *to* Cell A/Position 3. A *maximum quantity* of 1,000 of these parts is allowed at the work position. The kanban card will be sent to Stockroom A for replenishment when the on-hand balance at the work position falls to the *reorder point* of 200. The Stockroom is then authorized to *replenish* a *maximum quantity* of 800. It can transfer less if the supplier package quantity makes it more convenient, but it is not authorized to move more.

that you can concentrate on more critical items. If the package quantity is too large, discuss it with the supplier. Initially, however, the line is usually replenished by the stockroom rather than the external supplier.

When we began using Just-in-Time at Hewlett-Packard, it seemed impractical to have minor items delivered directly from the supplier to each person on the production line. We assumed these pieces would always have to go through the stockroom before being placed at the point of use. However, Barry Wooley, of HP/Vancouver found a way to have even these minor items delivered directly to the point of use.

To understand his approach, picture a soft-drink machine. The supplier regularly comes in and reloads the drinks directly into the dispenser columns in the machine. At HP/Vancouver, today, small items are delivered in what look like half-pint through half-gallon milk cartons and are stored in a column at the work position. Anyone can step back and see if a dispenser is two pints low. Material comes directly from the supplier, packaged in these boxes, and is placed in the dispensers just as with a soft-drink machine. The first person to touch one of the minor items in the carton is the person who uses them. We can learn a lot about how material should be handled in manufacturing by observing how it is handled in the retail grocery business. (see figure A.3)

Appendix B
Problem-Solving Storyboard

As we begin to reduce the inventory in the manufacturing pipeline, the velocity of material moving through the pipeline increases. We get faster feedback on quality problems, delivery responsiveness improves, and costs begin to decrease due to reduced inventory. But costs, responsiveness, and quality also begin to feel a negative constraint in the form of material handling. We find ourselves making more frequent trips through the stockroom in order to issue the materials required for the smaller and smaller lots. Just-in-Time drives us to make more frequent issues at less total cost; at the same time it exposes the constraint to higher velocities as material handling. Just-in-Time drives us to "have our cake and eat it too." How can we make more trips through the stockroom and decrease material handling? Certainly this is impossible with our current approach. We must change the material-handling process to eliminate the constraint to higher velocities (see figure B.1). Just-in-Time will drive us to store material at the point of use. Even if it does not all fit there today, the point of use is the primary location; material left behind in the stockroom is now considered to be located in the overflow stock area. Moving material to the point of use may seem impractical, but the opportunity is exposed, and a more competitive position awaits those who can break through the constraint.

Let us assume our people accept the challenge, and we plan to move material to the point of use. In so doing, we anticipate that material accuracy will suffer. In general, when we store material at the point of use we should expect lower inventory-record accuracy, right? Wrong— particularly if we want to make use of computer-based planning tools

Figure B.1
Just-in-Time

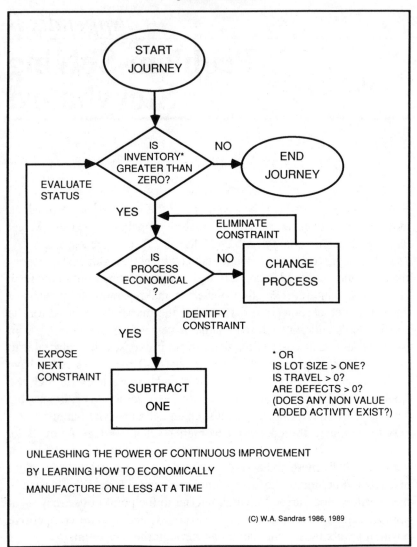

UNLEASHING THE POWER OF CONTINUOUS IMPROVEMENT
BY LEARNING HOW TO ECONOMICALLY
MANUFACTURE ONE LESS AT A TIME

such as Manufacturing Resource Planning. It is reasonable to expect an initial fluctuation in inventory accuracy levels. Wishful thinking, however, will not suffice if we wish to restore the required accuracy levels. We must understand the causes of the problems and correct them at the source. Just-in-Time drives us to put material at the point of use. Total Quality Control is used to eliminate the causes of inaccuracy.

PROBLEM-SOLVING STORYBOARD

Referring to the Problem-Solving Storyboard[1] presented in Figures B.2, B.3 and B.4, we see that the *problem* is assigned to the Just-in-Time/Total Quality Control production area for resolution. Production is now responsible for the material stored in its area. Stock remains responsible for material stored in the "overflow" stockroom.

Responsibility for resolution is assigned to Bill Sandras. If someone asks, "Who has responsibility for inventory-record accuracy for material stored at the point of use?" there should be no doubt in Bill's mind that he must immediately raise his hand. Few problems of any significance will be resolved by only one person, but on October 18, 1988, Bill assumed responsibility for seeing this problem through to a satisfactory conclusion and committed himself to initiating action with the appropriate people. The person responsible should be at the appropriate organizational level and possess, or be able to influence, adequate authority to see the job through. He is also expected to prioritize his time as required.

The *Problem* is stated verbally in the next portion of the storyboard. The problem can be one we are currently experiencing or, as in this instance, one that we expect and are attempting to control. In this section, "feeling" words may be used if necessary. But this is the last time emotions will be allowed; from now on the process requires facts!

In figure B.3, in the *solution* section, we see that on October 18, 1988, a team is formed. Members of the team would likely include someone from a JIT/TQC production area, someone from the stockroom who is familiar with the problems of maintaining inventory-record accuracy, and perhaps people from accounting, purchasing, and information systems. On October 20, 1988, the key performance measures

[1] Note that this Storyboard has a slightly different format from those presented in chapter 11, figures 11.15, 11.16.

are determined. The team decides how to measure inventory-record accuracy for items stored at the point of use, and the data to be collected is determined. Up to this point, no entries are likely to have been made in the *history* section. The sequence of the form is seldom followed exactly. It is a working document and the various sections are repeatedly referred to. Where "team" is shown as responsible, it indicates Bill is responsible for gathering the team inputs.

In the *history* section, a graph is constructed to show the key process-performance measures identified during the October 20 meeting. The data should show whether or not the process is under control and provide an indication of the magnitude of the problem. In this instance, on October 20, the team decides that count errors per million will be appropriate and consistent with production-parts-per-million (PPM) measures. Note that 95 percent inventory-record accuracy is the same as 50,000 errors per million counts. Certainly we can uncover a significant reason for 50,000 errors. Sometimes more than one graph is used to quantify the top level of the problem. For example, a storyboard on part shortages may graph the number of shortages and the duration of shortages. The *history* section is used to display the magnitude of the problem in quantifiable terms. (In the *cause* section, we will show data designed to isolate the root cause of the problem.)

In this case, we are following the Total Quality Control process in anticipation of moving material to the point of use on January 1, 1989. Moving material to the point of use is difficult, and we know that we can correct the causes of error quickly only if we approach the potential problems in a scientific manner. The Problem-Solving Storyboard is an ongoing working document, and as time progresses, data begins to arrive and is graphed in the *history* section.

In the *goal* section we state that we will continue to work on this opportunity until we can sustain an acceptable level of inventory-record accuracy. Sometimes, when there is no *history* data we find we cannot state a goal. When we don't even know how to quantify the problem we often can't express an intelligent goal. In these instances, we must first decide on the appropriate performance measures and track the data. Once we have become more knowledgeable about the problem, we can set a goal. In this instance, even though we have no preexisting data, experience has shown that to effectively operate a Manufacturing Resource Planning system, at least 95 percent inventory-record accuracy is required.

The *priority* section is used to indicate the relative importance of this problem or opportunity. No one ever seems to have enough time to analyze a problem. It is just too easy to complain, jump to conclusions and shoot from the hip. But if the problem continues, we must follow the Total Quality Control process to eliminate it. Total Quality Control may be time-consuming, but it is effective. Generally, available time limits a person to simultaneously leading one or two difficult storyboards and perhaps assisting on a couple of others. The *priority* statement may indicate that this problem just does not compete adequately for our time at the present. If the problem deserves a low priority, the analysis may be temporarily postponed, or data may be tracked only at the *history* level. But what if the *priority* statement indicates that this problem is critical? We may be busy, but we are foolish if we are too busy to eliminate our biggest problems. If something on our list of things to do is going to be ignored, it certainly should not be our number-one problem. Whenever you think you are too busy to solve a problem correctly, reread the entry in this section.

The *cause* section is where we begin to determine and quantify the causes of inaccurate records. Numerous techniques can be employed here. As the *Solution* entry on October 28 shows, the team met to identify possible causes of inaccurate records when material is stored at the point of use. The results of that meeting are shown in the fishbone diagram in the *cause* section. Later meetings initiated development of data-collection forms and checksheets and training in their use. The data collected on the first-level checksheet resulted in the level-one Pareto chart. Then a checksheet was developed to break down the largest bar on the level-one Pareto, resulting in the level-two Pareto. A checksheet was subsequently developed to break down the largest bar on the level-two Pareto, resulting in the level-three Pareto, and so on. It is important to recognize that the root cause of most significant problems is found four to six levels deep. When one bar is all that remains on the Pareto chart, the root cause has been determined. Once this has been isolated, then corrective action must follow; the *Solutions* entry for March 16 shows that changes were implemented.

We continually *check* to see if our corrective actions are effective; if they are, the data in the *history* section should improve. If it does not improve enough to meet the *goal,* we must return to the *cause* step to study other bars in the Pareto chart tree. Then we go back to the *solution* section to document and implement more countermeasures, and again,

Figure B.2

Problem Solving Storyboard

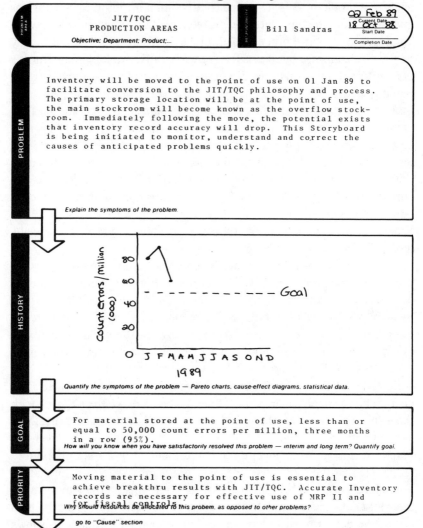

JIT/TQC
PRODUCTION AREAS
Objective; Department; Product;...

Bill Sandras

02 Feb 89
Current Date
18 Oct 88
Start Date

Completion Date

PROBLEM

Inventory will be moved to the point of use on 01 Jan 89 to facilitate conversion to the JIT/TQC philosophy and process. The primary storage location will be at the point of use, the main stockroom will become known as the overflow stockroom. Immediately following the move, the potential exists that inventory record accuracy will drop. This Storyboard is being initiated to monitor, understand and correct the causes of anticipated problems quickly.

Explain the symptoms of the problem.

HISTORY

Quantify the symptoms of the problem — Pareto charts. cause-effect diagrams. statistical data.

GOAL

For material stored at the point of use, less than or equal to 50,000 count errors per million, three months in a row (95%).
How will you know when you have satisfactorily resolved this problem — interim and long term? Quantify goal.

PRIORITY

Moving material to the point of use is essential to achieve breakthru results with JIT/TQC. Accurate Inventory records are necessary for effective use of MRP II and for fiscal controls
Why should resources be allocated to this probem. as opposed to other problems?

go to "Cause" section

Figure B.3

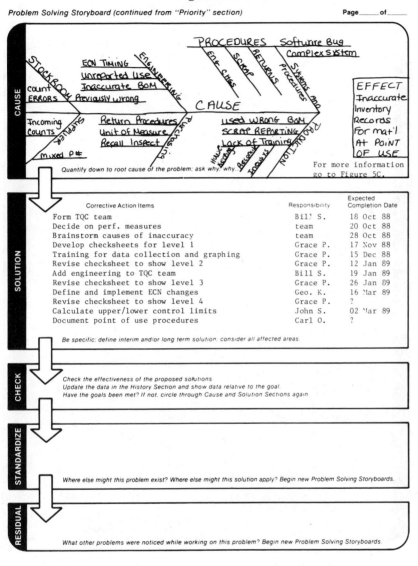

CAUSE

PROCEDURES   Software Bug
                      Complex System

STOCKROOM
count ERRORS
ECN Timing
Unreported Use
Inaccurate BOM
Previously Wrong
ENGINEERING
ENF. Cities
SCRAP
RETURNS
Systems and Procedures

CAUSE

Incoming Counts
vendors
Return Procedures
Unit of Measure
Recall Inspect
Mixed P#

USED WRONG BOM
SCRAP REPORTING
Lack of Training

EFFECT
Inaccurate
Inventory
Records
For mat'l
At Point
OF USE

Quantify down to root cause of the problem; ask why, why...

For more information go to Figure 5C.

SOLUTION

Corrective Action Items	Responsibility	Expected Completion Date
Form TQC team	Bill S.	18 Oct 88
Decide on perf. measures	team	20 Oct 88
Brainstorm causes of inaccuracy	team	28 Oct 88
Develop checksheets for level 1	Grace P.	17 Nov 88
Training for data collection and graphing	Grace P.	15 Dec 88
Revise checksheet to show level 2	Grace P.	12 Jan 89
Add engineering to TQC team	Bill S.	19 Jan 89
Revise checksheet to show level 3	Grace P.	26 Jan 89
Define and implement ECN changes	Geo. K.	16 Mar 89
Revise checksheet to show level 4	Grace P.	?
Calculate upper/lower control limits	John S.	02 Mar 89
Document point of use procedures	Carl O.	?

Be specific: define interim and/or long term solution, consider all affected areas.

CHECK

Check the effectiveness of the proposed solutions.
Update the data in the History Section and show data relative to the goal.
Have the goals been met? If not, circle through Cause and Solution Sections again.

STANDARDIZE

Where else might this problem exist? Where else might this solution apply? Begin new Problem Solving Storyboards.

RESIDUAL

What other problems were noticed while working on this problem? Begin new Problem Solving Storyboards.

Figure B.4

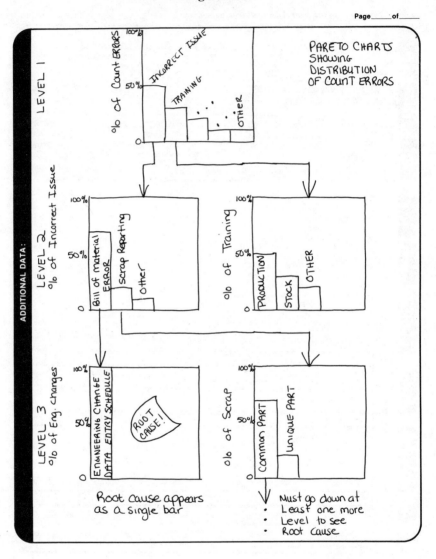

we must *check* the results. We progress through the *cause, solution, check,* and *history* sections again and again until the *goal* is met.

It is important to mention two practical points here. First, the Problem-Solving Storyboard shown in figures B.2, B.3 and B.4 makes use of a two-page form. As additional space was needed, a graph page (Figure B.4) was added. Fifty pages do not demonstrate a better understanding of the problem; nor do reams of level-one information. If the problem cannot be expressed succinctly, it is probably not well understood. While the person responsible for the project may have significant backup data, a storyboard should consist of no more than about six pages.

The second point involves aesthetics and intimidation. Some people have access to personal computers and desktop publishing software. Their storyboards are elegant. Unfortunately, sometimes more time is spent on presentation graphics than on analysis. In addition, sophisticated formats, even when done economically, can be intimidating to those who prefer to handwrite or type their storyboards. Be careful to ensure that the problem, not the aesthetics, remains the primary focus of your company's problem-solving efforts.

Once the *goal* is achieved, we are still not finished. We must *standardize.* We have worked hard to penetrate to the depths of the problem. We have developed and implemented effective countermeasures. The power of the process is maximized when we apply what we have learned to other areas. Everyone else should not need to duplicate our time to understand and develop countermeasures for the root cause of similar problems. They can benefit from our efforts and spend the time they save on other opportunities.

Finally, once the *goal* is met, the team members must decide if they should remain together to achieve a higher goal for inventory-record accuracy at the point of use, or disband to free up time that could be better spent in other teams working on other opportunities. If they disband, the *residual* section asks them to comment on any lingering inventory accuracy problems, and to document any other opportunities they noticed during the development of the storyboard.

The Problem-Solving Storyboard technique is applicable for a wide variety of problems and opportunities, including departmental objectives. However, when first learning the Total Quality Control Plan, Do, Check, Action process and the storyboard technique, it is useful to pick easily quantifiable problems; these need not necessarily be easy. Problems that are readily quantified and less subjective make it simpler to become familiar with the process. Good choices for the first few go-arounds include forecast errors, engineering changes, billing errors, filing errors, product defects, part shortages on the production lines, and, of course, inventory-record accuracy.

Most people must force themselves to follow the Total Quality Control and Problem-Solving Storyboard process through to conclusion on three or four problems before it begins to seem natural. And each significant problem may take from three to nine months, if not longer, to understand and correct. So get started now. There is a lot to learn!

JIT/TQC Implementation Checklist

Information systems
  plan changes for no work orders, purchase orders,
  periodic A/P and A/R
  consider multiple on-hand balance/part capability
Incoming inspection
  who reports to
  kanban queue
Preventive maintenance
  routine vs repair responsibilities
  define what can be done by operator
  set up schedule of needed services
Training program schedule
  direct
  indirect
  overhead
  support
  management
  suppliers
  customers
  literature library, circulate memos
  those not involved yet
Production
  process flow chart
  alternate routings

times, shifts
lot sizes
average current inv. at each step
resource needs
   man
   mach. and equip.
   acquire additional/place excess
material handling
   kits, on station, . . .
   sequence of parts
   storage of material at point of use
   rapid changeover
how to handle subcontract and preform parts
factory layout
   job shop or assembly line
   (generic or dedicated processes)
   material storage on line
   line balance
   "U" shape, straight, . . .
decide how to rotate people in line
   regular members
   cross-training of other "associates"
define cross-training plan
   within own area for multiple parts
   to customer/vendor jobs
   project board for other depts
      define if/how to charge
   setup reductions
      strategy
      schedule
Engineering
   define ECO procedures
      (back-flush, incorporation into production, MRP II, lot tracking, . . .)
Bills of material & item master considerations
   use of phantom structures
   adjustment of lead-time offsets
   coding of workstation, kit, cell

Material tracking
  issue from stock
  scrap and rework
  expensive, bulky, cheap/common
  eliminate work orders
  define how to receive at line directly
  move vs issue from stock to production
      new form?

Labor collection
  collect by exception
  eliminate work order
  use of payroll form

Performance measures
  how will you know you are successful (short & longer term)?
  keep it simple, minimal and macro
  establish baseline measures
  post in area
  key topics: quality, delivery, and cost
      cost of quality, ppm overall
      shipment linearity, to orig. promise date
      asset turnover, hard, soft, inventory, . . .
  throughput time
  inventory levels, turns, days of supply
  space
  machine downtime
  scrap/rework
  quality
  shipment delivery
  customer-delivery performance
      caution on using: standard hours vs actual, labor or machine
      efficiency, utilization or realization, purchase-part price vari-
      ances, . . .
  # kanbans, overall graph in areas
  morale
  absenteeism
  # suggestions, # used, . . .
  downtime

caution on: efficiencies of labor, M&E, . . .
    actual to standard time
understand additional duties not in standards
    hard to quantify exactly
    baseline disconnect, expect variances

Material planning
    examine build plan in light of implementation excesses
    decide how to bleed off excess
    consider D/L, I/L, and supplier implications

Photos
    before, after
    publicity
    memos, newsletter, tours
    jealousy

Train production on cycle count of RM
    record accuracy before/after

TQC
    training, PSSB, I/E
    flip chart on floor
    establish daily production floor meeting
        decide who should attend
    consider Problem-Solving Storyboards on:
        part shortages
        changes to p/o, c/o, b/m
        inventory-record accuracy
        errors: machine, workmanship, materials, test, returns
        shipment linearity
        variances in labor, material

Inspection
    done by QA or production
    part inspection or process audit

Engineering
    design for manufacturability
    build prototypes, early runs
    line feedback channels

Marketing
   consider changes in acknowledge practices
   impact on customer lead time, available to promise
   organization changes with MPS
   kanban FGI levels at factory, at customer, distribution ctr
Downtime
   keep record of why
   what did with time
Purchasing
   vendor consolidation
         ID multiple-vendor parts
         select likely candidates to begin consolidation
         and deliveries A', B', C'
   part consolidation
   open house
   no back orders
   inventory pressure
   JIT deliveries
   where to start
   pickup/consolidate vs delivery
   supplier selection team
   buyer-professionalism upgrade plan
   determine strategy to link to suppliers
   supplier open house
   direct suppliers for education

Appendix D

JIT/TQC Proven Path Detailed Implementation Plan

Just-in-Time/Total Quality Control (JIT/TQC)
Proven Path Detailed Implementation Plan

TASK	RESPONSIBLE	COMMENTS
1. AUDIT/ASSESSMENT I	Top Mgmt. Middle Mgmt.	Assess the company's current situation. In most cases, this is done with the help of an outside consultant with Class A credentials.
2. FIRST-CUT EDUCATION	Top Mgmt. Middle Mgmt.	Learn the philosophy and the process of JIT/TQC. Understand why it is essential to compete in the future. Have top managers attend the JIT/TQC Top Management Course. Key middle managers should attend the JIT/TQC Implementation Class.
3. VISION STATEMENT	Top Mgmt. Middle Mgmt.	A short, concise document defining what the company wants to accomplish in the JIT/TQC Breakthrough Pilot.
4. COST/BENEFIT	Top Mgmt. Middle Mgmt.	A clear estimate of the costs and benefits, developed by a cross-functional management team.
A. Prepare cost/benefit.	Top Mgmt. Middle Mgmt.	Cost/benefit analysis (typically begun in the JIT/TQC Implementation Class).
B. Commit to implementation.	Top Mgmt.	Approve the Breakthrough Pilot process. Communicate the commitment to JIT/TQC. Repeat clear, consistent messages.
5. PROJECT ORGANIZATION	Top Mgmt.	Create the appropriate management and operational teams. Even though JIT/TQC is a continuous effort, these teams are intended to manage the implementation until JIT/TQC becomes a way of life.
A. Executive Steering Committee.	Top Mgmt.	A group of selected top managers formed to provide strategic leadership and support for the JIT/TQC implementation. This committee must include the Executive Torchbearer (champion). Schedule review meetings once a month.

344

Just-in-Time/Total Quality Control (JIT/TQC)
Proven Path Detailed Implementation Plan

TASK	RESPONSIBLE	COMMENTS
B. Project Team (same group as the JIT Implementation Team).	Middle Mgmt.	This is the team that has the charter to implement the Breakthrough Pilot and drive JIT/TQC until it becomes a way of life at the company. Team Leader should be full-time.
C. Outside counsel.	Top Mgmt.	Benefit from the experience of an outside consultant with Class A experience to safely and economically accelerate competitive results.
6. PERFORMANCE GOALS	Top Mgmt. Middle Mgmt.	Using the ABCD Checklist and the Breakthrough Pilot criteria, agree on expected performance levels and measurements for the Breakthrough Pilot area. Typical performance measurements include: 1. Delivery: linearity, and delivery to customer promise dates. 2. Quality: parts per million, and cost of quality. 3. Inventory: days of supply and return on assets. 4. Velocity: days of lead time manufacturing, purchase, customer, and design.
7. INITIAL EDUCATION	Team Leader	Provide the necessary understanding to all people who will be involved in JIT/TQC. Everyone should be exposed to the basics of JIT/TQC at the onset of the program.
A. Outside education for the Project Team.	Team Leader	To be effective leaders, these people need to gain a detailed understanding of JIT/TQC principles at the JIT/TQC Implementation Course.
B. Steering Committee.	Team Leader	All members who have not previously attended should now complete the JIT Top Management Class.

345

Just-in-Time/Total Quality Control (JIT/TQC)
Proven Path Detailed Implementation Plan

TASK	RESPONSIBLE	COMMENTS
C. Video Education for Steering Committee and Project Team.	Team Leader	A series of business meetings where the managers apply the concepts to their company. While the initial focus is usually the implementation of the Breakthrough Pilot, these meetings may address the application of JIT/TQC throughout the entire business.
D. Pilot-level education and training.	Team Leader and Task Team Leader	A continuation of the business meetings where the general principles are translated into the specifics of operation for the Breakthrough Pilot. This education involves selecting implementation alternatives, and detailing the necessary changes. It also includes training in the mechanics of the new processes.
8. SALES, LOGISTICS, AND MANUFACTURING PROCESSES	Top Mgmt. Middle Mgmt.	Develop plans of how these operations will operate in relation to the Breakthrough Pilot.
9. PLANNING AND CONTROL PROCESSES		Identification of any changes that should be made to the planning and control systems in the Breakthrough Pilot area to support JIT/TQC.
10. DATA MANAGEMENT		These are the steps to maintain high levels of data integrity in the Breakthrough Pilot area.
A. Inventory Record Accuracy.	Stockroom Mgr. Mfg. Suprvsn.	Changes need to be made to maintain accuracy when using point-of-use and point-of-manufacture storage. Changes are also made in the who, how, and when of cycle counting.
B. Bill of Material Accuracy.	Engr. Mgr. Mfg. Suprvsn.	Typical areas of work include: 1. Flattening the bills of material as a result of simplifying the product and processes. 2. Noting where material is used, for use in postdeduct transactions (backflushing).

Just-in-Time/Total Quality Control (JIT/TQC)
Proven Path Detailed Implementation Plan

TASK	RESPONSIBLE	COMMENTS
C. Routing Accuracy.	Mfg. Engr. Mgr.	Typical activities include simplifying the routings to represent acceler-ated product flows and the creation of cells.
11. PROCESS IMPROVEMENT		Create a model of the future factory to help people understand and accept the forthcoming changes. Demonstrate the new procedures and breakthrough results.
A. Develop implementation plans for the Breakthrough Pilot	Project Team	Typical activities are listed below.
1. Establish performance mea-sures.	Project Team	Establish a benchmark to measure success based upon performance goals established.
2. Establish process layout.	Project Team	Determine manufacturing process and product flow within the pilot areas. Where economical, move equipment.
3. Establish material flow.	Project Team	Determine material flow to and from the pilot area from other areas not included in the pilot.
4. Establish kanban system for controlling production and material replenishment in the pilot area.	Project Team	Use of kanban is essential to the JIT process of "one less at a time." Establish kanban as the formal procedure for controlling production and authorizing material replenishment in the pilot area.
5. Define rules for common equipment.	Project Team	Some equipment may be required for traditional production as well as JIT production. Use information outlined in the implementation class to define how to share this equipment.

Just-in-Time/Total Quality Control (JIT/TQC)
Proven Path Detailed Implementation Plan

TASK	RESPONSIBLE	COMMENTS
6. Establish quantity and plan for control of material stored at point of use.	Project Team Production People	When material is stored at point of manufacture/use, responsibility for controlling this material shifts to production. Develop training and accuracy verification procedures.
7. Develop system interfaces.	Project Team	Develop procedural changes that will result in minimal software changes, yet will enable the pilot to operate according to the breakthrough specifications. An experienced consultant is critical at this stage.
8. Define points for material deduction.	Project Team	Determine where material will be postdeducted to maintain financial accountability.
9. Define engineering change procedure.	Project Team	When work orders are used, an engineering change is communicated to production via the work order. Without work orders, the changeover has to be done physically on the factory floor.
10. Define labor-collection procedures.	Project Team	Without work orders, how will labor be collected? Most companies use labor reporting by exception.
11. Decide how to bleed off excess inventory.	Project Team	When JIT/TQC is started, most companies quickly find they have more inventory in the pipeline than is required. The severity of the excess often dictates the need for a strategy to bleed off the excess while making constructive use of people's time.
12. SOFTWARE	MIS Mgr.	Make essential software changes identified by the Project Team that are needed to enable the pilot to operate according to the breakthrough specifications.

348

Just-in-Time/Total Quality Control (JIT/TQC)
Proven Path Detailed Implementation Plan

TASK	RESPONSIBLE	COMMENTS
13. PILOT AND CUTOVER	Project Team	Conversion of the current processes to the new processes using a pilot approach. Creating a model to demonstrate the effectiveness of the vision.
		The Breakthrough Pilot is the recommended approach to implementing JIT/TQC and should be ready to begin operation within 120 days.
A. Begin JIT/TQC in pilot area.	Project Team	Typical activities are listed below.
1. Practice JIT.	Project Team	Become familiar with the mechanics of the kanban technique, then begin to practice JIT's "one less at a time" process by carefully removing kanbans.
2. Practice TQC.	Project Team	When the JIT process exposes a constraint, eliminate the constraint using TQC's "Plan, Do, Check, Action" process.
3. Start formal set-up reduction process.	Production Task Team	Where equipment setups are or projected to be a constraint, follow the "SMED" process. Use videotaping.
4. Begin monitoring and displaying performance measurements.	Project Team	Post performance measurements in a prominent place in the pilot area. Use run type charts to show progress plus Pareto Charts to point the way to improvement.
5. Put flip chart in pilot area to collect problems/ suggestions.	Top Mgmt. Middle Mgmt. Project Team Production People	Provide an easy and efficient way for everyone to communicate ideas to eliminate waste. Management must ensure that a responsive answer is provided for each idea, but responsibility and authority should be delegated to the lowest level capable of responding to each idea.
6. Establish daily production floor meeting.	Project Team Production Supr.	Most people meet once per shift. Provides ability to communicate opportunities for improvement to those who can eliminate the root cause of the problem. Use problems documented on the flip chart as basis for discussion.

Just-in-Time/Total Quality Control (JIT/TQC)
Proven Path Detailed Implementation Plan

TASK	RESPONSIBLE	COMMENTS
14. PERFORMANCE MEASURE- MENTS	Dept. Heads	Compare actual results to the previously agreed-upon key measurements.
A. Evaluate results of pilot.	Top Mgmt.	"Go on/go back" checkpoint. Review actual results against expected performance levels.
15. AUDIT/ASSESSMENT II	Top Mgmt. Middle Mgmt.	Re-assess the company's situation. Is it now time to implement JIT/TQC across the company? When should suppliers and/or customers be involved? What's next? In most cases, this is done with the help of an outside consultant with Class A credentials.
16. ONGOING EDUCATION		Ongoing education for the Breakthrough Pilot typically means initial education for the next phase of implementation.
17. FIRST-CUT EDUCATION	Top Mgmt. Middle Mgmt.	In most cases, first-cut education was completed before the Breakthrough Pilot. Do any additional education as needed.
18. VISION STATEMENT	Top Mgmt. Middle Mgmt.	Prepare a "white paper," based on the insights gained from the Breakthrough Pilot. The document should thoroughly describe the company changes that will occur in the next five years as JIT/TQC drives continuous improvement.
19. COST/BENEFIT	Top Mgmt. Middle Mgmt.	Refine the cost/benefit analysis based on the results of the Breakthrough Pilot.
A. Prepare cost/benefit.	Top Mgmt. Middle Mgmt.	Revise as needed.
20. PROJECT ORGANIZATION	Top Mgmt.	Create the appropriate management and operational teams.

Just-in-Time/Total Quality Control (JIT/TQC)
Proven Path Detailed Implementation Plan

TASK	RESPONSIBLE	COMMENTS
A. Executive Steering Committee.	Top Mgmt.	Most companies keep the same Steering Committee created for the Breakthrough Pilot.
B. Project Team	Middle Mgmt.	Most companies keep the same Project Team created for the Breakthrough Pilot.
C. Outside counsel.	Top Mgmt.	Most companies continue to use the same outside consultant.
D. Execution teams.	Exec. Steering Committee	Identify the sequence of products and/or processes to be implemented.
21. PERFORMANCE GOALS	Top Mgmt. Middle Mgmt.	Using the ABCD Checklist, revise the expected performance levels and measurements based on the results of the Breakthrough Pilot.
22. INITIAL EDUCATION	Team Leader	Provide the necessary understanding to all people who will be involved in JIT/TQC.
A. Outside education for people who will be leaders at the in-house series of business meetings, and key managers.	Team Leader	To be effective discussion leaders, these managers need exposure at either the JIT/TQC Top Management Course or the JIT/TQC Implementation Course. The key managers mentioned here are people critical to the design or operation, but who have not been involved in either the first cut (Task #2) or initial education (Tasks #7A and #7B) for the Breakthrough Pilot.
B. Discussion Leaders video course.	Team Leader	A series of business meetings where the general principles are translated into the specifics of operation for your company. These people become the discussion leaders for the team specific meetings.

Just-in-Time/Total Quality Control (JIT/TQC)
Proven Path Detailed Implementation Plan

TASK	RESPONSIBLE	COMMENTS
C. Team specific video courses.	Discussion Leaders	Series of business meetings organized by execution teams. The objective is to determine specifically what changes need to be made to run the business differently.
D. Department-level education and training.	Dept. Mgrs.	This education is for the people doing the work in their areas. It involves selecting implementation alternatives, and detailing the necessary changes. It also includes training in the mechanics of the new processes.
23. SALES, LOGISTICS, AND MANUFACTURING PROCESSES	Top Mgmt. Middle Mgmt.	Refine the detailed statement of how these processes will operate following implementation (based on the results of the Breakthrough Pilot). The discussion leaders series of business meetings (Task #22B above) generally provides most of the information needed for this task.
24. PLANNING AND CONTROL PROCESSES		Identification of any further changes that should be made to the planning and control systems in order to support JIT/TQC.
A. Sales & Operations Planning.	Top Mgmt.	Do sales & operations planning on all products.
B. Demand Management.	Sales Mgr.	Focus on eliminating or reducing detailed forecasting wherever possible by using JIT/TQC to become more flexible in building different product configurations. May also involve DRP for some companies.
C. Master Production Scheduling.	P&IC Mgr.	Implement mixed-model master scheduling. Focus on linearity and responsiveness.
D. Capacity Planning.	P&IC Mgr. Mfg. Suprvsn.	In most companies, detailed Capacity Requirements Planning can be eliminated, using only Rough-Cut Capacity Planning.

Just-in-Time/Total Quality Control (JIT/TQC)
Proven Path Detailed Implementation Plan

TASK	RESPONSIBLE	COMMENTS
E. Shop Scheduling.	P&IC Mgr. Mfg. Suprvsn.	As kanban is implemented, traditional work-order-based shop floor control is gradually eliminated to the point where it may be completely replaced.
25. DATA MANAGEMENT		These are the steps to maintain high levels of data integrity, while also simplifying the manufacturing process by eliminating waste.
A. Inventory Record Accuracy.	Stockroom Mgr.	Changes need to be made to maintain accuracy when using point-of-use and point-of-manufacture storage. Changes are also made in the who, how, and when of cycle counting.
B. Bill of Material Accuracy.	Engr. Mgr. Mfg. Suprvsn.	Typical areas of work include: 1. Flattening the bills of material as a result of simplifying the product and processes. 2. Noting where material is used, for use in backflushing.
C. Routing Accuracy.	Mfg. Engr. Mgr.	Typical activities include simplifying the routings to represent simplified, accelerated product flows and the creation of cells.
26. PROCESS IMPROVEMENT		Extend the model of the future factory. Link segments of the pipeline from raw material to the end customer. Change mind-set from "pilot" to implementing a new way of life to ensure a competitive future.
A. Extend JIT/TQC implementation.	Execution Teams	Develop detailed plans to extend JIT/TQC to all areas of the company, into its supplier base, and, if applicable, into its customer base. Approach each new area in the same manner as the initial pilot. Examine measures and procedures used in the pilot. Reinforce or revise. Begin to standardize the procedures that were proven to be effective during the Breakthrough Pilot stage throughout the company.

Just-in-Time/Total Quality Control (JIT/TQC)
Proven Path Detailed Implementation Plan

TASK	RESPONSIBLE	COMMENTS
B. Link to suppliers.	Purchasing Mgr.	Typical activities include: 1. Begin supplier quality program. 2. Hold supplier open house (supplier education day).
C. Link to customers.	Sales Mgr.	If applicable.
D. Re-align personnel policies and procedures.	Personnel Mgr.	JIT/TQC is designed to strengthen people. Only when a company's people are thinking about the right constraints, and they are equipped to solve problems, can a company expect to compete. Human Resources must plan for the positive, yet significant, people issues surrounding JIT/TQC and our ability to compete in the future. These issues include compensation, labor grades, employment stability, and training.
E. Envision next steps.	Engr. Mgr.	JIT/TQC provides a fertile environment to successfully, economically, and knowledgeably implement other competitive tools. JIT/TQC provides stepping stones to automation, design for manufacturability, activity-based costing, benchmarking, and computer-integrated manufacturing.
27. SOFTWARE	MIS Mgr.	Develop programs and implement changes that will effectively support the direction JIT/TQC is leading the company.
A. Acquire necessary resources to evaluate system changes.	MIS Mgr.	Typical changes include manufacturing with no work orders, simplified reporting of production activity, collection of production labor by exception, multiple inventory locations, frequent replanning, mixed model scheduling, and purchasing without purchase orders.
B. Implement necessary modifications.	MIS Mgr.	See list above.

Just-in-Time/Total Quality Control (JIT/TQC)
Proven Path Detailed Implementation Plan

TASK	RESPONSIBLE	COMMENTS
C. Develop system interfaces.	MIS Mgr.	Procedural and software changes listed above typically require systems work to interface different business systems. Examine areas where the velocity of information is too slow to meet the needs of JIT/TQC.
28. EXTENSION OF INITIAL PILOT	Execution Teams	Conversion of the current processes to the new processes using a pilot approach.
		This phase can be thought of as a series of "Breakthrough Pilots" until all of the company is operating with JIT/TQC. The implementation of each of these areas uses the same steps as in the Breakthrough Pilot.
29. PERFORMANCE MEASUREMENTS	Dept. Heads	Compare actual results to the previously agreed-upon key measurements.
30. AUDIT/ASSESSMENT III	Top Mgmt. Middle Mgmt.	Re-assess the company's situation. Where are the current opportunities, where should the management focus be? How well are we practicing JIT/TQC? How can we improve? What are the next steps we should consider? In most cases, this is done with the help of an outside consultant with Class A credentials.
31. ONGOING EDUCATION	Dept. Heads	Develop a continuing program of outside education and business meetings to improve skill levels and company operating results.
A. Educate key managers new to the business.	Top Mgmt.	New managers in key positions need exposure at either the JIT/TQC Top Management Course or the JIT/TQC Implementation Course to continue achieving full operating benefits.
B. Continue the series of business meetings.	Dept. Heads	These meetings focus on how to improve the operating results of the business through the use of these tools. It's good to stand back and look at the situation from time to time. Sometimes new people are run through a special series of meetings; more typically, they are included into the ongoing series of business meetings.

Sources for Additional Information

Preparing yourself to implement a Class A MRP II system requires careful study of a huge amount of information, far more than could be included in this or any other book. The Oliver Wight Companies can provide further assistance in getting ready, including books on the subject, live education, and reviews of commercially available software packages.

OLIVER WIGHT LIMITED PUBLICATIONS, INC.

Oliver Wight Limited Publications, Inc. was created in 1981 to publish books on planning and scheduling, written by leading educators and consultants in the field.

A complete library of books on Manufacturing Resource Planning, Just-in-Time, and Distribution Resource Planning is available.

For more information, or to order publications, contact:

Oliver Wight Limited Publications, Inc.
5 Oliver Wight Drive
Essex Junction, VT 05452
800-343-0625 or 802-878-8161

OLIVER WIGHT EDUCATION ASSOCIATES

OWEA is made up of a group of independent MRP II educators and consultants around the world who share a common philosophy and common goals. Classes directed toward both upper- and middle-level management are being taught in various locations around the U.S. and Canada, as well as abroad. For a detailed class brochure, listing course descriptions, instructors, costs, dates, and locations, or for the name of a recommended consultant in your area, please contact:

Oliver Wight Education Associates
P.O Box 435
Newbury, NH 03255
800-258-3862 or 603-763-5926

OLIVER WIGHT VIDEO PRODUCTIONS, INC.

The Oliver Wight Video Library offers companies the video-based materials they need to teach the "critical mass" of their employees about the principles of MRP II and Just-in-Time. For more information on obtaining the Oliver Wight Video Library, contact:

Oliver Wight Video Productions, Inc.
5 Oliver Wight Drive
Essex Junction, VT 05452
800-343-0625 or 802-878-8161

Professional Societies

American Production and Inventory Control Society (APICS)
500 West Allendale Road
Falls Church, VA 22046-4274
(703) 237-8344

American Society for Quality Control
P.O. Box 555, Milwaukee, WI 53201
(414) 272-8575

Association for Manufacturing Excellence
P.O. Box 584 Elm Grove, WI 53122

Society of Manufacturing Engineers (SME)
One SME Drive, P.O. Box 930, Dearborn, MI 48121
(313) 271-1500

All of these societies have international branches.

Index